GRAHAM GREENE

Brighton Rock

VINTAGE BOOKS
London

Published by Vintage 2010

2 4 6 8 10 9 7 5 3 1

First published in Great Britain in 1938 by
William Heinemann

First published by Vintage in 2002

Vintage
Random House, 20 Vauxhall Bridge Road,
London SW1V 2SA

www.vintage-books.co.uk

Addresses for companies within The Random House Group
Limited can be found at: www.randomhouse.co.uk/offices.htm

The Random House Group Limited Reg. No. 954009

A CIP catalogue record for this book
is available from the British Library

ISBN 9780099541578

The
Stewa
certif
Green

BRIGHTON ROCK

Graham Greene was born in 1904. On coming down from Balliol College, Oxford, he worked for four years as sub-editor on *The Times*. He established his reputation with his fourth novel, *Stamboul Train*. In 1935 he made a journey across Liberia, described in *Journey Without Maps*, and on his return was appointed film critic of the *Spectator*. In 1926 he had been received into the Roman Catholic Church and visited Mexico in 1938 to report on the religious persecution there. As a result he wrote *The Lawless Roads* and, later, his famous novel *The Power and the Glory*. *Brighton Rock* was published in 1938 and in 1940 he became literary editor of the *Spectator*. The next year he undertook work for the Foreign Office and was stationed in Sierra Leone from 1941 to 1943. This later produced the novel *The Heart of the Matter*, set in West Africa.

As well as his many novels, Graham Greene wrote several collections of short stories, four travel books, six plays, three books of autobiography – *A Sort of Life*, *Ways of Escape* and *A World of My Own* (published posthumously) – two of biography and four books for children. He also contributed hundreds of essays, and film and book reviews, some of which appear in the collections *Reflections* and *Mornings in the Dark*. Many of his novels and short stories have been filmed and *The Third Man* was written as a film treatment. Graham Greene was a member of the Order of Merit and a Companion of Honour. He died in April 1991.

The Vintage ♥ Film series:

Alice in Wonderland Lewis Carroll

Atonement Ian McEwan

Brighton Rock Graham Greene

7

Catch-22 Joseph Heller

Death in Venice Thomas Mann

* *Fight Club* Chuck Palahniuk

The French Lieutenant's Woman John Fowles

3

Memoirs of a Geisha Arthur Golden

The Talented Mr Ripley Patricia Highsmith

1

Trainspotting Irvine Welsh

* not available in Australia and New Zealand

PART ONE

I

Hale knew, before he had been in Brighton three hours, that they meant to murder him. With his inky fingers and his bitten nails, his manner cynical and nervous, anybody could tell he didn't belong—belong to the early summer sun, the cool Whitsun wind off the sea, the holiday crowd. They came in by train from Victoria every five minutes, rocked down Queen's Road standing on the tops of the little local trams, stepped off in bewildered multitudes into fresh and glittering air: the new silver paint sparkled on the piers, the cream houses ran away into the west like a pale Victorian watercolour; a race in miniature motors, a band playing, flower gardens in bloom below the front, an aeroplane advertising something for the health in pale vanishing clouds across the sky.

It had seemed quite easy to Hale to be lost in Brighton. Fifty thousand people besides himself were down for the day, and for quite a while he gave himself up to the good day, drinking gins and tonics wherever his programme allowed. For he had to stick closely to a programme: from ten till eleven Queen's Road and Castle Square, from eleven till twelve the Aquarium and Palace Pier, twelve till one the front between the Old Ship and West Pier, back for lunch between one and two in any restaurant he chose round the Castle Square, and after that he had to make his way all down the parade to the West Pier and then to the station by the Hove streets. These were the limits of his absurd and widely advertised sentry-go.

Advertised on every *Messenger* poster: 'Kolley Kibber in Brighton today.' In his pocket he had a packet of cards to distribute in hidden places along his route; those who found them would receive ten shillings from the *Messenger*, but the big prize was reserved

3

for whoever challenged Hale in the proper form of words and with a copy of the *Messenger* in his hand: 'You are Mr Kolley Kibber. I claim the *Daily Messenger* prize.'

This was Hale's job to do sentry-go, until a challenger released him, in every seaside town in turn: yesterday Southend, today Brighton, tomorrow—

He drank his gin and tonic hastily as a clock struck eleven and moved out of Castle Square. Kolley Kibber always played fair, always wore the same kind of hat as in the photograph the *Messenger* printed, was always on time. Yesterday in Southend he had been unchallenged: the paper liked to save its guineas occasionally, but not too often. It was his duty today to be spotted—and it was his inclination too. There were reasons why he didn't feel too safe in Brighton, even in a Whitsun crowd.

He leant against the rail near the Palace Pier and showed his face to the crowd as it uncoiled endlessly past him, like a twisted piece of wire, two by two, each with an air of sober and determined gaiety. They had stood all the way from Victoria in crowded carriages, they would have to wait in queues for lunch, at midnight half asleep they would rock back in trains to the cramped streets and the closed pubs and the weary walk home. With immense labour and immense patience they extricated from the long day the grain of pleasure: this sun, this music, the rattle of the miniature cars, the ghost train diving between the grinning skeletons under the Aquarium promenade, the sticks of Brighton rock, the paper sailors' caps.

Nobody paid any attention to Hale; no one seemed to be carrying a *Messenger*. He deposited one of his cards carefully on the top of a little basket and moved on, with his bitten nails and his inky fingers, alone. He only felt his loneliness after his third gin; until then he despised the crowd, but afterwards he felt his kinship. He had come out of the same streets, but he was condemned by his higher pay to pretend to want other things, and all the time the piers, the peepshows pulled at his heart. He wanted to get back—but all he could do was to carry his sneer along the front, the badge of loneliness. Somewhere out of sight a woman was singing, 'When I came up from Brighton by the train': a rich Guinness voice, a voice from a public bar. Hale turned into the private

4

saloon and watched her big blown charms across two bars and through a glass partition.

She wasn't old, somewhere in the late thirties or the early forties, and she was only a little drunk in a friendly accommodating way. You thought of sucking babies when you looked at her, but if she'd borne them she hadn't let them pull her down: she took care of herself. Her lipstick told you that, the confidence of her big body. She was well-covered, but she wasn't careless; she kept her lines for those who cared for lines.

Hale did. He was a small man and he watched her with covetous envy over the empty glasses tipped up in the lead trough, over the beer handles, between the shoulders of the two serving in the public bar. 'Give us another, Lily,' one of them said and she began, 'One night—in an alley—Lord Rothschild said to me.' She never got beyond a few lines. She wanted to laugh too much to give her voice a chance, but she had an inexhaustible memory for ballads. Hale had never heard one of them before. With his glass to his lips he watched her with nostalgia: she was off again on a song which must have dated back to the Australian gold rush.

'Fred,' a voice said behind him, 'Fred.'

The gin slopped out of Hale's glass on to the bar. A boy of about seventeen watched him from the door—a shabby smart suit, the cloth too thin for much wear, a face of starved intensity, a kind of hideous and unnatural pride.

'Who are you Freding?' Hale said. 'I'm not Fred.'

'It don't make any difference,' the boy said. He turned back towards the door, keeping an eye on Hale over his narrow shoulder.

'Where are you going?'

'Got to tell your friends,' the boy said.

They were alone in the saloon bar except for an old commissionaire, who slept over a pint glass of old and mild. 'Listen,' Hale said, 'have a drink. Come and sit down over here and have a drink.'

'Got to be going,' the boy said. 'You know I don't drink, Fred. You forget a lot, don't you?'

'It won't make any difference having one drink. A soft drink.'

'It'll have to be a quick one,' the boy said. He watched Hale all the time closely and with wonder: you might expect a hunter searching through the jungle for some half-fabulous beast to look like that—at the spotted lion or the pygmy elephant—before the kill. 'A grape-fruit squash,' he said.

'Go on, Lily,' the voices implored in the public bar. 'Give us another, Lily,' and the boy took his eyes for the first time from Hale and looked across the partition at the big breasts and the blown charm.

'A double whisky and a grape-fruit squash,' Hale said. He carried them to a table, but the boy didn't follow. He was watching the woman with an expression of furious distaste. Hale felt as if hatred had been momentarily loosened like handcuffs to be fastened round another's wrists. He tried to joke, 'A cheery soul.'

'Soul,' the boy said. 'You've no cause to talk about souls.' He turned his hatred back on Hale, drinking down the grape-fruit squash in a single draught.

Hale said, 'I'm only here for my job. Just for the day. I'm Kolley Kibber.'

'You're Fred,' the boy said.

'All right,' Hale said, 'I'm Fred. But I've got a card in my pocket which'll be worth ten bob to you.'

'I know all about the cards,' the boy said. He had a fair smooth skin, the faintest down, and his grey eyes had an effect of heartlessness like an old man's in which human feeling has died. 'We were all reading about you,' he said, 'in the paper this morning,' and suddenly he sniggered as if he'd just seen the point of a dirty story.

'You can have one,' Hale said. 'Look, take this *Messenger*. Read what it says there. You can have the whole prize. Ten guineas,' he said. 'You'll only have to send this form to the *Messenger*.'

'Then they don't trust you with the cash,' the boy said, and in the other bar Lily began to sing, 'We met—'twas in a crowd—and I thought he would shun me.' 'Christ,' the boy said, 'won't anybody stop that buer's mouth?'

'I'll give you a fiver,' Hale said. 'It's all I've got on me. That and my ticket.'

'You won't want your ticket,' the boy said.

'I wore my bridal robe, and I rivall'd its whiteness.'

The boy rose furiously, and giving way to a little vicious spurt of hatred—at the song? at the man?—he dropped his empty glass on to the floor. 'The gentleman'll pay,' he said to the barman and swung through the door of the private lounge. It was then Hale realized that they meant to murder him.

> 'A wreath of orange blossoms,
> When next we met, she wore;
> The expression of her features
> Was more thoughtful than before.'

The commissionaire slept on and Hale watched her from the deserted elegant lounge. Her big breasts pointed through the thin vulgar summer dress, and he thought: I must get away from here, I must get away: sadly and desperately watching her, as if he were gazing at life itself in the public bar. But he couldn't get away, he had his job to do: they were particular on the *Messenger*. It was a good paper to be on, and a little flare of pride went up in Hale's heart when he thought of the long pilgrimage behind him: selling newspapers at street corners, the reporter's job at thirty bob a week on the little local paper with a circulation of ten thousand, the five years in Sheffield. He was damned, he told himself with the temporary courage of another whisky, if he'd let that mob frighten him into spoiling his job. What could they do while he had people round him? They hadn't the nerve to kill him in broad day before witnesses; he was safe with the fifty thousand visitors.

'Come on over here, lonely heart.' He didn't realize at first she was speaking to him, until he saw all the faces in the public bar grinning across at him, and suddenly he thought how easily the mob could get at him with only the sleeping commissionaire to keep him company. There was no need to go outside to reach the other bar, he had only to make a semicircle through three doors, by way of the saloon bar, the 'ladies only'. 'What'll you have?' he said, approaching the big woman with starved gratitude. She could save my life, he thought, if she'd let me stick to her.

'I'll have a port,' she said.

'One port,' Hale said.

'Aren't you having one?'

'No.' Hale said, 'I've drunk enough. I mustn't get sleepy.'

'Why ever not—on a holiday? Have a Bass on me.'

'I don't like Bass.' He looked at his watch. It was one o'clock. His programme fretted at his mind. He had to leave cards in every section: the paper in that way kept a check on him; they could always tell if he scamped his job. 'Come and have a bite,' he implored her.

'Hark at him,' she called to her friends. Her warm port-winey laugh filled all the bars. 'Getting fresh, eh? I wouldn't trust myself.'

'Don't you go, Lily,' they told her. 'He's not safe.'

'I wouldn't trust myself,' she repeated, closing one soft friendly cowlike eye.

There was a way, Hale knew, to make her come. He had known the way once. On thirty bob a week he would have been at home with her; he would have known the right phrase, the right joke, to cut her out from among her friends, to be friendly at a snack-bar. But he'd lost touch. He had nothing to say; he could only repeat, 'Come and have a bite.'

'Where shall we go, Sir Horace? To the Old Ship?'

'Yes,' Hale said. 'If you like. The Old Ship.'

'Hear that,' she told them in all the bars, the two old dames in black bonnets in the ladies, the commissionaire who slept on alone in the private, her own half dozen cronies. 'This gentleman's invited me to the Old Ship,' she said in a mock-refined voice. 'Tomorrow I shall be delighted, but today I have a prior engagement at the Dirty Dog.'

Hale turned hopelessly to the door. The boy, he thought, would not have had time to warn the others yet. He would be safe at lunch; it was the hour he had to pass after lunch he dreaded most.

The woman said, 'Are you sick or something?'

His eyes turned to the big breasts; she was like darkness to him, shelter, knowledge, common sense; his heart ached at the sight; but, in his little inky cynical framework of bone, pride bobbed up again, taunting him, 'Back to the womb . . . be a mother to you . . . no more standing on your own feet.'

'No,' he said, 'I'm not sick. I'm all right.'

'You look queer,' she said in a friendly concerned way.

'I'm all right,' he said. 'Hungry. That's all.'

'Why not have a bite here?' the woman said. 'You could do him a ham sandwich, couldn't you, Bell,' and the barman said, Yes, he could do a ham sandwich.

'No,' Hale said, 'I've got to be getting on.'

—Getting on. Down the front, mixing as quickly as possible with the current of the crowd, glancing to right and left of him and over each shoulder in turn. He could see no familiar face anywhere, but he felt no relief. He thought he could lose himself safely in a crowd, but now the people he was among seemed like a thick forest in which a native could arrange his poisoned ambush. He couldn't see beyond the man in flannels just in front, and when he turned his vision was blocked by a brilliant scarlet blouse. Three old ladies went driving by in an open horse-drawn carriage: the gentle clatter faded like peace. That was how some people still lived.

Hale crossed the road away from the front. There were fewer people there: he could walk faster and go further. They were drinking cocktails on the terrace of the Grand, a delicate pastiche of a Victorian sunshade twisted its ribbons and flowers in the sun, and a man like a retired statesman, all silver hair and powdered skin and double old-fashioned eyeglass, let life slip naturally, with dignity, away from him, sitting over a sherry. Down the broad steps of the Cosmopolitan came a couple of women with bright brass hair and ermine coats and heads close together like parrots, exchanging metallic confidences. '"My dear," I said quite coldly, "if you haven't learnt the Del Rey perm, all I can say—"' and they flashed their pointed painted nails at each other and cackled. For the first time for five years Kolley Kibber was late in his programme. At the foot of the Cosmopolitan steps, in the shadow the huge bizarre building cast, he remembered that the mob had bought his paper. They hadn't needed to watch the public house for him: they knew where to expect him.

A mounted policeman came up the road, the lovely cared-for chestnut beast stepping delicately on the hot macadam, like an expensive toy a millionaire buys for his children; you admired the finish, the leather as deeply glowing as an old mahogany table top, the bright silver badge; it never occurred to you that the toy was for use. It never occurred to Hale watching the policeman pass; he couldn't appeal to him. A man stood by the kerb selling objects on a tray; he had lost the whole of one side of the body: leg and arm and shoulder, and the beautiful horse as it paced by turned its head aside delicately like a dowager. 'Shoelaces,' the man said hopelessly to Hale, 'matches.' Hale didn't hear him. 'Razor blades.' Hale went by, the words lodged securely in his brain: the thought of the thin wound and the sharp pain. That was how Kite was killed.

Twenty yards down the road he saw Cubitt. Cubitt was a big man, with red hair cut *en brosse* and freckles. He saw Hale, but he made no sign of recognition, leaning carelessly against a pillar-box watching him. A postman came to collect and Cubitt shifted. Hale could see him exchanging a joke with the postman and the postman laughed and filled his bag and all the time Cubitt looked away from him down the street waiting for Hale. Hale knew exactly what he'd do; he knew the whole bunch; Cubitt was slow and had a friendly way with him. He'd simply link his arm with Hale's and draw him on where he wanted him to go.

But the old desperate pride persisted, a pride of intellect. He was scared sick, but he told himself, 'I'm not going to die.' He jested hollowly, 'I'm not front page stuff.' This was real: the two women getting into a taxi, the band playing on the Palace Pier, 'tablets' fading in white smoke on the pale pure sky; not red-haired Cubitt waiting by the pillar-box. Hale turned again and crossed the road, made back towards the West Pier walking fast; he wasn't running away, he had a plan.

He had only, he told himself, to find a girl: there must be hundreds waiting to be picked up on a Whitsun holiday, to be given a drink and taken to dance at Sherry's and presently home, drunk and affectionate, in the corridor carriage. That was the best way: to carry a witness round with him. It would be no good, even if his pride allowed him, to go to the station now. They would be watching it for certain, and it was always easy to kill a lonely man at a railway station: they had only to gather close round a carriage door or fix you in the crush at the barrier; it was at a station that Colleoni's mob had killed Kite. All down the front the girls sat in the twopenny deck-chairs, waiting to be picked, all who had not brought their boys with them; clerks, shop-girls, hairdressers—

you could pick out the hairdressers by their new and daring perms, by their beautifully manicured nails: they had all waited late at their shops the night before, preparing each other till midnight. Now they were sleepy and sleek in the sun.

In front of the chairs the men strolled in twos and threes, wearing their summer suits for the first time, knife-edged silver-grey trousers and elegant shirts; they didn't look as if they cared a damn whether they got a girl or not, and among them Hale went in his seedy suit and his string tie and his striped shirt and his inkstains, ten years older, and desperate for a girl. He offered them cigarettes and they stared at him like duchesses with large cold eyes and said, 'I don't smoke, thank you,' and twenty yards behind him, he knew, without turning his head, that Cubitt strolled.

It made Hale's manner strange. He couldn't help showing his desperation. He could hear the girls laughing at him after he'd gone, at his clothes and the way he talked. There was a deep humility in Hale; his pride was only in his profession: he disliked himself before the glass—the bony legs and the pigeon breast, and he dressed shabbily and carelessly as a sign—a sign that he didn't expect any woman to be interested. Now he gave up the pretty ones, the smart ones, and looked despairingly down the chairs for someone plain enough to be glad of even his attentions.

Surely he thought, *this* girl, and he smiled with hungry hope at a fat spotty creature in pink whose feet hardly touched the ground. He sat down in an empty chair beside her and gazed at the remote and neglected sea coiling round the piles of the West Pier.

'Cigarette?' he asked presently.

'I don't mind if I do,' the girl said. The words were sweet like a reprieve.

'It's nice here,' the fat girl said.

'Down from town?'

'Yes.'

'Well,' Hale said, 'you aren't going to sit here alone all day, are you?'

'Oh, I don't know,' the girl said.

'I thought of going to have something to eat, and then we might—'

'*We*,' the girl said, 'you're a fresh one.'

'Well, you aren't going to sit here alone all day, are you?'

'Who said I was?' the fat girl said. 'Doesn't mean I'm going with *you*.'

'Come and have a drink anyway and talk about it.'

'I wouldn't mind,' she said, opening a compact and covering her spots deeper.

'Come along then,' Hale said.

'Got a friend?'

'I'm all alone.'

'Oh then, I couldn't,' the girl said. 'Not possibly. I couldn't leave my friend all alone,' and for the first time Hale observed in the chair beyond her a pale bloodless creature waiting avidly for his reply.

'But you'd like to come,' Hale implored.

'Oh, yes, but I couldn't possibly.'

'Your friend won't mind. She'll find someone.'

'Oh, no. I couldn't leave her alone.' She stared pastily and impassively at the sea.

'You wouldn't mind, would you?' Hale leaned forward and begged the bloodless image, and it screeched with embarrassed laughter back at him.

'She doesn't know anyone,' the fat girl said.

'She'll find somebody.'

'Would you, Delia?' The pasty girl leant her head close to her friend's and they consulted together: every now and then Delia squealed.

'That's all right then,' Hale said, 'you'll come?'

'Couldn't you find a friend?'

'I don't know anyone here,' Hale said. 'Come along. I'll take you anywhere for lunch. All I want—' he grinned miserably—'is for you to stick close.'

'No,' the fat girl said. 'I couldn't possibly—not without my friend.'

'Well, both of you come along then,' Hale said.

'It wouldn't be much fun for Delia,' the fat girl said.

A boy's voice interrupted them. 'So there you are, Fred,' and Hale looked up at the grey inhuman seventeen-year-old eyes.

'Why,' the fat girl squealed, 'he said he hadn't got a friend.'

'You can't believe what Fred says,' the voice said.

'Now we can make a proper party,' the fat girl said. 'This is my friend Delia. I'm Molly.'

'Pleased to meet you,' the boy said. 'Where are we going, Fred?'

'I'm hungry,' the fat girl said. 'I bet you're hungry too, Delia?' and Delia wriggled and squealed.

'I know a good place,' the boy said.

'Do they have sundaes?'

'The best sundaes,' he reassured her in his serious dead voice.

'That's what I want, a sundae. Delia likes splits best.'

'We'll be going, Fred,' the boy said.

Hale rose. His hands were shaking. This was real now: the boy, the razor cut, life going out with the blood in pain: not the deck chairs and the permanent waves, the miniature cars tearing round the curve on the Palace Pier. The ground moved under his feet, and only the thought of where they might take him while he was unconscious saved him from fainting. But even then common pride, the instinct not to make a scene, remained overpoweringly strong; embarrassment had more force than terror, it prevented him crying his fear aloud, it even urged him to go quietly. If the boy had not spoken again he might have gone.

'We'd better get moving, Fred,' the boy said.

'No,' Hale said. 'I'm not coming. I don't know him. My name's not Fred. I've never seen him before. He's just getting fresh,' and he walked rapidly away, with his head down, hopeless now—there wasn't time—only anxious to keep moving, to keep out in the clear sun; until from far down the front he heard a woman's winey voice singing, singing of brides and bouquets, of lilies and mourning shrouds, a Victorian ballad, and he moved towards it like someone who has been lost a long while in a desert makes for the glow of a fire.

'Why,' she said, 'if it isn't lonely heart,' and to his astonishment she was all by herself in a wilderness of chairs. 'They've gone to the gents,' she said.

'Can I sit down?' Hale asked. His voice broke with relief.

'If you've got twopence,' she said. 'I haven't.' She began to laugh, the great breasts pushing at her dress. 'Someone pinched

my bag,' she said. 'Every penny I've got.' He watched her with as-
tonishment. 'Oh,' she said, 'that's not the funny part. It's the letters.
He'll have had all Tom's letters to read. Were they passionate?
Tom'll be crazy when he hears.'

'You'll be wanting some money,' Hale said.

'Oh,' she said, 'I'm not worrying. Some nice feller will lend me
ten bob—when they come out of the gents.'

'They your friends?' Hale asked.

'I met 'em in the pub,' she said.

'You think,' Hale said, 'they'll come back from the gents?'

'My,' she said, 'you don't think—' She gazed up the parade,
then looked at Hale and began to laugh again. 'You win,' she said.
'They've pulled my leg properly. But there was only ten bob—and
Tom's letters.'

'Will you have lunch with me now?' Hale said.

'I had a snack in the pub,' she said. 'They treated me to that, so
I got something out of my ten bob.'

'Have a little more.'

'No, I don't fancy any more,' she said, and leaning far back in
the deck-chair with her skirt pulled up to her knees exposing her fine
legs, with an air of ribald luxury, she added, 'What a day,' sparkling
back at the bright sea. 'All the same,' she said, 'they'll wish they'd
never been born. I'm a sticker where right's concerned.'

'Your name's Lily?' Hale asked. He couldn't see the boy any
more: he'd gone: Cubitt had gone. There was nobody he could
recognize as far as he could see.

'That's what *they* called me,' she said. 'My real name's Ida.' The
old and vulgarized Grecian name recovered a little dignity. She
said, 'You look poorly. You ought to go off and eat somewhere.'

'Not if you won't come,' Hale said. 'I only want to stay here
with you.'

'Why, that's a nice speech,' she said. 'I wish Tom could hear
you—he writes passionate, but when it comes to talking—'

'Does he want to marry you?' Hale asked. She smelt of soap
and wine: comfort and peace and a slow sleepy physical enjoy-
ment, a touch of the nursery and the mother, stole from the big
tipsy mouth, the magnificent breasts and legs, and reached Hale's
withered and frightened and bitter little brain.

'He *was* married to me once,' Ida said. 'But he didn't know when he was lucky. Now he wants to come back. You should see his letters. I'd show them to you if they hadn't been stolen. He ought to be ashamed,' she said, laughing with pleasure, 'writing such things. You'd never think. And he was such a quiet fellow too. Well, I always say it's fun to be alive.'

'Will you take him back?' Hale asked, peering out from the valley of the shadow with sourness and envy.

'I should think not,' Ida said. 'I know all about him. There'd be no thrill. If I wanted a man I could do better than that now.' She wasn't boastful: only a little drunk and happy. 'I could marry money if I chose.'

'And how do you live now?' Hale said.

'From hand to mouth,' she said and winked at him and made the motion of tipping a glass. 'What's your name?'

'Fred.' He said it automatically: it was the name he always gave to chance acquaintances. From some obscure motive of secrecy he shielded his own name, Charles. From childhood he had loved secrecy, a hiding place, the dark, but it was in the dark he had met Kite, the boy, Cubitt, the whole mob.

'And how do you live?' she asked cheerfully. Men always liked to tell, and she liked to hear. She had an immense store of masculine experiences.

'Betting,' he said promptly, putting up his barrier of evasion.

'I like a flutter myself. Could you give me a tip, I wonder, for Brighton on Saturday?'

'Black Boy,' Hale said, 'in the four o'clock.'

'He's twenty to one.'

Hale looked at her with respect. 'Take it or leave it.'

'Oh, I'll take it,' Ida said. 'I always take a tip.'

'Whoever gives it you?'

'That's my system. Will you be there?'

'No,' Hale said. 'I can't make it.' He put his hand on her wrist. He wasn't going to run any more risks. He'd tell the news-editor he was taken ill: he'd resign: he'd do anything. Life was here beside him, he wasn't going to play around with death. 'Come to the station with me,' he said. 'Come back to town with me.'

"On a day like this,' Ida said. 'Not me. You've had too much town. You look stuffed up. A blow along the front'll do you good. Besides, there's lots of things I want to see. I want to see the Aquarium and Black Rock and I haven't been on the Palace Pier yet today. There's always something new on the Palace Pier. I'm out for a bit of fun.'

'We'll do those and then—'

'When I make a day of it,' Ida said, 'I like to make a real day of it. I told you—I'm a sticker.'

'I don't mind,' Hale said, 'if you'll stay with me.'

'Well, *you* can't steal my bag,' Ida said. 'But I warn you—I like to spend. I'm not satisfied with a ring here and a shot there: I want all the shows.'

'It's a long walk,' Hale said, 'to the Palace Pier in this sun. We'd better take a taxi.' But he made no immediate pass at Ida in the taxi, sitting there bonily crouched with his eyes on the parade: no sign of the boy or Cubitt in the bright broad day sweeping by. He turned reluctantly back, and, with the sense of her great open friendly breasts, fastened his mouth on hers and received the taste of port wine on his tongue and saw in the driver's mirror the old 1925 Morris following behind, with its split and flapping hood, its bent fender and cracked and discoloured windscreen. He watched it with his mouth on hers, shaking against her as the taxi ground slowly along beside the parade.

'Give me breath,' she said at last, pushing him off and straightening her hat. 'You believe in hard work,' she said. 'It's you little fellows—' she could feel his nerves jumping under her hand, and she shouted quickly through the tube at the driver, 'Don't stop. Go on back and round again.' He was like a man with fever.

'You're sick,' she said. 'You oughtn't to be alone. What's the matter with you?'

He couldn't keep it in. 'I'm going to die. I'm scared.'

'Have you seen a doctor?'

'They are no good. They can't do anything.'

'You oughtn't to be out alone,' Ida said. 'Did they tell you that—the doctors, I mean?'

'Yes,' he said and put his mouth on hers again because when he kissed her he could watch in the mirror the old Morris vibrating after them down the parade.

She pushed him off but kept her arms round him. 'They're crazy. You aren't that sick. You can't tell me I wouldn't know if you were that sick,' she said. 'I don't like to see a fellow throw up the sponge that way. It's a good world if you don't weaken.'

'It's all right,' he said, 'long as you are here.'

'That's better,' she said, 'be yourself,' and letting down the window with a rush for the air to come in, she pushed her arm through his and said in a frightened gentle way, 'You were just kidding, weren't you, when you said that about the doctors? It wasn't true, was it?'

'No,' Hale said wearily, 'it wasn't true.'

'That's a boy,' Ida said. 'You nearly had me scared for a moment. Nice thing it would have been for me if you'd passed out in this taxi. Something for Tom to read about in the paper, I'd say. But men are funny with me that way. Always trying to make out there's something wrong, money or the wife or the heart. You aren't the first who said he was dying. Never anything infectious though. Want to make the most of their last hours and all the rest of it. It comes of me being so big, I suppose. They think I'll mother them. I'm not saying I didn't fall for it the first time. "The doctors only give me a month," he said to me—that was five years ago. I see him regular now in Henekey's. "Hullo, you old ghost," I always say to him, and he stands me oysters and a Guinness.'

'No, I'm not sick,' Hale said. 'You needn't be scared.' He wasn't going to let his pride down as much as that again, even in return for the peaceful and natural embrace. The Grand went by, the old statesman dozing out the day, the Metropole. 'Here we are,' Hale said. 'You'll stay with me, won't you, even if I'm not sick.'

'Of course I will,' Ida said, hiccuping gently as she stepped out. 'I like you, Fred. I liked you the moment I saw you. You're a good sport, Fred. What's that crowd, there?' she asked with joyful curiosity, pointing to the gathering of neat and natty trousers, of bright blouses and bare arms and bleached and perfumed hair.

'With every watch I sell,' a man was shouting in the middle of it all, 'I give a free gift worth twenty times the value of the watch. Only a shilling, ladies and gents, only a shilling. With every watch I sell . . .'

'Get me a watch, Fred,' Ida said, pushing him gently, 'and give me threepence before you go. I want to get a wash.' They stood on the pavement at the entrance to the Palace Pier; the crowd was thick around them, passing in and out of the turnstiles, watching the pedlar: there was no sign anywhere of the Morris car.

'You don't want a wash, Ida,' Hale implored her. 'You're fine.'

'I've got to get a wash,' she said, 'I'm sweating all over. You just wait here. I'll only be two minutes.'

'You won't get a good wash here,' Hale said. 'Come to a hotel and have a drink—'

'I can't wait, Fred. Really I can't. Be a sport.'

Hale said, 'That ten shillings. You'd better have that too while I remember it.'

'It's real good of you, Fred. Can you spare it?'

'Be quick, Ida,' Hale said. 'I'll be here. Just here. By this turnstile. You won't be long, will you? I'll be here,' he repeated, putting his hand on a rail of the turnstile.

'Why,' Ida said, 'anyone'd think you were in love,' and she carried the image of him quite tenderly in her mind down the steps of the ladies' lavatory: the small rather battered man with the nails bitten close (she missed nothing) and the inkstains and the hand clutching the rail. He's a good geezer, she said to herself, I liked the way he looked even in that bar if I did laugh at him, and she began to sing again, softly this time, in her warm winey voice, 'One night—in an alley—Lord Rothschild said to me . . .' It was a long time since she'd hurried herself so for a man, and it wasn't more than four minutes before, cool and powdered and serene, she mounted into the bright Whitsun afternoon to find him gone. He wasn't by the turnstile, he wasn't in the crowd by the pedlar; she forced herself into that to make sure and found herself facing the flushed, permanently irritated salesman. 'What? Not give a shilling for a watch, and a free gift worth exactly twenty times the watch. I'm not saying the watch is worth much more than a shilling, though it's worth that for the looks alone, but with it a free gift twenty times—' She held out the ten-shilling note and got her small package and the change, thinking: he's probably gone to the gents, he'll be back; and taking up her place by the turnstile, she opened the little envelope which wrapped the watch round.

'Black Boy,' she read, 'in the four o'clock at Brighton,' and thought tenderly and proudly, 'That was his tip. He's a fellow who knows things,' and prepared patiently and happily to wait for him to return. She was a sticker. A clock away in the town struck half-past one.

The Boy paid his threepence and went through the turnstile. He moved rigidly past the rows of deck-chairs four deep where people were waiting for the orchestra to play. From behind he looked younger than he was in his dark thin ready-made suit a little too big for him at the hips, but when you met him face to face he looked older, the slatey eyes were touched with the annihilating eternity from which he had come and to which he went. The orchestra began to play: he felt the music as a movement in his belly: the violins wailed in his guts. He looked neither right nor left but went on.

In the Palace of Pleasure he made his way past the peepshows, the slot-machines and the quoits to a shooting-booth. The shelves of dolls stared down with glassy innocence, like Virgins in a church repository. The Boy looked up: chestnut ringlets, blue orbs and painted cheeks: he thought—Hail Mary . . . in the hour of our death. 'I'll have six shots,' he said.

'Oh, it's you, is it?' the stall-holder said, eyeing him with uneasy distaste.

'Yes, it's me,' the Boy said. 'Have you got the time on you, Bill?'

'What do you mean—the time? There's a clock up there in the hall, isn't there?'

'It says nearly a quarter-to-two. I didn't think it was that late.'

'That clock's always right,' the man said. He came down to the end of the booth pistol in hand. 'It's always right, see,' he said. 'It doesn't stand for any phoney alibis. A quarter-to-two, that's the time.'

'That's all right, Bill,' the Boy said. 'A quarter-to-two. I just wanted to know. Give me that pistol.' He raised it: the young bony hand was steady as a rock: he put six shots inside the bull. 'That's worth a prize,' he said.

'You can take your bloody prize,' Bill said, 'and hop it. What do you want? Chocolates?'

'I don't eat chocolates,' the Boy said.

'Packet of Players?'

'I don't smoke.'

'You'll have to have a doll then or a glass vase.'

'The doll'll do,' the Boy said. 'I'll have that one—the one up there with the brown hair.'

'You getting a family?' the man said, but the Boy didn't answer, walking rigidly away past the other booths, with the smell of gun-powder on his fingers, holding the Mother of God by the hair. The water washed round the piles at the end of the pier, dark poison-bottle green, mottled with seaweed, and the salt wind smarted on his lips. He climbed the ladder on to the tea-terrace and looked around; nearly every table was full. He went inside the glass shelter and round into the long narrow tea-room which faced west, perched fifty feet above the slow withdrawing tide. A table was free and he sat down where he could see all the room and across the water to the pale parade.

'I'll wait,' he said to the girl who came for his order. 'I've got friends coming.' The window was open and he could hear the low waves beating at the pier and the music of the orchestra—faint and sad, borne away on the wind towards the shore. He said, 'They are late. What time is it?' His fingers pulled absent-mindedly at the doll's hair, detaching the brown wool.

'It's nearly ten-to-two,' the girl said.

'All the clocks on this pier are fast,' he said.

'Oh, no,' the girl said. 'It's real London time.'

'Take the doll,' the Boy said. 'It's no good to me. I just won it in one of those shooting booths. It's no good to me.'

'Can I really?' the girl said.

'Go on. Take it. Stick it up in your room and pray.' He tossed it at her, watching the door impatiently. His body was stiffly con-trolled. The only sign of nervousness he showed was a slight tick in his cheek through the soft chicken down, where you might have expected a dimple. It beat more impatiently when Cubitt appeared, and with him Dallow, a stout muscular man with a broken nose and an expression of brutal simplicity.

'Well?' the Boy said.

'It's all right,' Cubitt said.

'Where's Spicer?'

'He's coming,' Dallow said. 'He's just gone into the gents to have a wash.'

'He ought to have come straight,' the Boy said. 'You're late. I said a quarter-to-two sharp.'

'Don't take on so,' Cubitt said. 'All you'd got to do was to come straight across.'

'I had to tidy up,' the Boy said. He beckoned to the waitress. 'Four fish and chips and a pot of tea. There's another coming.'

'Spicer won't want fish and chips,' Dallow said. 'He's got no appetite.'

'He'd better have an appetite,' the Boy said, and leaning his face on his hands, he watched Spicer's pale-faced progress up the tearoom and felt anger grinding at his guts like the tide at the piles below. 'It's five-to-two,' he said. 'That's right, isn't it? It's five-to-two?' he called to the waitress.

'It took longer than we thought,' Spicer said, dropping into the chair, dark and pallid and spotty. He looked with nausea at the brown crackling slab of fish the girl set before him. 'I'm not hungry,' he said. 'I can't eat this. What do you think I am?' and they all three left their fish untasted as they stared at the Boy—like children before his ageless eyes.

The Boy poured anchovy sauce out over his chips. 'Eat,' he said. 'Go on. Eat.' Dallow suddenly grinned. 'He's got no appetite,' he said and stuffed his mouth with fish. They all talked low, their words lost to those around in the hubbub of plates and voices and the steady surge of the sea. Cubitt followed suit, picking at his fish: only Spicer wouldn't eat. He sat stubbornly there, grey-haired and sea-sick.

'Give me a drink, Pinkie,' he said. 'I can't swallow this stuff.'

'You aren't going to have a drink, not today,' the Boy said. 'Go on. Eat.'

Spicer put some fish to his mouth. 'I'll be sick,' he said, 'if I eat.'

'Spew then,' the Boy said. 'Spew if you like. You haven't any guts to spew.' He said to Dallow, 'Did it go all right?'

'It was beautiful,' Dallow said. 'Me and Cubitt planted him. We gave the cards to Spicer.'

'You put 'em out all right?' the Boy said.

'Of course I put 'em out,' Spicer said.

'All along the parade?'

'Of course I put 'em out. I don't see why you get so fussed about the cards.'

'You don't see much,' the Boy said. 'They're an alibi, aren't they?' He dropped his voice and whispered it over the fish. 'They prove he kept to programme. They show he died after two.' He raised his voice again. 'Listen. Do you hear that?'

Very faintly in the town a clock chimed and struck twice.

'Suppose they found him already?' Spicer said.

'Then that's just too bad for us,' the Boy said.

'What about that polony he was with?'

'She doesn't matter,' the Boy said. 'She's just a buer—he gave her a half. I saw him hand it out.'

'You take account of most things,' Dallow said with admiration. He poured himself a cup of black tea and helped himself to five lumps of sugar.

'I take account of what I do myself,' the Boy said. 'Where did you put the cards?' he said to Spicer.

'I put one of 'em in Snow's,' Spicer said.

'What do you mean? Snow's?'

'He had to eat, hadn't he?' Spicer said. 'The paper said so. You said I was to follow the paper. It'd look odd, wouldn't it, if he didn't eat, and he always put one where he eats.'

'It'd look odder,' the Boy said, 'if the waitress spotted your face wasn't right and she found it soon as you left. Where did you put it in Snow's?'

'Under the table-cloth,' Spicer said. 'That's what he always does. There'll have been plenty at that table since me. She won't know it wasn't him. I don't suppose she'll find it before night, when she takes off the cloth. Maybe it'll even be another girl.'

'You go back,' the Boy said, 'and bring that card here. I'm not taking chances.'

'I'll not go back.' Spicer's voice rose above a whisper, and once again they all three stared at the Boy in silence.

'You go, Cubitt,' the Boy said. 'Maybe it had better not be him again.'

'Not me,' Cubitt said. 'Suppose they'd found the card and saw me looking. Better take a chance and leave it alone,' he urged in a whisper.

'Talk natural,' the Boy said, 'talk natural,' as the waitress came back to the table.

'Do you boys want any more?' she asked.

'Yes,' the Boy said, 'we'll have ice-cream.'

'Stow it, Pinkie,' Dallow protested when the girl had left them, 'we don't want ice-cream. We ain't a lot of tarts, Pinkie.'

'If you don't want ice-cream, Dallow,' the Boy said, 'you go to Snow's and get that card. You've got guts, haven't you?'

'I thought we was done with it all,' Dallow said. 'I've done enough. I've got guts, you know that, but I was scared stiff . . . Why, if they've found him before time, it'd be crazy to go into Snow's.'

'Don't talk so loud,' the Boy said. 'If nobody else'll go,' he said, 'I'll go. I'm not scared. Only I get tired sometimes of working with a mob like you. Sometimes I think I'd be better alone.' Afternoon moved across the water. He said, 'Kite was all right, but Kite's dead. Which was your table?' he asked Spicer.

'Just inside. On the right of the door. A table for one. It's got flowers on it.'

'What flowers?'

'I don't know what flowers,' Spicer said. 'Yellow flowers.'

'Don't go, Pinkie,' Dallow said, 'better leave it alone. You can't tell what'll happen,' but the Boy was already on his feet, moving stiffly down the long narrow room above the sea. You couldn't tell if he was scared; his young ancient poker-face told nothing.

In Snow's the rush was over and the table free. The wireless droned a programme of weary music, broadcast by a cinema organist—a great *vox humana* trembled across the crumby stained desert of used cloths: the world's wet mouth lamenting over life. The waitress whipped the cloths off as soon as the tables were free and laid tea things. Nobody paid any attention to the Boy; they turned their back when he looked at them. He slipped his hand under the cloth and found nothing there. Suddenly the little spurt of vicious anger rose again in the Boy's brain and he smashed a salt sprinkler down on the table so hard that the base cracked. A waitress detached herself from the gossiping group and came towards him, cold-eyed, acquisitive, ash-blonde. 'Well?' she said, taking in the shabby suit, the too young face.

'I want service,' the Boy said.

'You're late for the Lunch.'

'I don't want lunch,' the Boy said. 'I want a cup of tea and a plate of biscuits.'

'Will you go to one of the tables laid for tea, please?'

'No,' the Boy said. 'This table suits me.'

She sailed away again, superior and disapproving, and he called after her, 'Will you take that order?'

'The waitress serving your table will be here in a minute,' she said and moved away to the gossips by the service door. The Boy shifted his chair, the nerve in his cheek twitched, again he put his hand under the cloth: it was a tiny action, but it might hang him if he was observed. But he could feel nothing, and he thought with fury of Spicer: he'll muddle once too often, we'd be better without him.

'Was it tea you wanted, sir?' He looked sharply up with his hand under the cloth: one of those girls who creep about, he thought, as if they were afraid of their own footsteps: a pale thin girl younger than himself.

He said, 'I gave the order once.'

She apologized abjectly. 'There's been such a rush. And it's my first day. This was the only breathing spell. Have you lost something?'

He withdrew his hand, watching her with dangerous and unfeeling eyes. His cheek twitched again; it was the little things which tripped you up, he could think of no reason at all for having his hand under the table. She went on helpfully, 'I'll have to change the cloth again for tea, so if you've lost—' In no time she had cleared the table of pepper and salt and mustard, the cutlery and the O.K. sauce, the yellow flowers, had nipped together the corners of the cloth and lifted it in one movement from the table, crumbs and all.

'There's nothing there, sir,' she said. He looked at the bare table-top and said, 'I hadn't lost anything.' She began to lay a fresh cloth for tea. She seemed to find something agreeable about him which made her talk, something in common perhaps—youth and shabbiness and a kind of ignorance in the dapper café. Already she had apparently forgotten his exploring hand. But would she remember, he wondered, if later people asked her questions? He despised her quiet, her pallor, her desire to please: did she also observe, remember . . . ? 'You wouldn't guess,' she said, 'what I found here only ten minutes ago. When I changed the cloth.'

'Do you always change the cloth?' the Boy asked.

'Oh, no,' she said, putting out the tea things, 'but a customer upset his drink and when I changed it, there was one of Kolley Kibber's cards, worth ten shillings. It was quite a shock,' she said, lingering gratefully with the tray, 'and the others don't like it. You see it's only my second day here. They say I was a fool not to challenge him and get the prize.'

'Why didn't you challenge him?'

'Because I never thought. He wasn't a bit like the photograph.'

'Maybe the card had been there all the morning.'

'Oh, no,' she said, 'it couldn't have been. He was the first man at this table.'

'Well,' the Boy said, 'it don't make any odds. You've *got* the card.'

'Oh yes, I've got it. Only it don't seem quite fair—you see what I mean—him being so different. I *might* have got the prize. I can tell you I ran to the door when I saw the card: I didn't wait.'

'And did you see him?'

She shook her head.

'I suppose,' the Boy said, 'you hadn't looked at him close. Else you'd have known.'

'I always look at you close,' the girl said, 'the customer, I mean. You see, I'm new. I get a bit scared. I don't want to do anything to offend. Oh,' she said aghast, 'like standing here talking when you want a cup of tea.'

'That's all right,' the Boy said. He smiled at her stiffly; he couldn't use those muscles with any naturalness. 'You're the kind of girl I like—' The words were the wrong ones; he saw it at once and altered them. 'I mean,' he said, 'I like a girl who's friendly. Some of these here—they freeze you.'

'They freeze me.'

'You're sensitive, that's what it is,' the Boy said, 'like me.' He said abruptly, 'I suppose you wouldn't recognize that newspaper man again? I mean, he may be still about.'

'Oh, yes,' she said, 'I'd know him. I've got a memory for faces.'

The Boy's cheek twitched. He said, 'I see you and I've got a bit in common. We ought to get together one evening. What's your name?'

'Rose.'

He put a coin on the table and got up. 'But your tea,' she said.

'Here we been talking, and I had an appointment at two sharp.'

'Oh, I'm so sorry,' Rose said. 'You should've stopped me.'

'That's all right,' the Boy said. 'I liked it. It's only ten-past anyway—by your clock. When do you get off of an evening?'

'We don't close till half-past ten except on Sundays.'

'I'll be seeing you,' the Boy said. 'You an' me have things in common.'

3

Ida Arnold broke her way across the Strand; she couldn't be bothered to wait for the signals, and she didn't trust the Belisha beacons. She made her way under the radiators of the buses; the drivers ground their brakes and glared at her, and she grinned back at them. She was always a little flushed as the clock struck eleven and she reached Henekey's, as if she had emerged from some adventure which had given her a better opinion of herself. But she wasn't the first in Henekey's. 'Hullo, you old ghost,' she said, and the sombre thin man in black with a bowler hat sitting beside a wine barrel said, 'Oh, forget it, Ida. Forget it.'

'You in mourning for yourself?' Ida asked, cocking her hat at a better angle in a mirror which advertised White Horse: she didn't look a day over forty.

'My wife's dead. Have a Guinness, Ida?'

'Yes. I'll have a Guinness. I didn't even know you had a wife.'

'We don't know much about each other, that's what it is, Ida,' he said. 'Why, I don't even know how you live or how many husbands you've had.'

'Oh, there's only been one Tom,' Ida said.

'There's been more than Tom in *your* life.'

'You ought to know,' Ida said.

'Give me a glass of Ruby,' the sombre man said. 'I was just thinking when you came in, Ida, why shouldn't we two come together again?'

'You and Tom always want to start again,' Ida said. 'Why don't you keep tight hold when you've got a girl?'

'What with my little bit of money and yours—'

'I like to start something fresh,' Ida said. 'Not off with the new and on with the old.'

'But you've a kind heart, Ida.'

'That's what you call it,' Ida said, and in the dark depth of her Guinness kindness winked up at her, a bit sly, a bit earthy, having a good time. 'Do you ever have a bit on the horses?' she asked.

'I don't believe in betting. It's a mug's game.'

'That's it,' Ida said. 'A mug's game. You never know whether you'll be up or down. I like it,' she said with passion, looking across the wine barrel at the thin pale man, her face more flushed than ever, more young, more kind. 'Black Boy,' she said softly.

'Eh, what's that?' the ghost said sharply, snatching a glance at his face in the White Horse mirror.

'It's the name of a horse,' she said, 'that's all. A fellow gave it me at Brighton. I was wondering if maybe I'd see him at the races. He got lost somehow. I liked him. You didn't know whatever he'd be saying next. I owe him money, too.'

'You saw about this Kolley Kibber at Brighton the other day?'

'Found him dead, didn't they? I saw a poster.'

'They've had the inquest.'

'Did he kill himself?'

'Oh, no. Just his heart. The heat knocked him over. But the paper's paid the prize to the man who found him. Ten guineas,' the ghost said, 'for finding a corpse.' He laid the paper bitterly down on the wine barrel. 'Give me another Ruby.'

'Why,' Ida said. 'Is that picture the man who found him? The little rat. That's where he went to. No wonder he didn't need his money back.'

'No, no, that's not *him*,' the ghost said. 'That's Kolley Kibber.' He took a little wooden pick out of a paper packet and began to scrape his teeth.

'Oh,' Ida said. It was like a blow. 'Then he wasn't trying it on,' she said. 'He *was* sick.' She remembered how his hand had shaken in the taxi and how he had implored her not to leave him, just as if he had known he was going to die before she came back. But he hadn't made a scene. 'He was a gentleman,' she said gently. He must have fallen there by the turnstile as soon as she had turned her back, and she had gone on down without knowing into the ladies. A sense of tears came to her now in Henekey's; she measured those polished white steps down to the wash-basins as if they were the slow stages of a tragedy.

'Ah well,' the ghost said gloomily, 'we've all got to die.'

'Yes,' Ida said, 'but he wouldn't've wanted to die any more than I want to die.' She began to read and exclaimed almost at once: 'What made him walk all that way in that heat?' For he hadn't dropped at the turnstile: he'd gone back all the way they'd come, sat in a shelter . . .

'He'd got his job to do.'

'He didn't say anything to me about a job. He said, "I'll be here. I'll stay right here by this turnstile." He said, "Be quick, Ida. I'll be just here,"' and as she repeated what she could remember of his words she had a feeling that later, in an hour or two, when things got straightened out, she would want to cry a bit for the death of that scared passionate bag of bones who called himself—

'Why,' she said, 'whatever do they mean? Read here.'

'What about it?' the man said.

'The bitches,' Ida said, 'what would they go and tell a lie like that for?'

'What lie? Have another Guinness. You don't want to fuss about that.'

'I don't mind if I do,' Ida said, but when she had taken a long draught she returned to the paper. She had instincts, and now her instincts told her there was something odd, something which didn't smell right. 'These girls,' she said, 'he tried to pick up, they say a man came along who called him "Fred", and he said he wasn't Fred and he didn't know the man.'

'What about it? Listen, Ida, let's go to the pictures.'

'But he *was* Fred. He told me he was Fred.'

'He was Charles. You can read it there. Charles Hale.'

'That don't signify,' Ida said. 'A man always has a different name for strangers. You aren't telling me your real name's Clarence. And a man don't have a different name for every girl. He'd get confused. You know you always stick to Clarence. You can't tell me much about men I don't know.'

'It don't mean anything. You can read how it was. They just happened to mention it. Nobody took any notice of that.'

She said sadly, 'Nobody's taken any notice of anything. You can read it here. He hadn't got any folks to make a fuss. "The Coroner asked if any relation of the deceased was present, and the police witness stated that they could trace no relations other than a second cousin in Middlesbrough." It sounds sort of lonely,' she said. 'Nobody there to ask questions.'

'I know what loneliness is, Ida,' the sombre man said. 'I've been alone a month now.'

She took no notice of him: she was back at Brighton on Whit Monday, thinking how while she waited there, he must have been dying, walking along the front to Hove, dying, and the cheap drama and pathos of the thought weakened her heart towards him. She was of the people, she cried in cinemas at *David Copperfield*, when she was drunk all the old ballads her mother had known came easily to her lips, her homely heart was touched by the word 'tragedy'. 'The second cousin in Middlesbrough—he was represented by counsel,' she said. 'What does that mean?'

'I suppose if this Kolly Kibber hasn't left a will, he gets any money there is. He wouldn't want any talk of suicide because of the life assurance.'

'He didn't ask any questions.'

'There wasn't any need. No one made out he'd killed himself.'

'Perhaps he did all the same,' Ida said. 'There was something queer about him. I'd like to 'ave asked some questions.'

'What about? It's plain enough.'

A man in plus-fours and a striped tie came to the bar. 'Hullo, Ida,' he called.

'Hullo, Harry,' she said sadly, staring at the paper.

'Have a drink?'

'I've got a drink, thank you.'

'Swallow it down and have another.'

'No, I don't want any more, thank you,' she said. 'If I'd been there—'

'What'd have been the good?' the sombre man said.

'I could've asked questions.'

'Questions, questions,' he said irritably. 'You keep on saying questions. What about beats me.'

'Why he said he wasn't Fred.'

'He wasn't Fred. He was Charles.'

'It's not natural.' The more she thought about it the more she wished she had been there: it was like a pain in the heart, the thought that no one at the inquest was interested, the second cousin stayed in Middlesbrough, his counsel asked no questions, and Fred's own paper only gave him half a column. On the front page was another photograph—the new Kolley Kibber: he was going to be at Bournemouth tomorrow. They might have waited, she thought, a week. It would have shown respect.

'I'd like to have asked them why he left me like that, to go scampering down the front in that sun.'

'He had his job to do. He had to leave those cards.'

'Why did he tell me he'd wait?'

'Ah,' the sombre man said, 'you'd have to ask him that,' and at the words it was almost as if he *was* trying to answer her, answer her in his own kind of hieroglyphics, in the obscure pain, speaking in her nerves as a ghost would have to speak. Ida believed in ghosts.

'There's a lot he'd say if he could,' she said. She took up the paper again and read slowly. 'He did his job to the end,' she said tenderly. She liked men who did their jobs: there was a kind of vitality about it. He'd dropped his cards all the way down the front: they'd come back to the office: from under a boat, from a litter-basket, a child's pail. He had only a few left when 'Mr Alfred Jefferson, described as a chief clerk, of Clapham' found him. 'If he did kill himself,' she said (she was the only counsel to represent the dead), 'he did his job first.'

'But he didn't kill himself,' Clarence said. 'You've only got to read. They cut him up and they say he died natural.'

'That's queer.' Ida said. 'He went and left one in a restaurant. I knew he was hungry. He kept on wanting to eat, but whatever made him slip away like that all by himself and leave me waiting. It sounds crazy.'

'I suppose he changed his mind about you, Ida.'

'I don't like it,' Ida said. 'It sounds strange to me. I wish I'd been there. I'd have asked 'em a few questions.'

'What about you and me going across to the flickers, Ida?'

'I'm not in the mood,' Ida said. 'It's not every day you lose a friend. And you oughtn't to be in the mood either with your wife just dead.'

"She's been gone a month now,' Clarence said. 'You can't expect anyone to go on mourning for ever.'

'A month's not so long,' Ida said sadly, brooding over the paper. A day, she thought, that's all he's been gone, and I dare say there's not another soul but me thinking about him: just someone he picked up for a drink and a cuddle, and again the easy pathos touched her friendly and popular heart. She wouldn't have given it all another thought if there had been other relations, besides the second cousin in Middlesbrough, if he hadn't been so alone as well as dead. But there *was* something fishy to her nose, though there was nothing she could put her finger on except that 'Fred'— and everyone would say the same: 'He wasn't Fred. You've only to read. Charles Hale.'

'You oughtn't to fuss about that, Ida. It's none of your business.'

'I know,' she said. 'It's none of mine.' But it's none of anybody's, her heart repeated to her: that was the trouble: no one but her to ask questions. She knew a woman once who'd seen her husband after he was dead standing by the wireless set trying to twiddle the knob: she twiddled the way he wanted and he disappeared and immediately she heard an announcer say on Midland Regional: 'Gale Warning in the Channel.' She had been thinking of taking one of the Sunday trips to Calais, that was the point. It just showed: you couldn't laugh at the idea of ghosts. And if Fred, she thought, wanted to tell someone something, it wouldn't be to his second cousin in Middlesbrough that he'd go; why shouldn't he come to me? He had left her waiting there; she had waited nearly half an hour: perhaps he wanted to tell her why. 'He was a gentleman,' she said aloud, and with bolder resolution she cocked her hat and smoothed her hair and rose from the wine barrel. 'I've got to be going,' she said. 'So long, Clarence.'

'Where to? I've never known you in such a hurry, Ida,' he complained bitterly over the Guinness.

Ida put her finger on the paper. 'Someone ought to be *there*,' she said, 'even if second cousins aren't.'

'He won't care who's putting him in the ground.'

'You never know,' Ida said, remembering the ghost by the radio set. 'It shows respect. Besides—I *like* a funeral.'

But he wasn't exactly being put in the ground in the bright new flowery suburb where he had lodged. There were no unhygienic buryings in that place. Two brick towers like those of a Scandinavian town hall, cloisters with little plaques along the walls like school war memorials, a bare cold secular chapel which could be adapted quietly and conveniently to any creed: no cemetery, wax flowers, impoverished jam-pots of wilting wild flowers. Ida was late. Hesitating a moment outside the door for fear the place might be full of Fred's friends, she thought someone had turned on the National Programme. She knew that cultured inexpressive voice, but when she opened the door, a man, not a machine, stood up in a black cassock saying 'Heaven'. There was nobody there but someone who looked like a landlady, a servant who had parked a pram outside, two men impatiently whispering.

'Our belief in heaven,' the clergyman went on, 'is not qualified by our disbelief in the old medieval hell. We believe,' he said, glancing swiftly along the smooth polished slipway towards the New Art doors through which the coffin would be launched into the flames, 'we believe that this our brother is already at one with the One.' He stamped his words like little pats of butter with his personal mark. 'He has attained unity. We do not know what that One is with whom (or with which) he is now at one. We do not retain the old medieval beliefs in glassy seas and golden crowns. Truth is beauty and there is more beauty for us, a truth-loving generation, in the certainty that our brother is at this moment reabsorbed in the universal spirit.' He touched a little buzzer, the New Art doors opened, the flames flapped and the coffin slid smoothly down into the fiery sea. The doors closed, the nurse rose and made for the door, the clergyman smiled gently from behind the slipway, like a conjurer who has produced his nine hundred and fortieth rabbit without a hitch.

It was all over. Ida squeezed out with difficulty a last tear into a handkerchief scented with Californian Poppy. She liked a funeral—but it was with horror—as other people like a ghost story. Death shocked her, life was so important. She wasn't religious. She didn't believe in heaven or hell, only in ghosts, ouija boards, tables which rapped and little inept voices speaking plaintively of flowers. Let Papists treat death with flippancy: life wasn't so important perhaps to them as what came after: but to her death was the end of everything. At one with the One—it didn't mean a thing beside a glass of Guinness on a sunny day. She believed in ghosts, but you couldn't call that thin transparent existence life eternal: the squeak of a board, a piece of ectoplasm in a glass cupboard at the psychical research headquarters, a voice she'd heard once at a séance saying, 'Everything is very beautiful on the upper plane. There are flowers everywhere.'

Flowers, Ida thought scornfully; that wasn't life. Life was sunlight on brass bedposts, Ruby port, the leap of the heart when the outsider you have backed passes the post and the colours go bobbing up. Life was poor Fred's mouth pressed down on hers in the taxi, vibrating with the engine along the parade. What was the sense of dying if it made you babble of flowers? Fred didn't want flowers, he wanted—and the enjoyable distress she had felt in Henekey's returned. She took life with a deadly seriousness: she was prepared to cause any amount of unhappiness to anyone in order to defend the only thing she believed in. To lose your lover—'broken hearts,' she would say, 'always mend,' to be maimed or blinded—'lucky,' she'd tell you, 'to be alive at all.' There was something dangerous and remorseless in her optimism, whether she was laughing in Henekey's or weeping at a funeral or a marriage.

She came out of the crematorium, and there from the twin towers above her head fumed the very last of Fred, a thin stream of grey smoke from the ovens. People passing up the flowery suburban road looked up and noted the smoke; it had been a busy day at the furnaces. Fred dropped in indistinguishable grey ash on the pink blossoms: he became part of the smoke nuisance over London, and Ida wept.

But while she wept a determination grew; it grew all the way to the tram lines which would lead her back to her familiar territory, to the bars and the electric signs and the variety theatres. Man is made by the places in which he lives, and Ida's mind worked with the simplicity and the regularity of a sky sign: the ever-tipping glass, the ever-revolving wheel, the plain question flashing on and off: 'Do You Use Forhams for the Gums?' I'd do as much for Tom, she thought, for Clarence, that old deceitful ghost in Henekey's, for Harry. It's the least you can do for anyone—ask questions, questions at inquests, questions at séances. Somebody had made Fred unhappy, and somebody was going to be made unhappy in turn. An eye for an eye. If you believed in God, you might leave vengeance to him, but you couldn't trust the One, the universal spirit. Vengeance was Ida's, just as much as reward was Ida's, the soft gluey mouth affixed in taxis, the warm handclasp in cinemas, the only reward there was. And vengeance and reward—they both were fun.

The train tingled and sparked down the Embankment. If it was a woman who had made Fred unhappy, she'd tell her what she thought. If Fred had killed himself, she'd find it out, the papers would print the news, someone would suffer. Ida was going to begin at the beginning and work right on. She was a sticker.

The first stage (she had held the paper in her hand all through the service) was Molly Pink, 'described as a private secretary', employed by Messrs Carter & Galloway.

Ida came up from Charing Cross Station, into the hot and windy light in the Strand flickering on the carburettors; in an upper room of Stanley Gibbons a man with a long grey Edwardian moustache sat in a window examining a postage stamp through a magnifying glass; a great dray laden with barrels stamped by, and the fountains played in Trafalgar Square, a cool translucent flower blooming and dropping into the drab sooty basins. It'll cost money, Ida repeated to herself, it always costs money if you want to know the truth, and she walked slowly up St Martin's Lane calculating, while all the time beneath the melancholy and the resolution, her heart beat faster to the refrain: it's exciting, it's fun, it's living. In Seven Dials the negroes were hanging round the public house doors in tight natty suitings and old school ties, and Ida recognized one of them and passed the time of day. 'How's business, Joe?' The great white teeth went on like a row of lights in the darkness above the bright striped shirt. 'Fine, Ida, fine.'

'And the hay fever?'

'Tur'ble, Ida, tur'ble.'

'So long, Joe.'

'So long, Ida.'

It was a quarter of an hour's walk to Messrs Carter & Galloway who lived at the very top of a tall building on the outskirts of Grays Inn. She had to economize now: she wouldn't even take a bus, and when she got to the dusty antiquated building, there wasn't a lift. The long flights of stone stairs wearied Ida. She'd had a long day and nothing to eat but a bun at the station. She sat down on a window-sill and took off her shoes. Her feet were hot, she wiggled her toes. An old gentleman came down. He had a long moustache and a sidelong raffish look. He wore a check coat, a yellow waistcoat and a grey bowler. He took off his bowler. 'In distress, madam?' he asked peering down at Ida with little bleary eyes. 'Be of assistance?'

'I don't allow anyone else to scratch my toes,' Ida said.

'Ha, ha,' the old gentleman said, 'a card. After my own heart. Up or down?'

'Up. All the way to the top.'

'Carter & Galloway. Good firm. Tell 'em I sent you.'

'What's your name?'

'Moyne. Charlie Moyne. Seen you here before.'

'Never.'

'Some place else. Never forget fine figure of a woman. Tell 'em Moyne sent you. Give you special terms.'

'Why don't they have a lift in this place?'

'Old-fashioned people. Old-fashioned myself. Seen you at Epsom.'

'You might have.'

'Always tell a sporting woman. Ask you round the corner to split a bottle of fizz if those beggars hadn't taken the last fiver I came out with. Wanted to go and lay a couple. Have to go home first. Odds'll go down while I'm doing it. You'll see. You couldn't oblige me, I suppose? Two quid, Charlie Moyne.' The bloodshot eyes watched her without hope, a little aloof and careless; the buttons on the yellow waistcoat stirred as the old heart hammered.

'Here,' Ida said, 'you can have a quid; now run along.'

'Awfully kind of you. Give me your card. Post you a cheque tonight.'

'I haven't got a card,' Ida said.

'Came out without mine, too. Never mind. Charlie Moyne. Care of Carter & Galloway. All know me here.'

'That's all right,' Ida said. 'I'll see you again. I've got to be going on up.'

'Take my arm.' He helped her up. 'Tell 'em Moyne sent you. Special terms.' She looked back at the turn of the stairs. He was tucking the pound note away in his waistcoat, smoothing the moustache which was still golden at the tips, like a cigarette smoker's fingers, setting his bowler at an angle. Poor old geezer, Ida thought, he never expected to get that, watching him go down the stairs in his jaunty and ancient despair.

There were only two doors on the top landing. She opened one marked 'Enquiries', and there without a doubt was Molly Pink. In a little room hardly larger than a broom cupboard she sat beside a gas-ring sucking a sweet. A kettle hissed at Ida as she entered. A swollen spotty face glared back at her without a word.

'Excuse me,' Ida said.

'The partners is out.'

'I came to see *you*.'

The mouth fell a little open, a lump of toffee stirred on the tongue, the kettle whistled.

'Me?'

'Yes,' Ida said. 'You'd better look out. The kettle'll boil over. You *are* Molly Pink?'

'You want a cup?' The room was lined from floor to ceiling with files. A little window disclosed through the undisturbed dust of many years another block of buildings with the same arrangement of windows staring dustily back like a reflection. A dead fly hung in a broken web.

'I don't like tea,' Ida said.

'That's lucky. There's only one cup,' Molly said, filling a thick brown teapot with a chipped spout.

'A friend of mine called Moyne . . .' Ida began.

'Oh, him!' Molly said. 'We just turned him out of house and home.' A copy of *Woman and Beauty* was propped open on her typewriter, and her eyes slid continually back to it.

'Out of house and home?'

'House and home. He came to see the partners. He tried to blarney.'

'Did he see them?'

'The partners is out. Have a toffee?'

'It's bad for the figure,' Ida said.

'I make up for it. I don't eat breakfast.'

Over Molly's head Ida could see the labels on the files: 'Rents of 1–6 Mud Lane.' 'Rents of Wainage Estate, Balham.' 'Rents of . . .' They were surrounded by the pride of ownership, property . . .

'I came here,' Ida said, 'because you met a friend of mine.'

'Sit down.' Molly said. 'That's the client's chair. I has to entertain 'em. Mr Moyne's not a friend.'

'Not Moyne. Someone called Hale.'

'I don't want any more to do with that business. You ought to 'ave seen the partners. They was furious. I had to have a day off for the inquest. They kept me hours late next day.'

'I just want to hear what happened.'

'What happened! The partners is awful when roused.'

'I mean about Fred—Hale.'

'I didn't exactly know him.'

'That man you said at the inquest came up—'

'He wasn't a man. He was just a kid. He knew Mr Hale.'

'But in the paper it said—'

'Oh, Mr Hale *said* he didn't know him. I didn't tell them different. They didn't ask me. Except was there anything odd in his manner? Well, there wasn't anything you'd call odd. He was just scared, that's all. We get lots like that in here.'

'But you didn't tell them that?'

'That's nothing uncommon. I knew what it was at once. He owed the kid money. We get lots like that. Like Charlie Moyne.'

'He was scared was he? Poor old Fred.'

' "I'm not Fred," he said, sharp as you please. But I could tell all right. So could my friend.'

'What was the kid like?'

'Oh, just a kid.'

'Tall?'

'Not particularly.'

'Fair?'

'I couldn't say that.'

'How old was he?'

'—Bout my age, I dessay.'

'What's that?'

'Eighteen,' Molly said, staring defiantly across the typewriter and the steaming kettle, sucking a toffee.

'Did he ask for money?'

'He didn't have time to ask for money.'

'You didn't notice anything else?'

'He was awful anxious for me to go along with him. But I couldn't, not with my friend there.'

'Thanks,' Ida said, 'it's something learnt.'

'You a woman detective?' Molly asked.

'Oh, no, I'm just a friend of his.'

There *was* something fishy: she was convinced of it now. She remembered again how scared he'd been in the taxi, and going down Holborn towards her digs behind Russell Square, in the late afternoon sun, she thought again of the way in which he had handed her the ten shillings before she went down into the ladies. He was a real gentleman: perhaps it was the last few shillings he had: and those people—that boy—dunning him for money. Perhaps he was another one ruined like Charlie Moyne, and now that her memory of his face was getting a bit dim, she couldn't help lending him a few of Charlie Moyne's features, the bloodshot eyes if nothing else. Sporting gentlemen, free-handed gentlemen, real gentlemen. The dewlaps of the commercials drooped in the hall of the Imperial, the sun lay flat across the plane trees, and a bell rang and rang for tea in a boarding-house in Coram Street.

I'll try the Board, Ida thought, and then I'll know.

When she got in, there was a card on the hall table, a card of Brighton Pier: if I was superstitious, she thought, if I was superstitious. She turned it over. It was only from Phil Corkery, asking her to come down. She had the same every year from Eastbourne, Hastings and once from Aberystwyth. But she never went. He wasn't someone she liked to encourage. Too quiet. Not what she called a man.

She went to the basement stairs and called Old Crowe. She needed two sets of fingers for the Board and she knew it would give the old man pleasure. 'Old Crowe,' she called, peering down the stone stairs. 'Old Crowe.'

'What is it, Ida?'

'I'm going to have a turn at the Board.'

She didn't wait for him, but went on up to her bed-sitting-room to make ready. The room faced east and the sun had gone. It was cold and dusk. Ida turned on the gas-fire and drew the old scarlet velvet curtains to shut out the grey sky and the chimney-pots. Then she patted the divan bed into shape and drew two chairs to the table. In a glass-fronted cupboard her life stared back at her—a good life: pieces of china bought at the seaside, a photograph of Tom, an Edgar Wallace, a Netta Syrett from a second-hand stall, some sheets of music, *The Good Companions,* her mother's picture, more china, a few jointed animals made of wood and elastic, trinkets given her by this, that and the other, *Sorrell and Son,* the Board.

She took the Board gently down and locked the cupboard. A flat oval piece of polished wood on tiny wheels, it looked like something which had crept out of a cupboard in a basement kitchen. But in fact it was Old Crowe who had done that, knocking gently on the door, sidling in, white hair, grey face, short-sighted pit-pony eyes, blinking at the bare globe in Ida's reading-lamp. Ida tossed a pink netty scarf over the light and dimmed it for him.

'You got something to ask it, Ida?' Old Crowe said. He shivered a little, frightened and fascinated. Ida sharpened a pencil and inserted it in the prow of the little board.

'Sit down, Old Crowe. What you been doing all day?'

'They had a funeral at twenty-seven. One of those Indian students.'

'I been to a funeral, too. Was yours a good one?'

'There aren't any good funerals these days. Not with plumes.' Ida gave the little board a push. It slid sideways across the polished table more than ever like a beetle. 'The pencil's too long,' Old Crowe said. He sat, hugging his hands between his knees, bent forward watching the board. Ida screwed the pencil a little higher. 'Past or future?' Old Crowe asked, panting a little.

'I want to get into touch today,' Ida said.

'Dead or alive?' Old Crowe said.

'Dead. I seen him burnt this afternoon. Cremated. Come on, Old Crowe, put your fingers on.'

'Better take off your rings,' Old Crowe said. 'Gold confuses it.'

Ida unclothed her fingers, laid the tips on the board which squeaked away from her across the sheet of foolscap. 'Come on, Old Crowe,' she said.

Old Crowe giggled. He said, 'It's naughty,' and placed his bony digits on the very rim, where they throbbed a tiny nervous tattoo. 'What you going to ask it, Ida?'

'Are you there, Fred?'

The board squeaked away under their fingers drawing long lines across the paper this way and that 'It's got a will of its own,' Ida said.

'Hush,' said Old Crowe.

The board bucked a little with its hind wheel and came to a stop. 'We might look now,' Ida said. She pushed the board to one side, and they stared together at the network of pencilling.

'You might make out a Y there,' Ida said.

'Or it might be an N.'

'Anyway something's there. We'll try again.' She put her fingers firmly on the board. 'What happened to you, Fred?' and immediately the board was off and away. All her indomitable will worked through her fingers: she wasn't going to have any nonsense this time, and across the board the grey face of Old Crowe frowned with concentration.

'It's writing—real letters,' Ida said with triumph, and as her own fingers momentarily loosened their grip she could feel the board slide firmly away as if on another's errand.

'Hush,' said Old Crowe, but it bucked and stopped. They pushed the board away, and there, unmistakably, in large thin letters was a word, but not a word they knew: 'SUKILL'.

'It looks like a name,' Old Crowe said.

'It must mean something,' Ida said. 'The Board always means something. We'll try again,' and again the wooden beetle scampered off, drawing its tortuous trail. The globe burnt red under the scarf, and Old Crowe whistled between his teeth. 'Now,' Ida said and lifted the Board. A long ragged word ran diagonally across the paper: 'FRESUICILLEYE'.

'Well,' Old Crowe said, 'that's a mouthful. You can't make any-thing of that, Ida.'

'Can't I though,' Ida said. 'Why, it's clear as clear. *Fre* is short for Fred and *Suici* for Suicide and Eye; that's what I always say—an eye for an eye and a tooth for a tooth.'

'What about those two L's?'

'I don't know yet, but I'll bear them in mind.' She leant back in her chair with a sense of power and triumph. 'I'm not supersti-tious,' she said, 'but you can't get over that. The Board knows.'

'She knows,' Old Crowe said, sucking his teeth.

'One more try?' The board slid and squeaked and abruptly stopped. Clear as clear the name stared up at her: 'PHIL'.

'Well,' Ida said, 'well.' She blushed a little. 'Like a sugar bis-cuit?'

'Thank you, Ida, thank you.'

Ida took a tin out of the cupboard drawer and pushed it over to Old Crowe. 'They drove him to death,' Ida said happily. 'I knew there was something fishy. See that *Eye*. That as good as tells me what to do.' Her eye lingered on *Phil*. 'I'm going to make those people sorry they was ever born.' She drew in her breath luxuri-ously and stretched her monumental legs. 'Right and wrong,' she said. 'I believe in right and wrong,' and delving a little deeper, with a sigh of happy satiety, she said, 'It's going to be exciting, it's going to be fun, it's going to be a bit of life, Old Crowe,' giving the highest praise she could give to anything, while the old man sucked his tooth and the pink light wavered on the Warwick Deeping.

PART TWO

I

The Boy stood with his back to Spicer staring out across the dark wash of sea. They had the end of the pier to themselves; everyone else at that hour and in that weather was in the concert hall. The lightning went on and off above the horizon and the rain dripped. 'Where've you been?' the Boy asked.

'Walking around,' Spicer said.

'You been There?'

'I wanted to see it was all safe, that there wasn't anything you'd forgotten.'

The Boy said slowly, leaning out across the rail into the doubtful rain, 'When people do one murder, I've read they sometimes have to do another—to tidy up.' The word murder conveyed no more to him than the word 'box', 'collar', 'giraffe'. He said, 'Spicer, you keep away from there.'

The imagination hadn't awoken. That was his strength. He couldn't see through other people's eyes, or feel with their nerves. Only the music made him uneasy, the catgut vibrating in the heart; it was like nerves losing their freshness, it was like age coming on, other people's experience battering on the brain. 'Where are the rest of the mob?'

'In Sam's, drinking.'

'Why aren't you drinking too?'

'I'm not thirsty, Pinkie, I wanted some fresh air. This thunder makes you feel queer.'

'Why don't they stop that bloody noise in there?' the Boy said.

'You not going to Sam's?'

'I've got a job of work to do,' the Boy said.

'It's all right, Pinkie, ain't it? After that verdict it's all right? Nobody asked questions.'

'I just want to be sure,' the Boy said.

'The mob won't stand for any more killing.'

'Who said there was going to be any killing?' The lightning flared up and showed his tight shabby jacket, the bunch of soft hair at the nape. 'I've got a date, that's all. You be careful what you say, Spicer. You aren't milky, are you?'

'I'm not milky. You got me wrong, Pinkie. I just don't want another killing. That verdict sort of shook us all. What did they mean by it? We *did* kill him, Pinkie?'

'We got to go on being careful, that's all.'

'What did they mean by it, though? I don't trust the doctors. A break like that's *too* good.'

'We got to be careful.'

'What's that in your pocket, Pinkie?'

'I don't carry a gun,' the Boy said. 'You're fancying things.' In the town a clock struck eleven: three strokes were lost in the thunder coming down across the Channel. 'You better be off,' the Boy said. 'She's late already.'

'You've got a razor there, Pinkie.'

'I don't need a razor with a polony. If you want to know what it is, it's a bottle.'

'You don't drink, Pinkie.'

'Nobody would want to drink this.'

'What is it, Pinkie?'

'Vitriol,' the Boy said, 'It scares a polony more than a knife.' He turned impatiently away from the sea and complained again, 'That music.' It moaned in his head in the hot electric night, it was the nearest he knew to sorrow, just as a faint secret sensual pleasure he felt, touching the bottle of vitriol with his fingers, as Rose came hurrying by the concert-hall, was his nearest approach to passion. 'Get out,' he said to Spicer. 'She's here.'

'Oh,' Rose said, 'I'm late. I've run all the way,' she said. 'I thought you might have thought—'

'I'd have waited,' the Boy said.

'It was an awful night in the café,' the girl said. 'Everything went wrong. I broke two plates. And the cream was sour.' It all came out in a breath. 'Who was your friend?' she asked, peering into the darkness.

'He don't matter,' the Boy said.

'I thought somehow—I couldn't see properly—'

'He don't matter,' the Boy repeated.

'What are we going to do?'

'Why, I thought we'd talk a little here first,' the Boy said, 'and then go on somewhere—Sherry's? I don't care.'

'I'd love Sherry's,' Rose said.

'You got your money yet for that card?'

'Yes. I got it this morning.'

'Nobody came and asked you questions?'

'Oh no. But wasn't it dreadful, his being dead like that?'

'You saw his photograph?'

Rose came close to the rail and peered palely up at the Boy. 'But it wasn't him. That's what I don't understand.'

'People look different in photographs.'

'I've got a memory for faces. It wasn't him. They must have cheated. You can't trust the newspapers.'

'Come here,' the Boy said. He drew her round the corner until they were a little farther from the music, more alone with the lightning on the horizon and the thunder coming closer. 'I like you,' the Boy said, an unconvincing smile forking his mouth, 'and I want to warn you. This fellow Hale, I've heard a lot about him. He got himself mixed up with things.'

'What sort of things?' Rose whispered.

'Never mind what things,' the Boy said. 'Only I'd warn you for your own good—you've got the money—if I was you I'd forget it, forget all about that fellow who left the card. He's dead, see. You've got the money. That's all that matters.'

'Anything you say,' Rose said.

'You can call me Pinkie if you like. That's what my friends call me.'

'Pinkie,' Rose repeated, trying it shyly out as the thunder cracked overhead.

'You read about Peggy Baron, didn't you?'

'No, Pinkie.'

'It was in all the papers.'

'I didn't see any papers till I got this job. We couldn't afford papers at home.'

'She got mixed up with a mob,' the Boy said, 'and people came asking her questions. It's not safe.'

'I wouldn't get mixed up with a mob like that,' Rose said.

'You can't always help it. It sort of comes that way.'

'What happened to her?' Rose said.

'They spoilt her looks. She lost one eye. They splashed vitriol on her face.'

Rose whispered, 'Vitriol? What's vitriol?' and the lightning showed a strut of tarred wood, a wave breaking and her pale, bony, terrified face.

'You never seen vitriol?' the Boy said, grinning through the dark. He showed her the little bottle. 'That's vitriol.' He took the cork out and spilled a little on the wooden plank of the pier: it hissed like steam. 'It burns,' the Boy said. 'Smell it,' and he thrust the bottle under her nose.

She gasped at him. 'Pinkie, *you* wouldn't—' and 'I was pulling your leg,' he smoothly lied to her. 'That's not vitriol, that's just spirit. I wanted to warn you, that's all. You and me's going to be friends. I don't want a friend with her skin burned off. You tell me if anyone asks questions. Anyone—mind. Get me on the blower at Frank's straight off. Three sixes. You can remember that.' He took her arm and propelled her away from the lonely pier-end, back by the lit concert-hall, the music drifting landwards, grief in the guts. 'Pinkie,' she said, 'I wouldn't want to interfere. I don't interfere in anyone's business. I've never been nosy. Cross my heart.'

'You're a good kid,' he said.

'You know an awful lot about things, Pinkie,' she said with horror and admiration, and suddenly at the stale romantic tune the orchestra was playing—'lovely to look at, beautiful to hold, and heaven itself—' a little venom of anger and hatred came out on the Boy's lips: 'You've got to know a lot,' he said, 'if you get around. Come on, we'll go to Sherry's.'

Once off the pier they had to run for it; taxis splashed them with water; the strings of coloured bulbs down the Hove parade gleamed like pools of petrol through the rain. They shook the water off on to the floor of Sherry's and Rose saw the queue waiting all the way upstairs for the gallery. 'It's full,' she said, with disappointment.

'We'll go on the floor,' the Boy said, paying his three shillings as carelessly as if he always went there, and walked out among the little tables, the dancing partners with bright metallic hair and little black bags, while the coloured lights flashed green and pink and blue. Rose said, 'It's lovely here. It reminds me,' and all the way to their table she counted over aloud all the things of which it reminded her, the lights, the tune the band was playing, the crowd on the floor trying to rumba. She had an immense store of trivial memories and when she wasn't living in the future she was living in the past. As for the present—she got through that as quickly as she could, running away from things, running towards things, so that her voice was always a little breathless, her heart pounding at an escape or an expectation. 'I whipped the plate under the apron and she said, "Rose, what are you hiding there?"' and a moment later she was turning wide unfledged eyes back to the Boy with a look of the deepest admiration, the most respectful hope.

'What'll you drink?' the Boy said.

She didn't even know the name of a drink. In Nelson Place from which she had emerged like a mole into the daylight of Snow's restaurant and the Palace Pier, she had never known a boy with enough money to offer her a drink. She would have said 'beer', but she had had no opportunity of discovering whether she liked beer. A twopenny ice from an Everest tricycle was the whole extent of her knowledge of luxury. She goggled hopelessly at the Boy. He asked her sharply, 'What d'you like? *I* don't know what you like.'

'An ice,' she said with disappointment, but she couldn't keep him waiting.

'What kind of an ice?'

'Just an ordinary ice,' she said. Everest hadn't in all the slum years offered her a choice.

'Vanilla?' the waiter said. She nodded; she supposed that that was what she had always had, and so it proved—only a size larger; otherwise she might just as well have been sucking it between wafers by a tricycle.

'You're a soft sort of kid,' the Boy said. 'How old are you?'

'I'm seventeen,' she said defiantly; there was a law which said a man couldn't go with you before you were seventeen.

'I'm seventeen too,' the Boy said, and the eyes which had never been young stared with grey contempt into the eyes which had only just begun to learn a thing or two. He said, 'Do you dance?' and she replied humbly, 'I haven't danced much.'

'It don't matter,' the Boy said. 'I'm not one for dancing.' He eyed the slow movement of the two-backed beasts: pleasure, he thought, they call it pleasure: he was shaken by a sense of loneliness, an awful lack of understanding. The floor was cleared for the last cabaret of the evening. A spotlight picked out a patch of floor, a crooner in a dinner jacket, a microphone on a long black movable stand. He held it tenderly as if it were a woman, swinging it gently this way and that, wooing it with his lips while from the loudspeaker under the gallery his whisper reverberated hoarsely over the hall, like a dictator announcing victory, like the official news following a long censorship. 'It gets you,' the Boy said, 'it gets you,' surrendering himself to the huge brazen suggestion.

> 'Music talks, talks of our love.
> The starling on our walks, talks, talks of our love.
> The taxis tooting,
> The last owl hooting,
> The tube train rumbling,
> Busy bee bumbling,
>   Talk of our love.
>
> Music talks, talks of our love,
> The west wind on our walks, talks, talks of our love.
> The nightingale singing,
> The postmen ringing,
> Electric drill groaning,
> Office telephoning,
>   Talk of our love.'

The Boy stared at the spotlight: music, love, nightingale, postmen: the words stirred in his brain like poetry: one hand caressed the vitriol bottle in his pocket, the other touched Rose's wrist. The inhuman voice whistled round the gallery and the Boy sat silent. It was he this time who was being warned; life held the vitriol bottle and warned him: I'll spoil your looks. It spoke to him in the music, and when he protested that he for one would never get mixed up, the music had its own retort at hand: 'You can't always help it. It sort of comes that way.'

'The watchdog on our walks, talks, talks of our love.'

The crowd stood at attention six deep behind the tables (there wasn't enough room on the floor for so many). They were dead quiet. It was like the anthem on Armistice Day when the King has deposited his wreath, the hats off, and the troops turned to stone. It was love of a kind, music of a kind, truth of a kind they listened to.

'Gracie Fields funning,
The gangsters gunning,
Talk of our love.'

The music pealed on under the Chinese lanterns and the pink spotlight featured the singer holding the microphone closer to his starched shirt. 'You been in love?' the Boy asked sharply and uneasily.

'Oh yes,' Rose said.

The Boy retorted with sudden venom, 'You would have been. You're green. You don't know what people do.' The music came to an end and in the silence he laughed aloud. 'You're innocent.' People turned in their chairs and looked at them: a girl giggled. His fingers pinched her wrist. 'You're green,' he said again. He was working himself into a little sensual rage, as he had done with the soft kids at the council school. 'You don't know anything,' he said, with contempt in his nails.

'Oh no,' she protested. 'I know a lot.'

The Boy grinned at her, 'Not a thing,' pinching the skin of her wrist until his nails nearly met. 'You'd like me for your boy, eh? We'll keep company?'

'Oh,' she said, 'I'd love it.' Tears of pride and pain pricked behind her lids. 'If you like doing that,' she said, 'go on.'

The Boy let go. 'Don't be soft,' he said. 'Why should I like it? You think you know too much,' he complained. He sat there, anger like a live coal in his belly, as the music came on again: all the good times he'd had in the old days with nails and splinters: the tricks he'd learnt later with a razor blade: what would be the fun if people didn't squeal? He said furiously, 'We'll be going. I can't stand this place,' and obediently Rose began to pack her handbag, putting back her Woolworth compact and her handkerchief. 'What's that?' the Boy said when something clinked in her bag; she showed him the end of a string of beads.

'You a Roman?' the Boy asked.

'Yes,' Rose said.

'I'm one too,' the Boy said. He gripped her arm and pushed her out into the dark dripping street. He turned up the collar of his jacket and ran as the lightning flapped and the thunder filled the air. They ran from doorway to doorway until they were back on the parade in one of the empty glass shelters. They had it to themselves in the noisy stifling night. 'Why, I was in a choir once,' the Boy confided and suddenly he began to sing softly in his spoilt boy's voice: 'Agnus dei qui tollis peccata mundi, dona nobis pacem.' In his voice a whole lost world moved—the lighted corner below the organ, the smell of incense and laundered surplices, and the music. Music—it didn't matter what music—'Agnus dei', 'lovely to look at, beautiful to hold', 'the starling on our walks', 'credo in unum Dominum'—any music moved him, speaking of things he didn't understand.

'Do you go to Mass?' he asked.

'Sometimes,' Rose said. 'It depends on work. Most weeks I wouldn't get much sleep if I went to Mass.'

'I don't care what you do,' the Boy said sharply. 'I don't go to Mass.'

'But you believe, don't you,' Rose implored him, 'you think it's true?'

'Of course it's true,' the Boy said. 'What else could there be?' he went scornfully on. 'Why,' he said, 'it's the only thing that fits.

These atheists, they don't know nothing. Of course there's Hell. Flames and damnation,' he said with his eyes on the dark shifting water and the lightning and the lamps going out above the black struts of the Palace Pier, 'torments.'

'And Heaven too,' Rose said with anxiety, while the rain fell interminably on.

'Oh, maybe,' the Boy said, 'maybe.'

Wet to the skin, the trousers sticking to his thin legs the Boy went up the long unmatted flight to his bedroom at Frank's. The banister shook under his hand, and when he opened the door and found the mob there, sitting on his brass bedstead smoking, he said furiously, 'When's that banister going to be mended? It's not safe. Someone'll take a fall one day.' The curtain wasn't drawn, the window was open, and the last lightning flapped across the grey roofs stretching to the sea. The Boy went to his bed and swept off the crumbs of Cubitt's sausage roll. 'What's this,' he said, 'a meeting?'

'There's trouble about the subscriptions, Pinkie,' Cubitt said. 'There's two not come in. Brewer and Tate. They say now Kite's dead—'

'Do we carve 'em up, Pinkie?' Dallow asked. Spicer stood at the window watching the storm. He said nothing, staring out at the flames and chasms of the sky.

'Ask Spicer,' the Boy said. 'He's been doing a lot of thinking lately.' They all turned and watched Spicer. Spicer said, 'Maybe we ought to lay off a while. You know a lot of the boys cleared out when Kite got killed.'

'Go on,' the Boy said. 'Listen to him. He's what they call a philosopher.'

'Well,' Spicer said angrily, 'there's free speech in this mob, ain't there? Those that cleared out, they didn't see how a kid could run this show.'

The Boy sat on the bed watching him with his hands in his damp pockets. He shivered once.

'I was always against murder,' Spicer said. 'I don't care who knows it.'

'Sour and milky,' the Boy said.

Spicer came into the middle of the room. 'Listen, Pinkie,' he said. 'Be reasonable.' He appealed to them all, 'Be reasonable.'

'There's things in what he says,' Cubitt suddenly put in. 'We had a lucky break. We don't want to draw attention to ourselves. We'd better let Brewer and Tate be for a while.'

The Boy got up. A few crumbs stuck to his wet suit. 'You ready, Dallow?' he said.

'What you say, Pinkie,' Dallow said, grinning like a large friendly dog.

'Where you going, Pinkie?' Spicer asked.

'I'm going to see Brewer.'

Cubitt said, 'You act as if it was last year we killed Hale, not last week. We got to act cautious.'

'That's over and done,' the Boy said. 'You heard the verdict. Natural causes,' he said, looking out at the dying storm.

'You forget that girl in Snow's. She could hang us.'

'I'm looking after the girl. She won't talk.'

'You're marrying her, aren't you?' Cubitt said. Dallow laughed.

The Boy's hands came out of his pockets, the knuckles clenched white. He said, 'Who told you I was marrying her?'

'Spicer,' Cubitt said.

Spicer backed away from the Boy. He said, 'Listen, Pinkie. I only said as it would make her safe. A wife can't give evidence . . .'

'I don't need to marry a squirt to make her safe. How do we make you safe, Spicer?' His tongue came out between his teeth, licking the edges of his dry cracked lips. 'If carving'd do it . . .'

'It was just a joke,' Cubitt said. 'You don't need to take it so solemn. You want a sense of humour, Pinkie.'

'You think that was funny, eh?' the Boy said. 'Me—marrying—that cheap polony.' He croaked 'Ha, ha,' at them. 'I'll learn. Come on, Dallow.'

'Wait till morning,' Cubitt sad. 'Wait till some of the other boys come in.'

'You milky too?'

'You don't believe that, Pinkie. But we got to go slow.'

'You with me, Dallow?' the boy asked.

'I'm with you, Pinkie.'

'Then we'll be going,' the Boy sad. He went across to the wash-stand and opened the little door where the jerry stood. He felt at the back behind the jerry and pulled out a tiny blade, like the blades women shave with, but blunt along one edge and mounted with sticking-plaster. He stuck it under his long thumb-nail, the only nail not bitten close, and drew on his glove. He said, 'We'll be back with the sub. in half an hour,' and led the way bang straight down Frank's stairs. The cold of his drenching had got under his skin: he came out on to the front a pace ahead of Dallow, his face contorted with ague, a shiver twisting the narrow shoulders. He said over his shoulder to Dallow, 'We'll go to Brewer's. One lesson'll be enough.'

'What you say, Pinkie,' Dallow said, plodding after. The rain had stopped: it was low tide and the shallow edge of the sea scraped far out at the rim of the shingle. A clock struck midnight. Dallow suddenly began to laugh.

'What's got you, Dallow?'

'I was just thinking,' Dallow said. 'You're a grand little geezer, Pinkie. Kite was right to take you on. You go straight for things, Pinkie.'

'You're all right,' the Boy said, staring ahead, the ague wringing his face. They passed the Cosmopolitan, the lights on here and there all the way up the tall front to the turrets against the clouded moving sky. In Snow's when they passed a single light went out. They turned up the Old Steyne. Brewer had a house near the tram lines on the Lewes road almost under the railway viaduct.

'He's gone to bed,' Dallow said. Pinkie rang the bell, holding his finger on the switch. Low shuttered shops ran off on either hand, a tram went by with nobody in it, labelled 'Depot Only', ringing and swinging down the empty road, the conductor drows-ing on a seat inside, the roof gleaming from the storm. Pinkie kept his finger on the bell.

'What made Spicer say that—about me marrying?' the Boy asked.

'He just thought it'd close her clapper,' Dallow said.

'She's not what keeps me awake,' the Boy said, pressing on the bell. A light went on upstairs, a window creaked up, and a voice called, 'Who's that?'

'It's me,' the Boy said. 'Pinkie.'

'What do you want? Why don't you come around in the morning?'

'I want to talk to you, Brewer.'

'I've got nothing to talk about, Pinkie, that can't wait.'

'You'd better open up, Brewer. You don't want the mob along here.'

'The old woman's awful sick, Pinkie. I don't want any trouble. She's asleep. She hasn't slept for three nights.'

'This'll wake her,' the Boy said with his finger on the bell. A slow goods train went by across the viaduct, shaking smoke down into the Lewes road.

'Leave off, Pinkie, and I'll open up.'

Pinkie shivered as he waited, his gloved hand deep in his damp pocket. Brewer opened the door, a stout elderly man in soiled white pyjamas. The bottom button was missing and the coat swung from the bulging belly and the deep navel. 'Come in, Pinkie,' he said, 'and walk quiet. The old woman's bad. I've been worrying my head off.'

'That why you haven't paid your subscription, Brewer?' the Boy said. He looked with contempt down the narrow hall—the shell case converted into an umbrella-stand, the moth-eaten stag's head bearing on one horn a bowler hat, a steel helmet used for ferns. Kite ought to have got them into better money than this. Brewer had only just graduated from the street corner, saloon-bar betting. A welsher. It was no good trying to draw more than ten per cent of his bets.

Brewer said, 'Come in here and be snug. It's warm in here. What a cold night.' He had a hollow cheery manner even in pyjamas. He was like a legend on a racing card—The Old Firm. You can Trust Bill Brewer. He lit the gas-fire, turned on a stand lamp in a red silk shade with a bobble fringe. The light glowed on a silver-plated biscuit-box, a framed wedding group. 'Have a spot of Scotch?' Brewer invited them.

'You know I don't drink,' the Boy said.

'Ted will,' Brewer said.

'I don't mind a spot,' Dallow said. He grinned and said, 'Here's how.'

'We've called for that subscription, Brewer,' the Boy said.

The man in white pyjamas hissed soda into his glass. His back turned he watched Pinkie in the glass above the sideboard until he caught the other's eye. He said, 'I been worried, Pinkie. Ever since Kite was croaked.'

'Well?' the Boy said.

'It's like this. I said to myself if Kite's mob can't even protect—' he stopped suddenly and listened. 'Was that the old woman?' Very faintly from the room above came the sound of coughing. Brewer said, 'She's woke up. I got to go and see her.'

'You stay here,' the Boy said, 'and talk.'

'She'll want turning.'

'When we've finished you can go.'

Cough, cough, cough: it was like a machine trying to start and failing. Brewer said desperately, 'Be human. She won't know where I've got to. I'll only be a minute.'

'You don't need to be longer than a minute here,' the Boy said. 'All we want's what's due to us. Twenty pounds.'

'I haven't got it in the house. Honest I haven't.'

'That's too bad for you.' The Boy draw off his right glove.

'It's like this, Pinkie. I paid it all out yesterday. To Colleoni.'

'What in Jesus' name,' the Boy said, 'has Colleoni to do with it?'

Brewer went rapidly and desperately on, listening to the cough, cough, cough upstairs. 'Be reasonable, Pinkie. I can't pay both of you. I'd have been carved if I hadn't paid Colleoni.'

'Is he in Brighton?'

'He's stopping at the Cosmopolitan.'

•'And Tate—Tate's paid Colleoni too?'

'That's right, Pinkie. He's running the business in a big way.' A big way—it was like an accusation, a reminder of the brass bed-stead at Frank's, the crumbs on the mattress.

'You think I'm finished?' the Boy said.

'Take my advice, Pinkie, and go in with Colleoni.'

The Boy suddenly drew his hand back and slashed with his ra-zored nail at Brewer's cheek. He struck blood out along the cheek bone. 'Don't,' Brewer said, 'don't,' backing against the sideboard, upsetting the biscuit-box. He said, 'I've got protection. You be careful. I've got protection.'

The Boy laughed. Dallow refilled his glass with Brewer's whisky. The Boy said, 'Look at him. He's got protection.' Dallow took a splash of soda.

'You want any more?' the Boy said. 'That was just to show you who's protecting you.'

'I can't pay you both, Pinkie. God's sake, keep back.'

'Twenty pounds is what we've come for, Brewer.'

'Colleoni'll have my blood, Pinkie.'

'You needn't worry. We'll protect you.'

Cough, cough, cough went the woman upstairs, and then a faint cry like a sleeping child's. 'She's calling me,' Brewer said.

'Twenty pounds.'

'I don't keep my money in here. Let me fetch it.'

'You go with him, Dallow,' the Boy said. 'I'll wait here,' and he sat down on a straight carved dining-room chair and stared out—at the mean street, the dustbins along the pavement, the vast shadow of the viaduct. He sat perfectly still with his grey ancient eyes giving nothing away.

A big way—Colleoni come into it in a big way—he knew there wasn't a soul in the mob he could trust—except perhaps Dallow. That didn't matter. You couldn't make mistakes when you trusted nobody. A cat coasted cautiously round a bin on the pavement, stopped suddenly, crouched back, and in the semi-dark its agate eyes stared up at the Boy. Boy and cat, they didn't stir, watching each other, until Dallow returned.

'I've got the money, Pinkie,' Dallow said. The Boy turned his head and grinned at Dallow. Suddenly his face was convulsed: he sneezed twice, violently. Overhead the coughing died away. 'He won't forget this visit,' Dallow said. He added anxiously, 'You ought to have a spot of whisky, Pinkie. You've caught cold.'

'I'm all right,' the Boy said. He got up. 'We won't stop and say good-bye.'

The Boy led the way down the middle of the empty road, between the tram lines. He said suddenly, 'Do you think I'm finished, Dallow?'

'You?' Dallow, said. 'Why, you haven't even begun.' They walked for a while in silence, the water from the gutters dripped on the pavement. Then Dallow spoke.

'You worrying about Colleoni?'

'I'm not worrying.'

Dallow said suddenly, 'You're worth a dozen Colleonis. The Cosmopolitan,' he exclaimed and spat.

'Kite thought he'd go in for the automatic machines. He learned different. Now Colleoni thinks the coast's clear. *He's* branching out.'

'He ought to have learned from Hale.'

'Hale died natural.'

Dallow laughed. 'Tell that to Spicer.' They turned the corner by the Royal Albion and the sea was with them again—the tide had turned—a movement, a splashing, a darkness. The Boy looked suddenly sideways and up at Dallow—he could trust Dallow—receiving from the ugly and broken face a sense of triumph and companionship and superiority. He felt as a physically weak but cunning schoolboy feels who has attached to himself in an indiscriminating fidelity the strongest boy in the school. 'You mug,' he said and pinched Dallow's arm. It was almost like affection.

A light still burned in Frank's, and Spicer was waiting in the hall. 'Anything happened?' he asked anxiously. His pale face had come out in spots round the mouth and nose.

'What do you think?' the Boy said, going upstairs. 'We brought the subscription.'

Spicer followed him into his bedroom. 'There was a call for you just after you'd gone.'

'Who from?'

'A girl called Rose.'

The Boy sat on the bed undoing his shoe. 'What did she want?' he asked.

'She said while she was out with you, somebody had been in asking for her.'

The Boy sat still with the shoe in his hand. 'Pinkie,' Spicer said, 'was it *the* girl? The girl from Snow's?'

'Of course it was.'

'I answered the phone, Pinkie.'

'Did she know your voice?'

'How do I know, Pinkie?'

'Who was asking for her?'

'She didn't know. She said tell you because you wanted to hear. Pinkie, suppose the bogies have got that far?'

'The bogies aren't as smart as that,' Pinkie said. 'Maybe it's one of Colleoni's men, poking around after their pal Fred.' He took off his other shoe. 'You don't need to turn milky, Spicer.'

'It was a woman, Pinkie.'

'I'm not troubling. Fred died natural. That's the verdict. You can forget it. There's other things to think of now.' He put his shoes side by side under the bed, took off his coat, hung it on a bed ball, took off his trousers, lay back in his pants and shirt on top of the bed. 'I'm thinking, Spicer, you oughter take a holiday. You look all in. I wouldn't want anyone seeing you like that.' He closed his eyes. 'You be off, Spicer, and take things easy.'

'If that girl ever knew *who* put the card . . .'

'She'll never know. Turn out the light and get.'

The light went out and the moon went on like a lamp outside, slanting across the roofs, laying the shadow of clouds across the downs, illuminating the white empty stands of the racecourse above Whitehawk Bottom like the monoliths of Stonehenge, shining across the tide which drove up from Boulogne and washed against the piles of the Palace Pier. It lit the washstand, the open door where the jerry stood, the brass balls at the bed end.

2

The Boy lay on the bed. A cup of coffee went cold on the washstand, and the bed was sprinkled with flakes of pastry. The Boy licked an indelible pencil, his mouth was stained purple at the corners, he wrote: 'Refer you to my previous letter,' and concluded it at last, 'P. Brown, Secretary, the Bookmakers' Protection . . .' The envelope addressed 'Mr J. Tate' lay on the washstand, the corner soiled with coffee. When he had finished writing he put his head back on the pillow and closed his eyes. He fell asleep at once: it was like the falling of a shutter, the pressure of the bulb which ends a time exposure. He had no dreams. His sleep was functional. When Dallow opened the door he woke at once. 'Well?' he said, lying there without moving, fully dressed among the pastry crumbs.

'There's a letter for you, Pinkie. Judy brought it up.'

The Boy took the letter. Dallow said, 'It's an elegant letter, Pinkie. Smell it.'

The Boy held the mauve envelope to his nose. It smelt like a cachou for bad breath. He said, 'Can't you keep off that bitch? If Frank knew . . .'

'Who'd be writing an elegant letter like that, Pinkie?'

'Colleoni. He wants me to call in for a talk at the Cosmopolitan.'

'The Cosmopolitan,' Dallow repeated with disgust. 'You won't go, will you?'

'Of course I'll go.'

'It's not the sort of place where you'd feel at home.'

'Elegant,' the Boy said, 'like his notepaper. Costs a lot of money. He thinks he can scare me.'

'Perhaps we'd better lay off Tate.'

'Take that jacket down to Frank. Tell him to sponge it quick and put an iron over it. Give these shoes a brush.' He kicked them out from under the bed and sat up. 'He thinks he'll have the laugh on us.' In the tipped mirror on the washstand he could see himself, but his eyes shifted quickly from the image of smooth, never shaven cheek, soft hair, old eyes: he wasn't interested. He had too much pride to worry about appearances.

So that later he was quite at ease waiting in the great lounge under the domed lights for Colleoni: young men kept on arriving in huge motoring coats accompanied by small tinted creatures, who rang like expensive glass when they were touched but who conveyed an impression of being as sharp and tough as tin. They looked at nobody, sweeping through the lounge as they had swept in racing models down the Brighton Road, ending on high stools in the American Bar. A stout woman in a white fox fur came out of a lift and stared at the Boy, then she got back into the lift again and moved weightily upwards. A little bitch sniffed at him and then talked him over with another little bitch on a settee. Mr Colleoni came across an acre of deep carpet from the Louis Seize writing room, walking on tiptoe in glacé shoes.

He was small with a neat round belly; he wore a grey double-breasted waistcoat, and his eyes gleamed like raisins. His hair was thin and grey. The little bitches on the settee stopped talking as he passed and concentrated. He clinked very gently as he moved; it was the only sound.

'You were asking for me?' he said.

'You asked for me,' the Boy said. 'I got your letter.'

'Surely,' Mr Colleoni said, making a little bewildered motion with his hands, 'you are not Mr P. Brown?' He explained, 'I expected someone a good deal older.'

'You asked for me,' the Boy said.

The little raisin eyes took him in: the sponged suit and the narrow shoulders, the cheap black shoes. 'I thought Mr Kite . . .'

'Kite's dead,' the Boy said. 'You know that.'

'I missed it,' Mr Colleoni said. 'Of course that makes a difference.'

'You can talk to me,' the Boy said, 'instead of Kite.'

Mr Colleoni smiled. 'I don't think it's necessary,' he said.

'You'd better,' the Boy said. Little chimes of laughter came from the American Bar and the chink, chink, chink of ice. A page came out of the Louis Seize writing room, called, 'Sir Joseph Montagu, Sir Joseph Montagu,' and passed into the Pompadour Boudoir. The spot of damp, where Frank's iron had failed to pass, above the Boy's breast-pocket was slowly fading out in the hot Cosmopolitan air.

Mr Colleoni put out a hand and gave him a quick pat, pat, pat on the arm. 'Come with me,' he said. He led the way, walking on glacé tiptoe past the settee, where the bitches whispered, past a little table where a man was saying 'I told him ten thousand's my limit' to an old man who sat with closed eyes above his chilling tea. Mr Colleoni looked over his shoulder and said gently, 'The service here is not what it used to be.'

He looked into the Louis Seize writing room. A woman in mauve with an untimely tiara was writing a letter in a vast jumble of chinoiserie. Mr Colleoni withdrew. 'We'll go where we can talk in peace,' he said and tiptoed back across the lounge. The old man had opened his eyes and was testing his tea with his finger. Mr Colleoni led the way to the gilt grill of the lift. 'Number Fifteen,' he said. They rose angelically towards peace. 'Cigar?' Mr Colleoni asked.

'I don't smoke,' the Boy said. A last squeal of gaiety came from below, from the American Bar, the last syllable of the page boy returning from the Pompadour Boudoir, 'Gue,' before the gates slid back and they were in the padded soundproof passage. Mr Colleoni paused and lit his cigar.

'Let's have a look at that lighter,' the Boy said.

Mr Colleoni's small shrewd eyes shone blankly under the concealed pervasive electric glow. He held it out. The Boy turned it over and looked at the hallmark. 'Real gold,' he said.

'I like things good,' Mr Colleoni said, unlocking a door. 'Take a chair.' The arm-chairs, stately red velvet couches stamped with crowns in gold and silver thread, faced the wide seaward windows and the wrought-iron balconies. 'Have a drink?'

'I don't drink,' the Boy said.

'Now,' Mr Colleoni said, 'who sent you?'

'No one sent me.'

'I mean, who's running your mob if Kite's dead?'

'I'm running it,' the Boy said.

Mr Colleoni politely checked a smile, tapping his thumbnail with the gold lighter.

'What happened to Kite?'

'You know that story,' the Boy said. He gazed across at the Napoleonic crowns, the silver thread. '*You* won't want to hear the details. It wouldn't have happened if we hadn't been crossed. A journalist thought he could put one over on us.'

'What journalist's that?'

'You oughter read the inquests,' the Boy said, staring out through the window at the pale arch of sky against which a few light clouds blew up.

Mr Colleoni looked at the ash on his cigar; it was half an inch long; he sat deep down in his arm-chair and crossed his little plump thighs contentedly.

'I'm not saying anything about Kite,' the Boy said. 'He trespassed.'

'You mean,' Mr Colleoni said, 'you aren't interested in automatic machines?'

'I mean,' the Boy said, 'that trespassing's not healthy.'

A little wave of musk came over the room from the handkerchief in Mr Colleoni's breast-pocket.

'It'd be you who'd need protection,' the Boy said.

'I've got all the protection I need,' Mr Colleoni said. He shut his eyes; he was snug; the huge moneyed hotel lapped him round; he was at home. The Boy sat on the edge of his chair because he didn't believe in relaxing during business hours; it was he who looked like an alien in this room, not Mr Colleoni.

'You are wasting your time, my child,' Mr Colleoni said. 'You can't do me any harm.' He laughed gently. 'If you want a job though, come to me. I like push. I dare say I could find room for you. The World needs young people with energy.' The hand with the cigar moved expansively, mapping out the World as Mr Colleoni visualized it: lots of little electric clocks controlled by Greenwich, buttons on a desk, a good suite on the first floor, accounts audited, reports from agents, silver, cutlery, glass.

'I'll be seeing you on the course,' the Boy said.

'You'll hardly do that,' Mr Colleoni said. 'I haven't been to a racecourse, let me see, it must be twenty years.' There wasn't a point, he seemed to be indicating, fingering his gold lighter, at which their worlds touched: the week-end at the Cosmopolitan, the portable dictaphone beside the desk, had not the smallest connection with Kite slashed quickly with razors on a railway platform, the grubby hand against the skyline signalling to the bookie from the stand, the heat, the dust fuming up over the half-crown enclosure, the smell of bottled beer.

'I'm just a business man,' Mr Colleoni softly explained. 'I don't need to see a race. And nothing you might try to do to my men could affect me. I've got two in hospital now. It doesn't matter. They have the best attention. Flowers, grapes . . . I can afford it. I don't have to worry. I'm a business man,' Mr Colleoni went expansively and good-humouredly on. 'I like you. You're a promising youngster. That's why I'm talking to you like a father. You can't damage a business like mine.'

'I could damage you,' the Boy said.

'It wouldn't pay. There wouldn't be any faked alibis for you. It would be *your* witnesses who'd be scared. I'm a business man.' The raisin eyes blinked as the sun slanted in across a bowl of flowers and fell on the deep carpet. 'Napoleon the Third used to have this room,' Mr Colleoni said, 'and Eugenie.'

'Who was she?'

'Oh,' Mr Colleoni said vaguely, 'one of those foreign polonies.' He plucked a flower and stuck it in his buttonhole, and something a little doggish peeped out of the black buttony eyes, a hint of the seraglio.

'I'll be going,' the Boy said. He rose and moved to the door.

'You do understand me, don't you?' Mr Colleoni said without moving; holding his hand very still he kept the cigar ash, quite a long ash now, suspended. 'Brewer's been complaining. You don't do that again. And Tate . . . you mustn't try tricks with Tate.' His old Italian face showed few emotions but a mild amusement, a mild friendliness; but suddenly sitting there in the rich Victorian room, with the gold lighter in his pocket and the cigar-case on his lap, he looked as a man might look who owned the whole world, the whole visible world that is, the cash registers and policemen and prostitutes, Parliament and the laws which say 'this is Right and this is Wrong.'

'I understand all right,' the Boy said. 'You think our mob's too small for you.'

'I employ a great many people,' Mr Colleoni said.

The Boy closed the door; a loose shoe-lace tapped all the way down the passage: the huge lounge was almost empty: a man in plus-fours waited for a girl. The visible world was all Mr Colleoni's. The spot where the iron hadn't passed was still a little damp over the Boy's breast.

A hand touched the Boy's arm. He looked round and recognized the man in a bowler hat. He nodded guardedly. 'Morning.'

'They told me at Frank's,' the man said, 'you'd come here.'

The Boy's heart missed a beat: for almost the first time it occurred to him that the law could hang him, take him out in a yard, drop him in a pit, bury him in lime, put an end to the great future . . .

'You want me?'

'That's right.'

He thought: Rose, the girl, someone asking questions. His memory flashed back: he remembered how she caught him with his hand under the table, feeling for something. He grinned dully and said, 'Well, they haven't sent the Big Four, anyway.'

'Mind coming round to the station?'

'Got a warrant?'

'It's only Brewer been complaining you hit him. You left your scar all right.'

The Boy began to laugh. 'Brewer? Me? I wouldn't touch him.'

'Come round and see the inspector?'

'Of course I will.'

They came out on to the parade. A pavement photographer saw them coming and lifted the cap from his camera. The Boy put his hands in front of his face and went by. 'You oughter put a stop to those things,' he said. 'Fine thing it'd be to have a picture postcard stuck up on the pier, you and me walking to the station.'

'They caught a murderer once in town with one of those snaps.'

'I read about it,' the Boy said and fell silent. This is Colleoni's doing, he thought, he's showing off: he put Brewer up to this.

'Brewer's wife's pretty bad they say,' the detective remarked softly.

'Is she?' the Boy said. 'I wouldn't know.'

'Got your alibi ready, I suppose?'

'How do I know? I don't know when he said I hit him. A geezer can't have an alibi for every minute of the day.'

'You're a wise kid,' the detective said, 'but you needn't get fussed about this. The inspector wants to have a friendly chat, that's all.'

He led the way through the charge-room. A man with a tired ageing face sat behind a desk. 'Sit down, Brown,' he said. He opened a cigarette box and pushed it across.

'I don't smoke,' the Boy said. He sat down and watched the inspector alertly. 'Aren't you going to charge me?'

'There's no charge,' the inspector said. 'Brewer thought better of it.' He paused. He looked more tired than ever. He said: 'I want to talk straight for once. We know more about each other than we admit. I don't interfere with you and Brewer: I've got more important things to do than prevent you and Brewer—arguing. But you know just as well as I do that Brewer wouldn't come here to complain if he hadn't been put up to it.'

'You've certainly got ideas,' the Boy said.

'Put up to it by someone who's not afraid of your mob.'

'There's not much escapes the bogies,' the Boy said, grimacing derisively.

'The races start next week, and I don't want to have any big scale mob fighting in Brighton. I don't mind you carving each other up in a quiet way, I don't give a penny for your worthless skins, but when two mobs start scrapping people who matter may get hurt.'

'Meaning who?' the Boy said.

'Meaning decent innocent people. Poor people out to put a shilling on the tote. Clerks, charwomen, dustmen. People who wouldn't be seen dead talking to you—or to Colleoni.'

'What are you getting at?' the Boy said.

'I'm getting at this. You aren't big enough for your job, Brown. You can't stand against Colleoni. If there's any fighting I shall come down like a ton of bricks on both of you—but it will be

Colleoni who'll have the alibis. No one's going to fake you an alibi against Colleoni. You take my advice. Clear out of Brighton.'

'Fine,' the Boy said. 'A bogy doing Colleoni's job for him.'

'This is private and unofficial,' the inspector said. 'I'm being human for once. I don't care if you get carved or Colleoni gets carved, but I'm not going to have innocent people hurt if I can help it.'

'You think I'm finished?' the Boy said. He grinned uneasily, looking away, looking at the walls plastered with notices. Dog Licences. Gun Licences. Found Drowned. A dead face met his eye staring from the wall, unnaturally pasty. Unbrushed hair. A scar by the mouth. 'You think Colleoni'll keep the peace better?' He could read the writing: 'one nickel watch, waistcoat of grey cloth, blue-striped shirt, aertex vest, aertex pants'.

'Well?'

'It's valuable advice,' the Boy said, grinning down at the polished desk, the box of Players, a crystal paperweight. 'I'll have to think it over. I'm young to retire.'

'You're too young to run a racket if you ask me.'

'So Brewer's not bringing a charge?'

'He's not afraid to. I talked him out of it. I wanted to have a chance to speak to you straight.'

'Well,' the Boy said, standing up, 'maybe I'll be seeing you: maybe not.' He grinned again, passing through the charge-room, but a bright spot of colour stood out on each cheek-bone. There was poison in his veins, though he grinned and bore it. He had been insulted. He was going to show the world. They thought because he was only seventeen . . . he jerked his narrow shoulders back at the memory that he'd killed his man, and these bogies who thought they were clever weren't clever enough to discover that. He trailed the clouds of his own glory after him: hell lay about him in his infancy. He was ready for more deaths.

PART THREE

I

Ida Arnold sat up in the boarding-house bed. For a moment she didn't know where she was. Her head ached with the thick night at Sherry's. It came slowly back to her as she stared at the thick ewer on the floor, the basin of grey water in which she had perfunctorily washed, the bright pink roses on the wallpaper, a wedding group—Phil Corkery dithering outside the front door, pecking at her lips, swaying off down the parade as if that was all he could expect, while the tide receded. She looked round the room; it didn't look so good in the morning light as when she had booked it, but 'it's homely,' she thought with satisfaction, 'it's what I like.'

The sun was shining; Brighton was at its best. The passage outside her room was gritty with sand, she felt it under her shoes all the way down stairs, and in the hall there was a pail, two spades, and a long piece of seaweed hanging by the door as a barometer. There were a lot of sandshoes lying about, and from the dining-room came a child's querulous voice repeating over and over, 'I don't want to dig. I want to go to the pictures. I don't want to dig.'

At one she was meeting Phil Corkery at Snow's. Before that there were things to do; she had to go easy on the money, not put away too much in the way of Guinness. It wasn't cheap living down at Brighton, and she wasn't going to take cash from Corkery—she had a conscience, she had a code, and if she took cash she gave something in return. Black Boy was the answer: she had to see about it first thing before the odds shortened: sinews of war, and she made her way towards Kemp Town to the only bookie she knew, old Jim Tate, 'Honest Jim' of the half-crown enclosure.

He bellowed at her as soon as she got inside his office, 'Here's Ida. Sit down, Mrs Turner,' getting her name wrong. He pushed a box of Gold Flake across to her. 'Inhale a cheroot.' He was a little more than life-size. His voice, after the race meetings of twenty years, could hit no tone which wasn't loud and hoarse. He was a man you needed to look at through the wrong end of a telescope if you were to believe him the fine healthy fellow he made himself out to be. When you were close to him, you saw the thick blue veins on the left forehead, the red money-spider's web across the eyeballs. 'Well, Mrs Turner—Ida—what is it you fancy?'

'Black Boy,' Ida said.

'Black Boy,' Jim Tate repeated. 'That's ten to one.'

'Twelve to one.'

'The odds have shortened. There's been quite a packet laid on Black Boy this week. You wouldn't get ten to one from anyone but your old friend.'

'All right,' Ida said. 'Put me on twenty pounds. And my name's not Turner. It's Arnold.'

'Twenty nicker. That's a fat bet for you, Mrs What-ever-you-are.' He licked his thumb and began to comb the notes. Half-way through he paused, sat still like a large toad over his desk, listening. A lot of noise came in through the open window, feet on stone, voices, distant music, bells ringing, the continuous whisper of the Channel. He sat quite still with half the notes in his hand. He looked uneasy. The telephone rang. He let it ring for two seconds, his veined eyes on Ida; then he lifted the receiver. 'Hullo. Hullo. This is Jim Tate.' It was an old-fashioned telephone. He screwed the receiver close into his ear and sat still while a low voice burred like a bee.

One hand holding the receiver to his ear, Jim Tate shuffled the notes together, wrote out a slip. He said hoarsely, 'That's all right, Mr Colleoni. I'll do that, Mr Colleoni,' and planked the receiver down.

'You've written Black Dog,' Ida said.

He looked across at her. It took him a moment to understand. 'Black Dog,' he said, and then laughed, hoarse and hollow. 'What was I thinking of? Black Dog, indeed.'

'That means Care,' Ida said.

'Well,' he barked with unconvincing geniality, 'we've always something to worry about.' The telephone rang again. Jim Tate looked as if it might sting him.

'You're busy,' Ida said. 'I'll be going.'

When she went out into the street she looked this way and that to see if she could see any cause for Jim Tate's uneasiness, but there was nothing visible: just Brighton about its own business on a beautiful day.

Ida went into a pub and had a glass of Douro port. It went down sweet and warm and heavy. She had another. 'Who's Mr Colleoni?' she asked the barman.

'You don't know who Colleoni is?'

'I never heard of him till just now.'

The barman said, 'He's taking over from Kite.'

'Who's Kite?'

'Who *was* Kite? You saw how he got croaked at St Pancras?'

'No.'

'I don't suppose they meant to do it,' the barman said. 'They just meant to carve him up, but a razor slipped.'

'Have a drink?'

'Thanks. I'll have a gin.'

'Cheeryo.'

'Cheeryo.'

'I hadn't heard all this,' Ida said. She looked over his shoulder at the clock: nothing to do till one: she might as well have another and gossip awhile. 'Give me another port. When did all this happen?'

'Oh, before Whitsun.' The word Whitsun always caught her ear now: it meant a lot of things, a grubby ten shilling note, the white steps down to the ladies', Tragedy in capital letters. 'And what about Kite's friends?' she asked.

'They don't stand a chance now Kite's dead. The mob's got no leader. Why, they tag round after a kid of seventeen. What's a kid like that going to do against Colleoni?' He bent across the bar and whispered, 'He cut up Brewer last night.'

'Who? Colleoni?'

'No, the kid.'

'I dunno who Brewer is,' Ida said, 'but things seem lively.'

'You wait till the races start,' the man said. 'They'll be lively all right then. Colleoni's out for a monopoly. Quick, look through the window there and you'll see him.'

Ida went to the window and looked out, and again she saw only the Brighton she knew; she hadn't seen anything different even the day Fred died: two girls in beach pyjamas arm-in-arm, the buses going by to Rottingdean, a man selling papers, a woman with a shopping basket, a boy in a shabby suit, an excursion steamer edging off from the pier, which lay long, luminous and transparent, like a shrimp in the sunlight. She said, 'I don't see anyone.'

'He's gone now.'

'Who? Colleoni?'

'No, the kid.'

'Oh,' Ida said, 'that boy,' coming back to the bar, drinking up her port.

'I bet he's worried plenty.'

'A kid like that oughtn't to be mixed up with things,' Ida said. 'If he was mine I'd just larrup it out of him.' With those words she was about to dismiss him to turn her attention away from him, moving her mind on its axis like a great steel dredger, when she remembered: a face in a bar seen over Fred's shoulder, the sound of a glass breaking: 'The gentleman will pay.' She had a royal memory. 'You ever come across this Kolley Kibber?' she asked.

'No such luck,' the barman said.

'It seemed odd his dying like that. Must have made a bit of gossip.'

'None I heard of,' the barman said. 'He wasn't a Brighton man. No one knew him round these parts. He was a stranger.'

A stranger: the word meant nothing to her: there was no place in the world where she felt a stranger. She circulated the dregs of the cheap port in her glass and remarked to no one in particular, 'It's a good life.' There was nothing with which she didn't claim kinship: the advertising mirror behind the barman's back flashed her own image at her: the beach girls went giggling across the parade: the gong beat on the steamer for Boulogne: it was a good life. Only the darkness in which the Boy walked, going from Frank's, going back to Frank's, was alien to her; she had no pity for something she didn't understand. She said, 'I'll be getting on.'

It wasn't one yet, but there were questions she wanted to ask before Mr Corkery arrived. She said to the first waitress she saw, 'Are you the lucky one?'

'Not that I know of,' the waitress said coldly.

'I mean the one who found the card—the Kolley Kibber card.'

'Oh, that was *her*,' the waitress said, nodding a pointed powdered contemptuous chin.

Ida changed her table. She said, 'I've got a friend coming. I'll have to wait for him, but I'll try to pick. Is the shepherd's pie good?'

'It looks lovely.'

'Nice and brown on top?'

'It's a picture.'

'What's your name, dear?'

'Rose.'

'Why, I do believe,' Ida said, 'you were the lucky one who found a card?'

'Did *they* tell you that?' Rose said. 'They haven't forgiven me. They think I didn't ought to be lucky like that my first day.'

'Your first day? That *was* a bit of luck. You won't forget that day in a hurry.'

'No,' Rose said, 'I'll remember that always.'

'I mustn't keep you here talking.'

'If you only would. If you'd sort of look as if you was ordering things. There's no one else wants to be attended to and I'm ready to drop with these trays.'

'You don't like the job?'

'Oh,' Rose said quickly, 'I didn't say that. It's a good job. I wouldn't have anything different for the world. I wouldn't be in a hotel, or in Chessman's, not if they paid me twice as much. It's elegant here,' Rose said, gazing over the waste of green-painted tables, the daffodils, the paper napkins, the sauce bottles.

'Are you a local?'

'I've always lived here—all my life,' Rose said, 'in Nelson Place. This is a fine situation for me because they have us sleep in. There's only three of us in my room, and we have two looking-glasses.'

'How old are you?'

Rose leant gratefully across the table. 'Sixteen,' she said. 'I don't tell them that. I say seventeen. They'd say I wasn't old enough if they knew. They'd send me—' she hesitated a long while at the grim word, 'home'.

'You must have been glad,' Ida said, 'when you found that card.'

'Oh, I was.'

'Do you think I could have a glass of stout, dear?'

'We have to send out,' Rose said. 'If you give me the money—'

Ida opened her purse. 'I don't suppose you'll ever forget the little fellow.'

'Oh, he wasn't so . . .' Rose began and suddenly stopped, staring out through Snow's window across the parade to the pier.

'He wasn't what?' Ida said. 'What was it you were going to say?'

'I don't remember.'

'I just asked if you'd ever forget the little fellow.'

'It's gone out of my head,' Rose said. 'I'll get your drink. Does it cost all that—a glass of stout?' she asked, picking up the two shilling pieces.

'One of them's for you, dear,' Ida said. 'I'm inquisitive. I can't help it. I'm made that way. Tell me how he looked?'

'I don't know. I can't remember. I haven't got any memory for faces.'

'You can't have, can you, dear, or you'd have challenged him. You must have seen his picture in the papers.'

'I know. I'm silly that way.' She stood there, pale and determined and out of breath and guilty.

'And then it would have been ten pounds not ten shillings.'

'I'll get your drink.'

'Perhaps I'll wait after all. The gentleman who's giving me lunch, he can pay.' Ida picked up the shillings again, and Rose's eyes followed her hand back to her bag. 'Waste not, want not,' Ida said gently, taking in the details of the bony face, the large mouth, the eyes too far apart, the pallor, the immature body, and then suddenly she was loud and cheerful again, calling out, 'Phil Corkery, Phil Corkery,' waving her hand.

Mr Corkery wore a blazer with a badge and a stiff collar underneath. He looked as if he needed feeding up, as if he was wasted with passions he had never had the courage to express.

'Cheer up, Phil. What are you having?'

'Steak and kidney,' Mr Corkery said gloomily. 'Waitress, we want a drink.'

'We have to send out.'

'Well, in that case, make it two large bottles of Guinness,' Mr Corkery said.

When Rose came back Ida introduced her to Mr Corkery. 'This is the lucky girl who found a card.'

Rose backed away, but Ida detained her, grasping firmly her black cotton sleeve. 'Did he eat much?' she asked.

'I don't remember a thing,' Rose said, 'really I don't.' Their faces, flushed a little with the warm summer sun, were like posters announcing danger.

'Did he look,' Ida said, 'as if he was going to die?'

'How can I tell?'

'I suppose you talked to him?'

'I didn't talk to him. I was rushed. I just fetched him a Bass and a sausage roll, and I never saw him again.' She snatched her sleeve from Ida's hand and was gone.

'You can't get much from her,' Mr Corkery said.

'Oh yes I can,' Ida said, 'more than I bargained for.'

'Why, whatever's wrong?'

'It's what that girl said.'

'She didn't say much.'

'She said enough. I always had a feeling it was fishy. You see he told me in the taxi he was dying and I believed him for a moment: it gave me quite a turn till he told me he was just spinning a tale.'

'Well, he *was* dying.'

'He didn't mean it that way. I have my instincts.'

'Anyway,' Mr Corkery said, 'there's the evidence, he died natural. I don't see as there's anything to worry about. It's a fine day, Ida. Let's go on the *Brighton Belle* and talk it over there. No closing hours at sea. After all, if he did kill himself, it's his business.'

'If he killed himself,' Ida said, 'he was driven to it. I heard what the girl said, and I know this—it wasn't him that left the ticket here.'

'Good God,' Mr Corkery said. 'What do you mean? You oughtn't to talk like that. It's dangerous.' He swallowed nervously and the Adam's apple bobbed up and down under the skin of his scrawny neck.

'It's dangerous all right,' Ida said, watching the thin sixteen-year-old body shrink by in its black cotton dress, hearing the clink, clink, clink of a glass on a tray carried by an unsteady hand, 'but who to's another matter.'

'Let's go out in the sun,' Mr Corkery said. 'It's not so warm here.' He hadn't got a vest on, or a tie; he shivered a little in his cricket shirt and blazer.

'I've got to think,' Ida repeated.

'I shouldn't get mixed up in anything, Ida. He wasn't anything to you.'

'He wasn't anything to anyone, that's the trouble,' Ida said. She dug down into her deepest mind, the plane of memories, instincts, hopes, and brought up from them the only philosophy she lived by. 'I like fair play,' she said. She felt better when she'd said that and added with terrible lightheartedness, 'An eye for an eye, Phil. Will you stick by me?'

The Adam's apple bobbed. A draught from which all the sun had been sifted swung through the revolving door and Mr Corkery felt it on his bony breast. He said, 'I don't know what's given you the idea, Ida, but I'm for law and order. I'll stick by you.' His daring went to his head. He put a hand on her knee. 'I'd do anything for you, Ida.'

'There's only one thing to do after what *she* told me,' Ida said.

'What's that?'

'The police.'

Ida blew into the police-station with a laugh to this man and a wave of the hand to that. She didn't know them from Adam. She was cheerful and determined, and she carried Phil along in her wake.

'I want to see the inspector,' she told the sergeant at the desk.

'He's busy, ma'am. What was it you wanted to see him about?'

'I can wait,' Ida said, sitting down between the police capes. 'Sit down, Phil.' She grinned at them all with brassy assurance. 'Pubs don't open till six,' she said. 'Phil and I haven't anything to do till then.'

'What was it you wanted to see him about, ma'am?'

'Suicide,' Ida said, 'right under your noses and you call it natural death.'

The sergeant stared at her, and Ida stared back. Her large clear eyes (a spot of drink now and then didn't affect them) told nothing, gave away no secrets. Camaraderie, good nature, cheeriness fall like shutters before a plate-glass window. You could only guess at the goods behind: sound old-fashioned hallmarked goods, justice, an eye for an eye, law and order, capital punishment, a bit of fun now and then, nothing nasty, nothing shady, nothing you'd be ashamed to own, nothing mysterious.

'You aren't pulling my leg, are you?' the sergeant said.

'Not this time, sarge.'

He passed through a door and shut it behind him, and Ida settled herself more firmly on the bench, made herself at home. 'Bit stuffy in here, boys,' she said. 'What about opening another window?' and obediently they opened one.

The sergeant called to her from the door. 'You can go in,' he said.

'Come on, Phil,' Ida said and bore him with her into the tiny cramped official room which smelt of French polish and fish glue.

'And so,' the inspector said, 'you wanted to tell me about a suicide, Mrs—?' He looked tired and old and shy. He had tried to hide a tin of fruit drops behind a telephone and a manuscript book.

'Arnold, Ida Arnold. I thought it might be your line, inspector,' she said with heavy sarcasm.

'This your husband?'

'Oh no, a friend. I wanted a witness, that's all.'

'And who is it you're concerned about, Mrs Arnold?'

'Hale's the name, Fred Hale. I beg your pardon. Charles Hale.'

'We know all about Hale, Mrs Arnold. He died quite naturally.'

'Oh no,' Ida said, 'you don't know all. You don't know he was with me, two hours before he was found.'

'You weren't at the inquest?'

'I didn't know it was him till I saw his picture.'

'And why do you think there's anything wrong?'

'Listen,' Ida said. 'He was with me and he was scared about something. We were at the Palace Pier. I had to have a wash and brush up, but he didn't want me to leave him. I was only away five minutes and he'd gone. Where'd he gone to? You say he went and had lunch at Snow's and then went on down the pier to the shelter in Hove. You think he just gave me the slip, but it wasn't Fred—I mean Hale—who had lunch at Snow's and left that card. I've just seen the waitress. Hale didn't like Bass—he wouldn't drink Bass—but the man at Snow's sent out for a bottle.'

'That's nothing,' the inspector said. 'It was a hot day. He was feeling bad, too. He got tired of doing all the things he'd got to do. I wouldn't be surprised if he cheated and got someone else to go into Snow's.'

'The girl won't say a thing about him. She knows but she won't say.'

'I can think of an explanation easily enough, Mrs Arnold. The man may have left a card on condition she didn't say anything.'

'It's not that. She's scared. Someone's scared her. Maybe the same person who drove Fred . . . And there are other things.'

'I'm sorry, Mrs Arnold. It's just a waste of time getting fussed like this. You see there was a post-mortem. The medical evidence shows without any doubt that he died naturally. He had a bad heart. The medical name for it is coronary thrombosis. I'd call it just heat and crowds and exertion—and a weak heart.'

'Could I see the report?'

'It wouldn't be usual.'

'I was a friend of his, you see,' Ida said softly. 'I'd like to be satisfied.'

'Well, to put your mind at rest, I'll stretch a point. It's here now on my desk.'

Ida read it carefully. 'This doctor,' she said, 'he knows his stuff?'

'He's a first-class doctor.'

'It seems clear, doesn't it?' Ida said. She began to read it all over again. 'They do go into details, don't they. Why, I wouldn't know more about him if I'd married him. Appendix scar, supernumerary nipples, whatever they are, suffered from wind—I do that myself on a Bank Holiday. It's almost disrespectful, isn't it? He wouldn't have liked this,' she brooded over the report with easy kindliness. 'Varicose veins. Poor old Fred. What's this mean about the liver?'

'Drank too much, that's all.'

'I wouldn't be surprised. Poor Fred. So he had ingrowing toe-nails. It doesn't seem right to know that.'

'You were a great friend of his?'

'Well, we only knew each other that day. But I liked him. He was a real gentleman. If I hadn't been a bit lit this wouldn't have happened.' She blew out her bust. 'He wouldn't have come to any harm with me.'

'Have you quite finished with the report, Mrs Arnold?'

'He does mention everything, this doctor of yours, doesn't he? Bruises, superficial whatever that means, on the arms. What do you think of that, inspector?'

'Nothing at all. Bank Holiday crowds, that's all. Pushed here and there.'

'Oh, come off it,' Ida said, 'come off it.' Her tongue flared up. 'Be human. Were *you* out on Bank Holiday? Where do you find a crowd like that? Brighton's big enough, isn't it? It's not a tube lift. I was here. I know.'

The inspector said stubbornly, 'You've got fancies, Mrs Arnold.'

'So the police won't do a thing? You won't question that girl in Snow's?'

'The case is closed, Mrs Arnold. And even if it had been suicide, why open old wounds?'

'Someone drove him . . . perhaps it wasn't suicide at all . . . perhaps . . .'

'I've told you, Mrs Arnold, the case is closed.'

'That's what you think,' Ida said. She rose to her feet; she summoned Phil with a jerk of the chin. 'Not half it isn't,' she said. 'I'll be seeing you.' She looked back from the door at the elderly man behind the desk and threatened him with her ruthless vitality. 'Or perhaps not,' she said. 'I can manage this my own way. I don't need your police' (the constables in the outer room stirred uneasily; somebody laughed; somebody dropped a tin of boot polish). 'I've got my friends.'

Her friends—they were everywhere under the bright glittering Brighton air. They followed their wives obediently into fishmongers, they carried the children's buckets to the beach, they lingered round the bars waiting for opening time, they took a penny peep on the pier at 'A Night of Love'. She had only to appeal to any of them, for Ida Arnold was on the right side. She was cheery, she was healthy, she could get a bit lit with the best of them. She liked a good time, her big breasts bore their carnality frankly down the Old Steyne, but you had only to look at her to know that you could rely on her. She wouldn't tell tales to your wife, she wouldn't remind you next morning of what you wanted to forget, she was honest, she was kindly, she belonged to the great middle law-abiding class, her amusements were their amusements, her superstitions their superstitions (the planchette scratching the French polish on the occasional table, and the salt over the shoulder), she had no more love for anyone than they had.

'Expenses mounting up,' Ida said. 'Never mind. Everything will be all right after the races.'

'You got a tip?' Mr Corkery asked.

'Straight from the horse's mouth. I shouldn't say that. Poor Fred.'

'Tell a pal,' Mr Corkery implored.

'All in good time,' Ida said. 'Be a good boy and you don't know what mayn't happen.'

'You don't still think, do you?' Mr Corkery sounded her. 'Not after what the doctor wrote?'

'I've never paid any attention to doctors.'

'But why?'

'We've got to find out.'

'And how?'

'Give me time. I haven't started yet.'

The sea stretched like a piece of gay common washing in a tenement square across the end of the street. 'The colour of your eyes,' Mr Corkery interjected thoughtfully and with a touch of nostalgia. He said, 'Couldn't we now—just go for a while on the pier, Ida?'

'Yes,' Ida said. 'The pier. We'll go to the Palace Pier, Phil,' but when they got there she wouldn't go through the turnstile, but took up her stand like a huckster facing the Aquarium, the ladies' lavatory. 'This is where I start from,' she said. 'He waited for me here, Phil,' and she stared out over the red and green lights, the heavy traffic of her battlefield, laying her plans, marshalling her cannon fodder, while five yards away Spicer stood too waiting for an enemy to appear. Only a slight doubt troubled her optimism. 'That horse has got to win, Phil,' she said. 'I can't hold out else.'

2

Spicer was restless these days. There was nothing for him to do. When the races began again he wouldn't feel so bad, he wouldn't think so much about Hale. It was the medical evidence which upset him: 'death from natural causes', when with his own eyes he'd seen the Boy . . . It was fishy, it wasn't straight. He told himself that he could face a police inquiry, but he couldn't stand this not knowing, the false security of the verdict. There was a catch in it somewhere, and all through the long summer sunlight Spicer wandered uneasily, watching out for trouble: the police-station, the Place where It had been done, even Snow's came into his promenade. He wanted to be satisfied that the cops were doing nothing (he knew every plain-clothes man in the Brighton force), that no one was asking questions or loitering where they had no reason to loiter. He knew it was just nerves. 'I'll be all right when the races start,' he told himself, like a man with a poisoned body who believes that all will be well when a single tooth is drawn.

He came up the parade cautiously, from the Hove end, from the glass shelter where Hale's body had been set, pale with bloodshot eyes and nicotined finger-ends. He had a corn on his left foot and limped a little, dragging after him a bright orange-brown shoe. He had come out in spots, too, round his mouth, and that also was caused by Hale's death. Fear upset his bowels, and the spots came: it was always the way.

He limped cautiously across the road when he was close to Snow's: that was another vulnerable place. The sun caught the great panes of plate-glass and flashed back at him like headlamps. He sweated a little passing by. A voice said, 'Well, if it isn't Spicey?' He had had his eyes on Snow's across the road, he hadn't noticed who was beside him on the parade, leaning on the green railing above the shingle. He turned his damp face sharply. 'What are you doing here, Crab?'

'It's good to be back,' Crab said, a young man in a mauve suit, with shoulders like coat-hangers and a small waist.

'We ran you out once, Crab. I thought you'd stay out. You've altered.' His hair was carroty, except at the roots, and his nose was straightened and scarred. He had been a Jew once, but a hair-dresser and a surgeon had altered that. 'Afraid we'd lamp you if you didn't change your mug?'

'Why, Spicey, me afraid of your lot? You'll be saying "sir" to me one of these days. I'm Colleoni's right-hand man.'

'I always heard as how he was left-handed,' Spicer said. 'Wait till Pinkie knows you're back.'

Crab laughed. 'Pinkie's at the police-station,' he said.

The police-station: Spicer's chin went down, he was off, his orange shoe sliding on the paving, his corn shooting. He heard Crab laugh behind him, the smell of dead fish was in his nostrils, he was a sick man. The police-station: the police-station: it was like an abscess jetting its poison through the nerves. When he got to Frank's there was no one there. He creaked his tortured way up the stairs, past the rotten banister, to Pinkie's room: the door stood open, vacancy stared in the swing mirror: no message, crumbs on the floor: it looked as a room would look if someone had been called suddenly away.

Spicer stood by the chest of drawers (the walnut stain splashed unevenly): no scrap of written reassurance in a drawer: no warn-ing. He looked up and down, the corn shooting through his whole body to the brain, and suddenly there was his own face in the glass—the coarse black hair greying at the roots, the small erup-tions on the face, the bloodshot eyeballs, and it occurred to him, as if he were looking at a close-up on a screen, that that was the kind of face a nark might have, a man who grassed to the bogies.

He moved away: flakes of pastry ground under his foot; he told himself he wasn't a man to grass: Pinkie, Cubitt and Dallow, they were his pals. He wouldn't let them down—even though it wasn't he who'd done the killing. He'd been against it from the first: he'd only laid the cards: he only *knew*. He stood at the head of the stairs looking down past the shaky banister. He would rather kill himself than squeal, he told the empty landing in a whisper, but he knew really that he hadn't got that courage. Better run for it: and he thought with nostalgia of Nottingham and a pub he knew, a pub he had once hoped to buy when he had made his pile. It was a good spot, Nottingham, the air was good, none of this salt smart on the dry mouth, and the girls were kind. If he could get away—but the others would never let him go: he knew too much about too many things. He was in the mob for life now, and he looked down the drop of the staircase to the tiny hall, the strip of linoleum, the old-fashioned telephone on a bracket by the door.

As he watched, it began to ring. He looked down at it with fear and suspicion. He couldn't stand any more bad news. Where had everybody gone to? Had they run and left him without a warning? Even Frank wasn't in the basement. There was a smell of scorching as if he'd left his iron burning. The bell rang on and on. Let them ring, he thought. They'll tire of it in time: why should I do all the work of this bloody gaff? On and on and on. Whoever it was didn't tire easily. He came to the head of the stairs and scowled down at the vulcanite spitting noise through the quiet house. 'The trouble is,' he said aloud, as if he were rehearsing a speech to Pinkie and the others, 'I'm getting too old for this game. I got to retire. Look at my hair. I'm grey, ain't I? I got to retire.' But the only answer was the regular ring, ring, ring.

'Why can't someone answer the bloody blower?' he shouted down the well of the stairs. 'I got to do all the work, have I?' and he saw himself dropping a ticket into the child's bucket, slipping a ticket under an upturned boat, tickets which could have hanged him. He suddenly ran down the stairs in a kind of simulated fury and lifted the receiver. 'Well,' he bellowed, 'well, who the hell's there?'

'Is that Frank's?' a voice said. He knew the voice now. It was the girl in Snow's. He lowered the receiver in a panic and waited, and a thin doll's voice came out at him from the orifice: 'Please, I've got to speak to Pinkie.' It was almost as if listening betrayed him. He listened again and the voice repeated with desperate anxiety, 'Is that Frank's?'

Keeping his mouth away from the phone, curling his tongue in an odd way, mouthing hoarsely and crookedly, Spicer in disguise replied, 'Pinkie's out. What do you want?'

'I've got to speak to him.'

'He's out I tell you.'

'Who's that?' the girl asked in a scared voice.

'That's what I want to know. Who are you?'

'I'm a friend of Pinkie's. I got to find him. It's urgent.'

'I can't help you.'

'Please. You've got to find Pinkie. He told me I was to tell him— if ever—' The voice died away.

Spicer shouted down the phone. 'Hullo. Where you gone? If ever what?' There was no reply. He listened, with the receiver pressed against his ear, to silence buzzing up the wires. He began to jerk at the hook: 'Exchange. Hullo. Hullo. Exchange,' and then suddenly the voice came on again as if somebody had dropped a needle into place on a record. 'Are you there? Please, are you there?'

'Of course I'm here. What did Pinkie tell you?'

'You got to find Pinkie. He said he wanted to know. It's a woman. She was in here with a man.'

'What do you mean—a woman?'

'Asking questions,' the voice said. Spicer put down the receiver; whatever else the girl had to say was strangled on the wire. Find Pinkie? What was the good of finding Pinkie? It was the others who had done the finding. And Cubitt and Dallow: they'd slipped away without even warning him. If he did squeal it would be only returning them their own coin. But he wasn't going to squeal. He wasn't a nark. They thought he was yellow. *They'd think* he'd squeal. He wouldn't even get the credit . . . a little moisture of self-pity came pricking out of the dry ageing ducts.

I got to think, he repeated to himself. I got to think. He opened the street door and went out. He didn't even wait to fetch his hat. His hair was thin on top, dry and brittle under the dandruff. He walked rapidly, going nowhere in particular, but every road in Brighton ended on the front. I'm too old for the game, I got to get out, Nottingham; he wanted to be alone, he went down the stone steps to the level of the beach; it was early closing and the small shops facing the sea under the promenade were closed. He walked on the edge of the asphalt, scuffling in the shingle. I wouldn't grass, he remarked dumbly to the tide as it lifted and withdrew, but it wasn't my doing, I never wanted to kill Fred. He passed into shadow under the pier, and a cheap photographer with a box camera snapped him as the shadow fell and pressed a paper into his hand. Spicer didn't notice. The iron pillars stretched down across the wet dimmed shingle holding up above his head the motor-track, the shooting booths and peep machines, mechanical models, 'the Robot Man will tell your fortune'. A seagull flew straight towards him between the pillars like a scared bird caught in a cathedral, then swerved out into the sunlight from the dark iron nave. I wouldn't grass, Spicer said, unless I had to. . . . He stumbled on an old boot and put his hand on the stones to save himself: they had all the cold of the sea and had never been warmed by sun under these pillars.

He thought: that woman—how does she know anything— what's she doing asking questions? I didn't want to have Hale killed; it wouldn't be fair if I took the drop with the others; I told 'em not to do it. He came out into the sunlight and climbed back on to the parade. It'll be this way the bogies will come, he thought, if they know anything; they always reconstruct the crime. He took up his stand between the turnstile of the pier and the ladies' lavatory. There weren't many people about: he could spot the bogies easily enough—if they came. Over there was the Royal Albion; he could see all the way up the Grand Parade to Old Steyne; the pale green domes of the Pavilion floated above the dusty trees; he could see anyone in the hot empty mid-week afternoon who went down below the Aquarium, the white deck ready for dancing, to the little covered arcade where the cheap shops stood between the sea and the stone wall, selling Brighton rock.

3

The poison twisted in the Boy's veins. He had been insulted. He had to show someone he was—a man. He went scowling into Snow's, young, shabby and untrustworthy, and the waitresses with one accord turned their backs. He stood there looking for a table (the place was full), and no one attended to him. It was as if they doubted whether he had the money to pay for his meal. He thought of Colleoni padding through the enormous rooms, the embroidered crowns on the chair-backs. He suddenly shouted aloud: 'I want service,' and the pulse beat in his cheek. All the faces round him shivered into motion, and then were still again like water. Everyone looked away. He was ignored. Suddenly a sense of weariness overtook him. He felt as if he had travelled a great many miles to be ignored like this.

A voice said, 'There isn't a table.' They were still such strangers that he didn't recognize the voice, until it added: 'Pinkie'. He looked round and there was Rose, dressed to go out in a shabby black straw which made her face look as it would look in twenty years' time, after the work and the child-bearing.

'They got to serve me,' the Boy said. 'Who do they think they are?'

'There isn't a table.'

Everyone was watching them now—with disapproval.

'Come outside, Pinkie.'

'What are you all dressed up for?'

'It's my afternoon off. Come outside.'

He followed her out and suddenly taking her wrist he brought the poison on to his lips. 'I could break your arm.'

'What have I done, Pinkie?'

'No table. They don't like serving me in there, I'm no class. They'll see—one day—'

'What?'

But his mind staggered before the extent of his ambitions. He said, 'Never mind—they'll learn—'

'Did you get the message, Pinkie?'

'What message?'

'I phoned you at Frank's. I told him to tell you.'

'Told who?'

'I don't know.' She added casually, 'I think it was the man who left the ticket.'

He gripped her wrist again. He said, 'The man who left the ticket's dead. You read it all.' But she showed no sign of fear this time. He'd been too friendly. She ignored his reminder.

'Did he find you?' she asked, and he thought to himself: she's got to be scared again.

'No one found me,' he said. He pushed her roughly forward. 'Come on. We'll walk. I'll take you out.'

'I was going home.'

'You won't go home. You'll come with me. I want exercise,' he said, looking down at his pointed shoes which had never walked further than the length of the parade.

'Where'll we go, Pinkie?'

'Somewhere,' Pinkie said, 'out in the country. That's where you go on a day like this.' He tried to think for a moment of where the country was: the racecourse, that was country; and then a bus came by marked Peacehaven, and he waved his hand to it. 'There you are,' he said, 'that's country. We can talk there. There's things we got to get straight.'

'I thought we were going to walk.'

'This is walking,' he said roughly, pushing her up the steps. 'You're green. You don't know a thing. You don't think people re-ally *walk*. Why—it's miles.'

'When people say, "Come for a walk," they mean a bus?'

'Or a car. I'd have taken you in the car, but the mob are out in it.'

'You got a car?'

'I couldn't get on without a car,' the Boy said, as the bus

climbed up behind Rottingdean: red-brick buildings behind a wall, a great stretch of parkland, one girl with a hockey-stick staring at something in the sky, with cropped expensive turf all round her. The poison drained back into its proper glands: he was admired, no one insulted him, but when he looked at the girl who admired him, the poison oozed out again. He said, 'Take off that hat. You look awful.' She obeyed him: her mousy hair lay flat on the small scalp: he watched her with distaste. That was what they'd joked about him marrying: that. He watched her with his soured virginity, as one might watch a draught of medicine offered that one would never, never take; one would die first—or let others die. The chalky dust blew up round the windows.

'You told me to ring up,' Rose said, 'so when . . .'

'Not here,' the Boy said. 'Wait till we're alone.' The driver's head rose slowly against a waste of sky: a few white feathers blown backward into the blue: they were on top of the downs and turned eastwards. The Boy sat with his pointed shoes side by side, his hands in his pockets, feeling the throb of the engine come up through the thin soles.

'It's lovely,' Rose said, 'being out here—in the country with you.' Little tarred bungalows with tin roofs paraded backwards, gardens scratched in the chalk, dry flower-beds like Saxon emblems carved on the downs. Notices read: 'Pull in Here', 'Mazawattee tea', 'Genuine Antiques', and hundreds of feet below the pale green sea washed into the scarred and shabby side of England. Peacehaven itself dwindled out against the downs: half-made streets turned into grass tracks. They walked down between the bungalows to the cliff-edge. There was nobody about: one of the bungalows had broken windows, in another the blinds were down for a death. 'It makes me giddy,' Rose said, 'looking down.' It was early closing and the store was shut; closing time and no drinks obtainable at the hotel; a vista of To Let boards running back along the chalky ruts of unfinished roads. The Boy could see over her shoulder the rough drop to the shingle. 'It makes me feel I'll fall,' Rose said, turning from the sea. He let her turn; no need to act prematurely; the draught might never be offered.

'Tell me,' he said, 'now—who rang up who and why?'

'I rang up *you*, but you weren't in. *He* answered.'

'He?' the Boy repeated.

'The one who left the ticket that day you came in. You remember—you were looking for something.' He remembered all right—the hand under the cloth, the stupid innocent face he had expected would so easily forget. 'You remember a lot,' he said, frowning at the thought.

'I wouldn't forget that day,' she said abruptly and stopped.

'You forget a lot, too. I just told you that wasn't the man you heard speak. That man's dead.'

'It doesn't matter anyway,' she said. 'What matters is—someone was in asking questions.'

'About the ticket?'

'Yes.'

'A man?'

'A woman. A big one with a laugh. You should have heard the laugh. Just as if she'd never had a care. I didn't trust her. She wasn't our kind.'

'Our kind': he frowned again towards the shallow wrinkled tide at the suggestion that they had something in common and spoke sharply. 'What did she want?'

'She wanted to know everything. What the man who left the card looked like.'

'What did you tell her?'

'I didn't tell her a thing, Pinkie.'

The Boy dug with his pointed shoe into the thin dry turf and sent an empty corned-beef tin rattling down the ruts. 'It's only you I'm thinking of,' he said. 'It don't matter to me. I'm not concerned. But I wouldn't want you getting mixed up in things that might be dangerous.' He looked quickly up at her, sideways. 'You don't seem scared. It's serious what I'm telling you.'

'I wouldn't be scared, Pinkie—not with you about.'

He dug his nails into his hands with vexation. She remembered everything she ought to forget, and forgot all that she should remember—the vitriol bottle. He'd scared her all right then: he'd been too friendly since: she really believed that he was fond of her. Why, this, he supposed, was 'walking out', and he thought again of Spicer's joke. He looked at the mousy skull, the bony body and the shabby dress, and shuddered—involuntarily, a goose flying across the final bed. 'Saturday,' he thought, 'today's Saturday,' remembering the room at home, the frightening weekly exercise of his parents which he watched from his single bed. That was what they expected of you, every polony you met had her eye on the bed: his virginity straightened in him like sex. That was how they judged you: not by whether you had the guts to kill a man, to run a mob, to conquer Colleoni. He said, 'We don't want to stay round here. We'll be getting back.'

'We've only just come,' the girl said. 'Let's stay a bit, Pinkie. I like the country,' she said.

'You've had a look,' he said. 'You can't *do* anything with the country. The pub's closed.'

'We could just sit. We've got to wait for the bus anyway. You're funny. You aren't scared of anything, are you?'

He laughed queerly, sitting awkwardly down in front of the bungalow with the shattered glass. 'Me scared? That's funny.' He lay back against the bank, his waistcoat undone, his thin frayed tie bright and striped against the chalk.

'This is better than going home,' Rose said.

'Where's home?'

'Nelson Place. Do you know it?'

'Oh, I've passed through,' he said airily, but he could have drawn its plan as accurately as a surveyor on the turf: the barred and battlemented Salvation Army gaff at the corner: his own home beyond in Paradise Piece: the houses which looked as if they had passed through an intensive bombardment, flapping gutters and glassless windows, an iron bedstead rusting in a front garden, the smashed and wasted ground in front where houses had been pulled down for model flats which had never gone up.

They lay on the chalk bank side by side with a common geography, and a little hate mixed with his contempt. He thought he had made his escape, and here his home was: back beside him, making claims.

Rose said suddenly, '*She's* never lived there.'

'Who?'

'That woman asking questions. Never a care.'

'Well,' he said, 'we can't all 'ave been born in Nelson Place.'

'You weren't born there—or somewhere round?'

'Me. Of course not. What do you think?'

'I thought—maybe you were. You're a Roman too. We were all Romans in Nelson Place. You believe in things. Like Hell. But you can see she don't believe a thing.' She said bitterly, 'You can tell the world's all dandy with her.'

He defended himself from any connection with Paradise Piece: 'I don't take any stock in religion. Hell—it's just there. You don't need to think of it—not before you die.'

'You might die sudden.'

He closed his eyes under the bright empty arch, and a memory floated up imperfectly into speech. 'You know what they say— "Between the stirrup and the ground, he something sought and something found".'

'Mercy.'

'That's right: Mercy.'

'It would be awful, though,' she said slowly, 'if they didn't give you time.' She turned her cheek on to the chalk towards him and added, as if he could help her, 'That's what I always pray. That I won't die sudden. What do you pray?'

'I don't,' he said, but he was praying even while he spoke to someone or something: that he wouldn't need to carry on any further with her, get mixed up again with that drab dynamited plot of ground they both called home.

'You angry about anything?' Rose asked.

'A man wants to be quiet sometimes,' he said, lying rigidly against the chalk bank, giving nothing away. In the silence a shutter flapped, and the tide lisped: two people walking out: that's what they were, and the memory of Colleoni's luxury, the crowned chairs at the Cosmopolitan, came back to taunt him. He said, 'Talk, can't you? Say something.'

'You wanted to be quiet,' she retorted with a sudden anger which took him by surprise. He hadn't thought her capable of that. 'If I don't suit you,' she said, 'you can leave me alone. I didn't ask to come out.' She sat with her hands round her knees and her cheeks burned on the tip of the bone: anger was as good as rouge on her thin face. 'If I'm not grand enough—your car and all—'

'Who said—'

'Oh,' she said, 'I'm not that dumb. I've seen you looking at me. My hat—'

It occurred to him suddenly that she might even get up and leave him, go back to Snow's with her secret for the first comer who questioned her kindly: he had to conciliate her, they were walking out, he'd got to do the things expected of him. He put out his hand with repulsion; it lay like a cold paddock on her knee. 'You took me wrong,' he said, 'you're a sweet girl. I've been worried, that's all. Business worries. You and me'—he swallowed painfully—'we suit each other down to the ground.' He saw the colour go, the face turn to him with a blind willingness to be deceived, saw the lips waiting. He drew her hand up quickly and put his mouth against her fingers: anything was better than the lips: the fingers were rough on his skin and tasted a little of soap. She said, 'Pinkie, I'm sorry. You're sweet to me.'

He laughed nervously, 'You and me,' and heard the hoot of a bus with the joy of a besieged man listening to the bugles of the relieving force. 'There,' he said, 'the bus. Let's be going. I'm not much of a one for the country. A city bird. You too.' She got up and he saw the skin of her thigh for a moment above the artificial silk, and a prick of sexual desire disturbed him like a sickness. That was what happened to a man in the end: the stuffy room, the wakeful children, the Saturday night movements from the other bed. Was there no escape—anywhere—for anyone? It was worth murdering a world.

'It's beautiful here all the same,' she said, staring up the chalky ruts between the To Let boards, and the Boy laughed again at the fine words people gave to a dirty act: love, beauty . . . All his pride coiled like a watch spring round the thought that *he* wasn't deceived, that *he* wasn't going to give himself up to marriage and the birth of children, he was going to be where Colleoni now was and higher . . . He knew everything, he had watched every detail of the act of sex, you couldn't deceive him with lovely words, there was nothing to be excited about, no gain to recompense you for what you lost; but when Rose turned to him again, with the expectation of a kiss, he was aware all the same of a horrifying ignorance. His mouth missed hers and recoiled. He'd never yet kissed a girl.

She said, 'I'm sorry. I'm stupid. I've never had—' and suddenly broke off to watch a gull rise from one of the little parched gardens and drop over the cliff towards the sea.

He didn't speak to her in the bus, sullen and ill-at-ease, sitting with his hands in his pockets, his feet close together, not knowing why he'd come this far out with her, only to go back again with nothing settled, the secret, the memory still lodged securely in her skull. The country unwound the other way: Mazawattee tea, antique dealers, pull-ins, the thin grass petering out on the first asphalt.

From the pier the Brighton anglers flung their floats. A little music ground mournfully out into the windy sunlight. They walked on the sunny side past 'A Night of Love', 'For Men Only', 'The Fan Dancer'. Rose asked, 'Is business bad?'

'There's always worries,' the Boy said.

'I wish I could help, be of use.' He said nothing, walking on. She put out a hand towards the thin rigid figure, seeing the smooth cheek, the fluff of fair hair at the nape. 'You're so young, Pinkie, to get worries.' She put her hand through his arm. 'We're both young, Pinkie,' and felt his body stonily withdrawn.

A photographer said, 'Snap you together against the sea,' raising the cap from his camera, and the Boy flung up his hands before his face and went on.

'Don't you like being snapped, Pinkie? We might have had our pictures stuck up for people to see. It wouldn't have *cost* anything.'

'I don't mind what things cost,' the Boy said, rattling his pockets, showing how much cash he had.

'We might 'ave been stuck up there,' Rose said, halting at the photographer's kiosk, at the pictures of the bathing belles and the famous comedians and the anonymous couples, 'next—' and exclaimed with surprise, 'why—there *he* is.'

The Boy was staring over the side where the green tide sucked and slid like a wet mouth round the piles. He turned unwillingly to look and there was Spicer fixed in the photographer's window for the world to gaze at, striding out of the sunlight into the shadow under the pier, worried and hunted and in haste, a comic figure at which strangers could laugh and say, 'He's worried right enough. They caught *him* unawares.'

'The one who left the card,' Rose said. 'The one you said was dead. *He's* not dead. Though it almost looks—' she laughed with amusement at the blurred black-and-white haste—'that he's afraid he will be if he doesn't hurry.'

'An old picture,' the Boy said.

'Oh no, it's not. This is where today's pictures go. For you to buy.'

'You know a lot.'

'You can't miss it, can you?' Rose said. 'It's comic. Striding along. All fussed up. Not even seeing the camera.'

'Stay here,' the Boy said. Inside the kiosk it was dark after the sun. A man with a thin moustache and steel-rimmed spectacles sorted piles of prints.

'I want a picture that's up outside,' the Boy said.

'Slip, please,' the man said, and put out yellow fingers which smelt faintly of hypo.

'I haven't got a slip.'

'You can't have the picture without the slip,' the man said and held a negative up to the electric globe.

'What right have you,' the Boy said, 'to stick up pictures with-out a by-your-leave? You let me have that picture,' but the steel rims glittered back at him, without interest—a fractious boy. 'You bring that slip,' the man said, 'and you can have the picture. Now run along. I'm busy.' Behind his head were framed snapshots of King Edward VIII (Prince of Wales) in a yachting cap and a back-ground of peep machines, going yellow from inferior chemicals and age; Vesta Tilley signing autographs; Henry Irving muffled against the Channel winds; a nation's history. Lily Langtry wore ostrich feathers, Mrs Pankhurst hobble skirts, the English Beauty Queen of 1923 a bathing dress. It was little comfort to know that Spicer was among the immortals.

4

'Spicer,' the Boy called, 'Spicer.' He climbed up from Frank's small dark hall towards the landing, leaving a smear of country, of the downs, white on the linoleum. 'Spicer.' He felt the broken banister tremble under his hand. He opened the door of Spicer's room and there he was upon the bed, asleep face down. The window was closed, an insect buzzed through the stale air, and there was a smell of whisky from the bed. Pinkie stood looking down on the greying hair. He felt no pity at all; he wasn't old enough for pity. He pulled Spicer round; the skin round his mouth was in eruption. 'Spicer.'

Spicer opened his eyes. He saw nothing for a while in the dim room.

'I want a word with you, Spicer.'

Spicer sat up. 'My God, Pinkie, I'm glad to see you.'

'Always glad to see a pal, eh, Spicer?'

'I saw Crab. He said you were at the police-station.'

'Crab?'

'You weren't at the station, then?'

'I was having a friendly talk—about Brewer.'

'Not about—?'

'About Brewer.' The Boy suddenly put his hand on Spicer's wrist. 'Your nerves are all wrong, Spicer. You want a holiday.' He sniffed with contempt the tainted air. 'You drink too much.' He went to the window and threw it open on the vista of grey wall. A leather-jacket buzzed up the pane and the Boy caught it in his hand. It vibrated like a tiny watchspring in his palm. He began to pull off the legs and wings one by one. 'She loves me,' he said, 'she loves me not. I've been out with my girl, Spicer.'

'The one from Snow's?'

The Boy turned the denuded body over on his palm and puffed it away over Spicer's bed. 'You know who I mean,' he said. 'You had a message for me, Spicer. Why didn't you bring it?'

'I couldn't find you, Pinkie. Honest I couldn't. And anyway it wasn't that important. Some old busybody asking questions.'

'It scared you all the same,' the Boy said. He sat down on the hard deal chair before the mirror, his hands on his knees, watching Spicer. The pulse beat in his cheek.

'Oh, it didn't scare me,' Spicer said.

'You went walking blind straight to There.'

'What do you mean—There?'

'There's only one There to you, Spicer. You think about it and you dream about it. You're too old for this life.'

'This life?' Spicer said, glaring back at him from the bed.

'This racket, of course I mean. You get nervous and then you get rash. First there was that card in Snow's and now you let your picture be stuck up on the pier for anyone to see. For Rose to see.'

'Honest to God, Pinkie, I never knew that.'

'You forget to walk on your toes.'

'She's safe. She's stuck on you, Pinkie.'

'I don't know anything about women. I leave that to you and Cubitt and the rest. I only know what you tell me. You've told me time and time again there never was a safe polony yet.'

'That's just talk.'

'You mean I'm a kid and you tell me good night stories. But I've got so I believe them, Spicer. It don't seem safe to me that you and Rose are in the same town. Apart from this other buer asking questions. You'll have to disappear, Spicer.'

'What do you mean?' Spicer said. 'Disappear?' he fumbled inside his jacket and the Boy watched him, his hands flat on his knees. 'You wouldn't do anything,' he said, fumbling in his pocket.

'Why,' the Boy said, 'what do you think I mean? I mean take a holiday, go away somewhere for a while.'

Spicer's hand came out of his pocket. He held out a silver watch towards the Boy. 'You can trust me, Pinkie. Look there, what the boys gave me. Read the inscription. "Ten Years a Pal. From the boys at the Stadium." I don't let people down. That was fifteen years ago, Pinkie. Twenty-five years on the tracks. You weren't born when I started.'

'You need a holiday,' the Boy said. 'That's all I said.'

'I'd be glad to take a holiday,' Spicer said, 'but I wouldn't want you to think I'm milky. I'll go at once. I'll pack a bag and clear out tonight. Why, I'd be glad to be gone.'

'No,' the Boy said, staring down at his shoes. 'There's not all that hurry.' He lifted a foot. The sole was worn through in a piece the size of a shilling. He thought again of the crowns on Colleoni's chairs at the Cosmopolitan. 'I'll need you at the races.' He smiled across the room at Spicer. 'A pal I can trust.'

'You can trust me, Pinkie.' Spicer's fingers smoothed the silver watch. 'What are you smiling at? Have I got a smut or something?'

'I was just thinking of the races,' the Boy said. 'They mean a lot to me.' He got up and stood with his back to the greying light, the tenement wall, the smut-smeared pane, looking down at Spicer with a kind of curiosity. 'And where will you go, Spicer?' he said. His mind was quite made up, and for the second time in a few weeks he looked at a dying man. He couldn't help feeling inquisitive. Why, it was even possible that old Spicer was not set for the flames, he'd been a loyal old geezer, he hadn't done as much harm as the next man, he might slip through the gates into—but the Boy couldn't picture any eternity except in terms of pain. He frowned a little in the effort: a glassy sea, a golden crown, old Spicer.

'Nottingham,' Spicer said. 'A pal of mine keeps the "Blue Anchor" in Union Street. A free house. High class. Lunches served. He's often said to me, "Spicer, why don't you come into partnership? We'd make the old place into a hotel with a few more nickers in the till." If it wasn't for you and the boys,' Spicer said, 'I wouldn't want to come back. I wouldn't mind staying away for keeps.'

'Well,' the Boy said, 'I'll be off. We know where we are now, anyway.' Spicer lay back on the pillow and put up the foot with the shooting corn. There was a hole in his woollen stocking, and a big toe showed through, hard skin calcined with middle age. 'Sleep well,' the Boy said.

He went downstairs, the front door faced east, and the hall was dark. He switched on a light by the telephone and then switched it out again: he didn't know why. Then he rang up the Cosmopolitan. When the hotel exchange answered he could hear the dance music in the distance, all the way from the Palm House (*thés dansants* three shillings), behind the Louis Seize lounge. 'I want Mr Colleoni.' 'The nightingale singing, the postman ringing'—the tune was abruptly cut off, and a low voice purred up the line. 'That Mr Colleoni?'

He could hear a glass chink and ice move in a shaker. He said, 'This is Mr P. Brown. I've been thinking things over, Mr Colleoni.' Outside the little dark linoleumed hall a bus slid by, the lights faint in the grey end of the day. The Boy put his mouth close to the mouth of the telephone and said: 'He won't listen to reason, Mr Colleoni.' The voice purred happily back at him. The Boy explained slowly and carefully, 'I'll wish him good luck and pat him on the back.' He stopped and asked sharply, 'What's that you say, Mr Colleoni? No. I just thought you laughed. Hullo. Hullo.' He banged the receiver down and turned with a sense of uneasiness towards the stairs. The gold cigar-lighter, the grey double-breasted waistcoat, the feeling of a racket luxuriously successful for a moment dominated him: the brass bedstead upstairs, the little pot of violet ink on the washstand, the flakes of sausage-roll. His board school cunning wilted for a while; then he turned on the light, he was at home. He climbed the stairs, humming softly: 'the nightingale singing, the postman ringing', but as his thoughts circled closer to the dark, dangerous and deathly centre the tune changed: 'Agnus dei qui tollis peccata mundi . . .' He walked stiffly, the jacket sagging across his immature shoulders, but when he opened the door of his room—'dona novis pacem'—his pallid face peered dimly back at him full of pride from the mirror over the ewer, the soap-dish, the basin of stale water.

PART FOUR

I

It was a fine day for the races. People poured into Brighton by the first train. It was like Bank Holiday all over again, except that these people didn't spend their money; they harboured it. They stood packed deep on the tops of the trams rocking down to the Aquarium, they surged like some natural and irrational migration of insects up and down the front. By eleven o'clock it was impossible to get a seat on the buses going out to the course. A negro wearing a bright striped tie sat on a bench in the Pavilion garden and smoked a cigar. Some children played touch wood from seat to seat, and he called out to them hilariously, holding his cigar at arm's length with an air of pride and caution, his great teeth gleaming like an advertisement. They stopped playing and stared at him, backing slowly. He called out to them again in their own tongue, the words hollow and unformed and childish like theirs, and they eyed him uneasily and backed farther away. He put his cigar patiently back between the cushiony lips and went on smoking. A band came up the pavement through Old Steyne, a blind band playing drums and trumpets, walking in the gutter, feeling the kerb with the edge of their shoes, in Indian file. You heard the music a long way off, persisting through the rumble of the crowd, the shots of exhaust pipes, and the grinding of the buses starting uphill for the racecourse. It rang out with spirit, marched like a regiment, and you raised your eyes in expectation of the tiger skin and the twirling drumsticks and saw the pale blind eyes, like those of pit ponies, going by along the gutter.

In the public school grounds above the sea the girls trooped solemnly out to hockey: stout goal-keepers padded like armadillos; captains discussing tactics with their lieutenants; junior girls running amok in the bright day. Beyond the aristocratic turf, through the wrought-iron main gates they could see the plebeian procession, those whom the buses wouldn't hold, plodding up the down, kicking up the dust, eating buns out of paper bags. The buses took the long way round through Kemp Town, but up the steep hill came the crammed taxicabs—a seat for anyone at ninepence a time—a Packard for the members' enclosure, old Morrises, strange high cars with family parties, keeping the road after twenty years. It was as if the whole road moved upwards like an Underground staircase in the dusty sunlight, a creaking, shouting, jostling crowd of cars moving with it. The junior girls took to their heels like ponies racing on the turf, feeling the excitement going on out-side, as if this were a day on which life for many people reached a kind of climax. The odds on Black Boy had shortened, nothing could ever make life quite the same after that rash bet of a fiver on Merry Monarch. A scarlet racing model, a tiny rakish car which carried about it the atmosphere of innumerable roadhouses, of totsies gathered round swimming pools, of furtive encounters in by-lanes off the Great North Road, wormed through the traffic with incredible dexterity. The sun caught it: it winked as far as the dining-hall windows of the girls' school. It was crammed tight: a woman sat on a man's knee, and another man clung on the run-ning board as it swayed and hooted and cut in and out uphill to-wards the downs. The woman was singing, her voice faint and disjointed through the horns, something traditional about brides and bouquets, something which went with Guinness and oysters and the old Leicester Lounge, something out of place in the little bright racing car. Upon the top of the down the words blew back along the dusty road to meet an ancient Morris rocking and re-ceding in their wake at forty miles an hour, with flapping hood, bent fender and discoloured windscreen.

The words came through the flap, flap, flap of the old hood to the Boy's ears. He sat beside Spicer who drove the car. Brides and bouquets: and he thought of Rose with sullen disgust. He couldn't get the suggestion of Spicer out of his mind; it was like an invisi-ble power working against him: Spicer's stupidity, the photograph on the pier, that woman—who the hell was she?—asking questions . . . If he married her, of course, it wouldn't be for long: only as a last resort to close her mouth and give him time. He didn't want *that* relationship with anyone: the double bed, the intimacy, it sickened him like the idea of age. He crouched in the corner away from where the ticking pierced the seat, vibrating up and down in bitter virginity. To marry—it was like ordure on the hands.

'Where's Dallow and Cubitt?' Spicer asked.

'I didn't want them here today,' the Boy said. 'We've got something to do today the mob are better out of.' Like a cruel child who hides the dividers behind him, he put his hand with spurious affection on Spicer's arm. 'I don't mind telling you. I'm going to make it up with Colleoni. I wouldn't trust *them*. They are violent. You and I, we'll handle it properly between us.'

'I'm all for peace,' Spicer said. 'I always have been.'

The Boy grinned through the broken windscreen at the long disorder of cars. 'That's what I'm going to arrange,' he said.

'A peace that lasts,' Spicer said.

'No one's going to break this peace,' the Boy said. The faint singing died in the dust and the bright sun: a final bride, a final bouquet, a word which sounded like 'wreath'. 'How do you set about getting married?' the Boy unwillingly asked. 'If you've got to in a hurry?'

'Not so easy for you,' Spicer said. 'There's your age.' He ground the old gears as they climbed a final spur towards the white enclosure on the chalky soil, the gipsy vans. 'I'd have to think about it.'

'Think quick,' the Boy said. 'You don't forget you're clearing out tonight.'

'That's right,' Spicer said. Departure made him a little sentimental. 'The eight-ten. You ought to see that pub. You'd be welcome. Nottingham's a fine town. It'll be good to rest up there a while. The air's fine, and you couldn't ask for a better bitter than you get at the "Blue Anchor".' He grinned. 'I forgot you didn't drink.'

'Have a good time,' the Boy said.

'You'll be always welcome, Pinkie.'

They rolled the old car up into the park and got out. The Boy passed his arm through Spicer's. Life was good walking outside the white sun-drenched wall, past the loud-speaker vans, the man who believed in a second coming, towards the finest of all sensations, the infliction of pain. 'You're a fine fellow, Spicer,' the Boy said, squeezing his arm, and Spicer began to tell him in a low friendly confiding way all about the 'Blue Anchor'. 'It's not a tied house,' he said, 'they've a reputation. I've always thought when I'd made enough money I'd go in with my friend. He still wants me to. I nearly went when they killed Kite.'

'You get scared easy, don't you?' the Boy said. The loud-speakers on the vans advised them whom to put their money with, and gipsy children chased a rabbit with cries across the trampled chalk. They went down into the tunnel under the course and came up into the light and the short grey grass sloping down by the bungalow houses to the sea. Old bookies' tickets rotted into the chalk: 'Barker for the Odds', a smug smiling nonconformist face printed in yellow: 'Don't Worry I Pay', and old tote tickets among the stunted plantains. They went through the wire fence into the half-crown enclosure. 'Have a glass of beer, Spicer,' the Boy said, pressing him on.

'Why, that's good of you, Pinkie. I wouldn't mind a glass,' and while Spicer drank it by the wooden trestles, the Boy looked down the line of bookies. There was Barker and Macpherson and George Beale ('The Old Firm') and Bob Tavell of Clapton, all the familiar faces, full of blarney and fake good humour. The first two races had been run: there were long queues at the tote windows. The sun lit the white Tattersall stand across the course, and a few horses cantered by to the start. 'There goes General Burgoyne,' a man said, 'he's restless,' starting off to Bob Tavell's stand to cover his bet. The bookies rubbed out and altered the odds as the horses went by, their hoofs padding like boxing gloves on the turf.

'You going to take a plunge?' Spicer asked, finishing his Bass, blowing a little gaseous malted breath towards the bookies.

'I don't bet,' the Boy said.

'It's the last chance for me,' Spicer said, 'in good old Brighton. I wouldn't mind risking a couple of nicker. Not more. I'm saving my cash for Nottingham.'

'Go on,' the Boy said, 'have a good time while you can.'

They walked down the row of bookies towards Brewer's stand; there were a lot of men about. 'He's doing good business,' Spicer said. 'Did you see the Merry Monarch? He's going up,' and while he spoke, all down the line the bookies rubbed out the old sixteen to one odds. 'Ten's,' Spicer said.

'Have a good time while you're here,' the Boy said.

'Might as well patronize the old firm,' Spicer said, detaching his arm and walking across to Tate's stand. The Boy smiled. It was as easy as shelling peas. 'Memento Mori,' Spicer said, coming away card in hand. 'That's a funny name to give a horse. Five to one, a place. What does Memento Mori mean?'

'It's foreign,' the Boy said. 'Black Boy's shortening.'

'I wish I'd covered myself on Black Boy,' Spicer said. 'There was a woman down there says she's backed Black Boy for a pony. It sounds crazy to me. But think if he wins,' Spicer said. 'My God, what wouldn't I do with two hundred and fifty pounds? I'd take a share in the "Blue Anchor" straight away. You wouldn't see me back here,' he added, staring round at the brilliant sky, the dust over the course, the torn betting cards and the short grass towards the dark sea beneath the down.

'Black Boy won't win,' the Boy said. 'Who was it put the pony on?'

'Some polony or other. She was over there at the bar. Why don't you have a fiver on Black Boy? Have a bet for once to celebrate?'

'Celebrate what?' the Boy asked quickly.

'I forgot,' Spicer said. 'This holiday's perked me up, so's I think everyone's got something to celebrate.'

'If I did want to celebrate,' the Boy said, 'it wouldn't be with Black Boy. Why, that used to be Fred's favourite. Said he'd be a Derby winner yet. I wouldn't call that a lucky horse,' but he couldn't help watching him canter up by the rails: a little too fresh, a little too restless. A man on top of the half-crown stand tic-tacked to Bob Tavell of Clapton and a tiny Jew, who was studying the ten shilling enclosure through binoculars, suddenly began to saw the air, to attract the attention of the Old Firm. 'There,' the Boy said, 'what did I tell you? Black Boy's going out again.'

'Hundred to eight, Black Boy, hundred to eight,' George Beale's representative called, and 'They're off,' somebody said. People pressed out from the refreshment booth towards the rails carrying glasses of Bass and currant buns. Barker, Macpherson, Bob Travell, all wiped the odds from their boards, but the Old Firm remained game to the last: 'Hundred to six Black Boy': while the little Jew made masonic passes from the top of the stand. The horses came by in a bunch, with a sharp sound like splintering wood, and were gone. 'General Burgoyne,' somebody said, and somebody said: 'Merry Monarch.' The beer drinkers went back to the trestle boards and had another glass, and the bookies put up the runners in the four o'clock and began to chalk a few odds.

'There,' the Boy said, 'what did I tell you? Fred never knew a good horse from a bad one. That crazy polony's dropped a pony. It's not *her* lucky day. Why'—but the silence, the inaction after a race is run and before the results go up, had a daunting quality. The queues waited outside the totes. Everything on the course was suddenly still, waiting for a signal to begin again; in the silence you could hear a horse whinny all the way across from the weighing-in. A sense of uneasiness gripped the Boy in the quiet and the brightness. The soured false age, the concentrated and limited experience of the Brighton slum drained out of him. He wished he had Cubitt there and Dallow. There was too much to tackle by himself at seventeen. It wasn't only Spicer. He had started something on Whit Monday which had no end. Death wasn't an end; the censer swung and the priest raised the Host, and the loud-speaker intoned the winners: 'Black Boy. Memento Mori. General Burgoyne.'

'By God,' Spicer said, 'I've won. Memento Mori for a place,' and remembering what the Boy had said, 'And she's won too. A pony. What a break. Now what about Black Boy?' Pinkie was silent. He told himself: Fred's horse. If I was one of those crazy geezers who touch wood, throw salt, won't go under ladders, I might be scared to—

Spicer plucked at him. 'I've won Pinkie. A tenner. What do you know about that?'

—to go on with what he'd planned with care. Somewhere from farther down the enclosure he heard a laugh, a female laugh, mellow and confident, perhaps the polony who'd put a pony on

Fred's horse. He turned on Spicer with secret venom, cruelty straightening his body like lust.

'Yes,' he said, putting his arm round Spicer's shoulder, 'you'd better collect now.'

They moved together towards Tate's stand. A young man with oiled hair stood on a wooden step paying out money. Tate himself was away in the ten shilling enclosure, but they both knew Samuel. Spicer called out to him quite jovially as he advanced, 'Well, Sammy, now the pay-off.'

Samuel watched them, Spicer and the Boy, come across the shallow threadbare turf, arm-in-arm like very old friends. Half a dozen men collected and stood round, waiting, the last creditor slipped away, they waited in silence, a little man holding an account book put out a tip of tongue and licked a sore lip.

'You're in luck, Spicer,' the Boy said, squeezing his arm. 'Have a good time with your tenner.'

'You aren't saying good-bye yet, are you?' Spicer asked.

'I'm not waiting for the four-thirty. I won't be seeing you again.'

'What about Colleoni?' Spicer said. 'Aren't you and I . . . ?' The horses cantered by for another start; the odds were going up; the crowd moved in towards the tote and left them a clear lane. At the end of the lane the little group waited.

'I've changed my mind,' the Boy said. 'I'll see Colleoni at his hotel. You get your money.' A hatless tout delayed them: 'A tip for the next race. Only a shilling. I've tipped two winners today.' His toes showed through his shoes. 'Tip yourself off,' the Boy said. Spicer didn't like good-byes: he was a sentimental soul: he shifted on his corn-sore foot. 'Why,' he said, looking down the lane to the fence, 'Tate's lot haven't written up the odds yet.'

'Tate always was slow. Slow in paying out, too. Better get your money.' He urged him nearer, his hand on Spicer's elbow.

'There's not anything wrong, is there?' Spicer asked. He looked at the waiting men: they stared through him.

'Well, this is good-bye,' the Boy said.

'You remember the address,' Spicer said. 'The "Blue Anchor", you remember, Union Street. Send me any news. I don't suppose there'll be any for *me* to send.'

The Boy put his hand up as if to pat Spicer on the back and let it fall again: the group of men stood in a bunch waiting. 'Maybe—' the Boy said: he looked round: there wasn't any end to what he had begun. A passion of cruelty stirred in his belly. He put up his hand again and patted Spicer on the back. 'Good luck to you,' he said in a high broken adolescent voice and patted him again.

The men with one accord came round them. He heard Spicer scream, 'Pinkie,' and saw him fall: a boot with heavy nails was lifted, and then he felt pain run like blood down his own neck.

The surprise at first was far worse than the pain (a nettle could sting as badly). 'You fools,' he said, 'it's not me, it's him you want,' and turned and saw the faces ringing him all round. They grinned back at him: every man had his razor out: and he remembered for the first time Colleoni laughing up the telephone wire. The crowd had scattered at the first sign of trouble; he heard Spicer call out, 'Pinkie. For Christ's sake'; an obscure struggle reached its climax out of his sight. He had other things to watch: the long cut-throat razors which the sun caught slanting low down over the downs from Shoreham. He put his hand to his pocket to get his blade, and the man immediately facing him leant across and slashed his knuckles. Pain happened to him, and he was filled with horror and astonishment as if one of the bullied brats at school had stabbed first with the dividers.

They made no attempt to come in and finish him. He sobbed at them, 'I'll get Colleoni for this.' He shouted 'Spicer' twice before he remembered that Spicer couldn't answer. The mob were enjoying themselves, just as he had always enjoyed himself. One of them leant forward to cut his cheek, and when he put up his hand to shield himself they slashed his knuckles again. He began to weep, as the four-thirty went by in a drumbeat of hooves beyond the rail.

Then somebody from the stand shouted 'Bogies' and they all moved together, coming quickly at him in a bunch. Somebody kicked him on the thigh, he clutched a razor in his hand and was cut to the bone. Then they scattered as the police ran up the edge of the course, slow in their heavy boots, and he broke through them. A few followed him, out of the wire gate and straight down the side of the Down towards the houses and the sea. He wept as he ran, lame in one leg from the kick, he even tried to pray. You could be saved between the stirrup and the ground, but you couldn't be saved if you didn't repent and he hadn't time, scrambling down the chalk down, to feel the least remorse. He ran awkwardly, tripping, bleeding down his face and from both hands.

Only two men followed him now, and they followed him for the fun of it, shooing him as they might shoo a cat. He reached the first houses in the bottom, but there was no one about. The races had emptied every house: nothing but crazy paving and little lawns, stained-glass doors and a lawn mower abandoned on a gravel path. He didn't dare to take refuge in a house; while he rang and waited they would reach him. He had his razor blade out now, but he had never yet used it on an armed enemy. He had to hide, but he left a track of blood along the road.

The two men were out of breath; they had wasted it on laughter, and he had young lungs. He gained on them; he wrapped his hand in a handkerchief and held his head back so that the blood ran down his clothes. He turned a corner and was into an empty garage before they had reached it. There he stood in the dusky interior with his razor out, trying to repent. He thought 'Spicer', 'Fred', but his thoughts would carry him no further than the corner where his pursuers might reappear: he discovered that he hadn't the energy to repent.

And when a long while later the danger seemed to be over, and there was a long dusk on his hands, it wasn't eternity he thought about but his own humiliation. He had wept, begged, run: Dallow and Cubitt would hear of it. What would happen to Kite's mob now? He tried to think of Spicer, but the world held him. He couldn't order his thoughts. He stood with weak knees against the concrete wall with the blade advanced and watched the corner. A few people passed, the faintest sound of music bit, like an abscess, into his brain from the Palace Pier, the lights came out in the neat barren bourgeois road.

The garage had never been used for a garage; it had become a kind of potting shed. Little green shoots crept, like caterpillars, out of shallow boxes of earth: a spade, a rusty lawn mower, and all the junk the owner had no room for in the tiny house: an old rocking horse, a pram which had been converted into a wheelbarrow, a pile of ancient records—'Alexander's Rag Time Band', 'Pack Up Your Troubles', 'If You Were the Only Girl'; they lay with the trowels, what was left of the crazy paving, a doll with one glass eye and a dress soiled with mould. He took it all in with quick glances, his razor blade ready, the blood clotting on his neck, dripping from his hand, where the handkerchief had slipped. Whatever jackdaw owned this house would have that much added to his possessions—the little drying stain on the concrete floor.

Whoever the owner was, he had come a long way to land up here. The pram-wheelbarrow was covered with labels—the marks of innumerable train journeys—Doncaster, Lichfield, Clacton (that must have been a summer holiday), Ipswich, Northampton—roughly torn off for the next journey they left, in the litter which remained, an unmistakable trail. And this, the small villa under the racecourse, was the best finish he could manage. You couldn't have any doubt that this was the end, the mortgaged home in the bottom; like the untidy tidemark on a beach, the junk was piled up here and would never go farther.

And the Boy hated him. He was nameless, faceless, but the Boy hated him, the doll, the pram, the broken rocking horse. The small pricked-out plants irritated him like ignorance. He felt hungry and faint and shaken. He had known pain and fear.

Now, of course, was the time, while darkness drained into the bottom, for him to make his peace. Between the stirrup and the ground there wasn't time: you couldn't break in a moment the habit of thought: habit held you closely while you died, and he remembered Kite, after they'd got him at St Pancras, passing out in the waiting-room, while a porter poured coal-dust on the dead grate, talking all the time about someone's tits.

But 'Spicer', the Boy's thoughts came inevitably back with a sense of relief, 'they've got Spicer'. It was impossible to repent of something which made him safe. The nosy woman hadn't got a witness now, except for Rose, and he could deal with Rose; and then, when he was thoroughly secure, he could begin to think of making peace, of going home, and his heart weakened with a faint nostalgia for the tiny dark confessional box, the priest's voice, and the people waiting under the statue, before the bright lights burning down in the pink glasses, to be made safe from eternal pain. Eternal pain had not meant much to him: now it meant the slash of razor blades infinitely prolonged.

He sidled out of the garage. The new raw street cut in the chalk was empty except for a couple pressed against each other out of the lamplight by a wooden fence. The sight pricked him with nausea and cruelty. He limped by them, his cut hand closed on the razor, with his cruel virginity which demanded some satisfaction different from theirs, habitual, brutish and short.

He knew where he was going. He wasn't going to return to Frank's like this with the cobwebs from the garage on his clothes, defeat cut in his face and hand. They were dancing in the open air on the white stone deck above the Aquarium, and he got down on to the beach where he was more alone, the dry seaweed left by last winter's gales cracking under his shoes. He could hear the music— 'The One I Love'. Wrap it up in cellophane, he thought, put it in silver paper. A moth wounded against one of the lamps crawled across a piece of driftwood and he crushed it out of existence under his chalky shoe. One day—one day—he limped along the sand with his bleeding hand hidden, a young dictator. He was head of Kite's gang, this was a temporary defeat. One confession, when he was safe, to wipe out everything. The yellow moon slanted up over Hove, the exact mathematical Regency Square, and he daydreamed, limping in the dry unwashed sand, by the closed bathing-huts: I'll give a statue.

He climbed up from the sand just past the Palace Pier and made his painful way across the parade. Snow's Restaurant was all lit up. A radio was playing. He stood on the pavement outside until he saw Rose serve a table close to the window, then went and pressed his face to it. She saw him at once; his attention rang in her brain as quickly as if he had dialled her. He took his hand from his pocket, but his wounded face was anxiety enough for her. She tried to tell him something through the glass: he couldn't understand her; it was as if he were listening to a foreign language. She had to repeat it three times, 'Go to the back,' before he could read her lips. The pain in his leg was worse; he trailed round the building, and as he turned, a car went by, a Lancia, a uniformed chauffeur, and Mr

Colleoni—Mr Colleoni in a dinner jacket with a white waistcoat, who leant back and smiled and smiled in the face of an old lady in purple silk. Or perhaps it was not Mr Colleoni at all, they went so smoothly and swiftly past, but any rich middle-aged tycoon returning to the Cosmopolitan after a concert in the Pavilion.

He bent and looked through the letter-box of the back door: Rose came down the passage towards him with her hands clenched and a look of anger on her face. He lost some of his confidence; she's noticed, he thought, how done in . . . he'd always known a girl looked at your shoes and coat: if she sends me away, he thought, I'll crack this vitriol bottle . . . but when she opened the door she was as dumb and devoted as ever she'd been. 'Who's done it?' she whispered. 'If I could get at them.'

'Never mind,' the Boy said and boasted experimentally, 'you can leave them to me.'

'Your dear face.' He remembered with disgust that they were always said to like a scar, that they took it as a mark of manhood, of potency.

'Is there somewhere,' he asked, 'where I can wash?'

She whispered, 'Come quietly. Through here's the cellar,' and she led the way into a little closet, where the hot pipes ran and a few bottles lay in a small bin.

'Won't they be coming here?' he asked.

'No one here orders wine,' she said. 'We haven't got a licence. It's what was left when we took over. The manageress drinks it for her health.' Every time she mentioned Snow's she said 'we' with faint self-consciousness. 'Sit down,' she said. 'I'll fetch some water. I'll have to put the light out or someone might see.' But the moon lit the room enough for him to look around; he could even read the labels on the bottles: Empire wines, Australian hocks and harvest Burgundies.

She was gone only a little while, but immediately she returned she began humbly to apologize, 'Someone wanted a bill and cook was watching.' She had a white pudding basin of hot water and three handkerchiefs. 'They're all I've got,' she said, tearing them up, 'the laundry's not back,' and added firmly, as she dabbed the long shallow cut, like a line drawn with a pin down his neck: 'If I could get at them . . .'

'Don't talk so much,' he said and held out his slashed hand. The blood was beginning to clot: she tied it unskillfully.

'Has anyone been around again talking, asking questions?'

'That man the woman was with.'

'A bogy?'

'I don't think so. He said his name was Phil.'

'*You* seem to have done the asking.'

'They all tell you things.'

'I don't understand it,' the Boy said. 'What do they want if they aren't bogies?' He put out his unwounded hand and pinched her arm. 'You don't tell them a thing?'

'Not a thing,' she said and watched him with devotion through the dark. 'Were you afraid?'

'They can't put anything on me.'

'I mean,' she said, 'when they did this,' touching his hand.

'Afraid,' he lied, 'of course I wasn't afraid.'

'Why did they do it?'

'I told you not to ask questions.' He got up, unsteady on his bruised leg. 'Brush my coat. I can't go out like this. I've got to be respectable.' He leant against the harvest Burgundy while she brushed him down with the flat of her hand. The moonlight shadowed the room, the small bin, the bottles, the narrow shoulders, the smooth scared adolescent face.

He was aware of an unwillingness to go out again into the street, back to Frank's and the unending calculations with Cubitt and Dallow of the next move. Life was a series of complicated tactical exercises, as complicated as the alignments at Waterloo, thought out on a brass bedstead among the crumbs of sausage roll. Your clothes continually needed ironing, Cubitt and Dallow quarrelled or else Dallow went after Frank's wife, the old box telephone under the stairs rang and rang, and the extras were always being brought in and thrown on the bed by Judy who smoked too much and wanted a tip—a tip—a tip. How could you think out a larger strategy under those conditions? He had a sudden nostalgia for the small dark cupboard room, the silence, the pale light on the harvest Burgundy. To be alone a while . . .

But he wasn't alone. Rose put her hand on his and asked him with fear, 'They aren't waiting for you, are they, out there?'

He shrank away and boasted. 'They aren't waiting anywhere. They got more than they gave. They didn't reckon on me, only on poor Spicer.'

'Poor Spicer?'

'Poor Spicer's dead,' and just as he spoke a loud laugh came down the passage from the restaurant, a woman's laugh, full of beer and good fellowship and no regrets. '*She's* back,' the Boy said.

'It's her all right.' One had heard that laugh in a hundred places: dry-eyed, uncaring, looking on the bright side, when boats drew out and other people wept: saluting the bawdy joke in music halls: beside sick beds and in crowded Southern Railway compartments: when the wrong horse won, a good sportswoman's laugh. 'She scares me,' Rose whispered. 'I don't know what she wants.'

The Boy pulled her up to him. Tactics, tactics, there was never any time for strategy, and in the grey night light he could see her face lifted for a kiss. He hesitated, with repulsion, but tactics. He wanted to strike her, to make her scream, but he kissed her inexpertly, missing her lips. He took his crinkling mouth away, and said, 'Listen.'

She said, 'You haven't had many girls, have you?'

'Of course I have,' he said, 'but listen . . .'

'You're my first,' she said. 'I'm glad.' When she said that, he began again to hate her. She wouldn't even be something to boast of: her first: he'd robbed nobody, he had no rival, no one else would look at her, Cubitt and Dallow wouldn't give her a glance: her indeterminate natural hair, her simpleness, the cheap clothes he could feel under his hand. He hated her as he had hated Spicer and it made him circumspect; he pressed her breasts awkwardly under his palms, with a grim opportunist pretence of another man's passion, and thought: it wouldn't be so bad if she was more dolled up, a bit of paint and henna, but this—the cheapest, youngest, least experienced skirt in all Brighton—to have *me* in her power.

'O God,' she said, 'you're sweet to me, Pinkie. I love you.'

'You wouldn't give me away—to *her*?'

Somebody in the passage shouted 'Rose'; a door slammed.

'I'll have to go,' she said. 'What do you mean—give you away?'

'What I said. Talk. Tell her who left that ticket. That it wasn't you know who.'

'I won't tell her.' A bus went by in West Street. The lights came through a little barred window straight on to her white determined face: she was like a child who crosses her fingers and swears her private oath. She said gently, 'I don't care what you've done' as she might have denied interest in a broken window-pane or a smutty word chalked on someone else's door. He was speechless; and some knowledge of the astuteness of her simplicity, the long experience of her sixteen years, the possible depths of her fidelity touched him like cheap music, as the light shifted from cheek-bone to cheek-bone and across the wall, as the gears ground outside.

He said, 'What do you mean? I've done nothing.'

'I don't know,' she said. 'I don't care.'

'Rose,' a voice cried, 'Rose.'

'It's her,' she said, 'I'm sure it's her. Asking questions. Soft as butter. What does she know about us?' She came closer. She said, 'I did something once too. A mortal sin. When I was twelve. But she—she doesn't know what a mortal sin is.'

'Rose. Where are you? Rose.'

The shadow of her sixteen-year-old face shifted in the moonlight on the wall. 'Right and wrong. That's what she talks about. I've heard her at the table. Right and wrong. As if she knew.' She whispered with contempt, 'Oh, she won't burn. She couldn't burn if she tried.' She might have been discussing a damp Catherine wheel. 'Molly Carthew burnt. She was lovely. She killed herself. Despair. That's mortal sin. It's unforgivable. Unless—what is it you said about the stirrup?'

He told her unwillingly. 'The stirrup and the ground. That doesn't work.'

'What you did,' she persisted, 'did you confess it?'

He said evasively, a dark stubborn figure resting his bandaged hand on the Australian hock, 'I haven't been to Mass for years.'

'I don't care,' she repeated. 'I'd rather burn with you than be like Her.' Her immature voice stumbled on the word, 'She's ignorant.'

'Rose.' The door opened on their hiding-place. A manageress in a sage-green uniform, glasses hanging from a button on her breast, brought in with her the light, the voices, the radio, the laugh, dispelled the dark theology between them. 'Child,' she said, 'what are you doing here? And who's the other child?' she added peering at the thin figure in the shadows, but when he moved into the light she corrected herself: 'This boy.' Her eye ran along the bottles counting them. 'You can't have followers here.'

'I'm going,' the Boy said.

The woman watched him with suspicion and distaste: the cobwebs had not all gone. 'If you weren't so young,' she said, 'I'd call the police.'

He said with the only flash of humour he ever showed, 'I'd have an alibi.'

'And as for you,' the manageress turned on Rose, 'we'll talk about you later.' She watched the Boy out of the room and said with disgust, 'You're both too young for this sort of thing.'

Too young—that was the difficulty. Spicer hadn't solved that difficulty before he died. Too young to close her mouth with marriage, too young to stop the police putting her in the witness box, if it ever came to that. To give evidence that—why, to say that Hale had never left the card, that Spicer had left it, that he himself had come and felt for it under the cloth. She remembered even that detail. Spicer's death would add suspicion. He'd got to close her mouth one way or another: he had to have peace.

He slowly climbed the stairs to the bed-sitting-room at Frank's. He had the sense that he was losing grip, the telephone rang and rang, and as he lost grip he began to realize all the things he hadn't years enough to know. Cubitt came out of a downstairs room, his cheek was stuffed with apple, he had a broken penknife in his hand. 'No,' he said, 'Spicer's not here. He's not back yet.'

The Boy called down from the first landing, 'Who wants Spicer?'

'She's rung off.'

'Who was she?'

'I don't know. Some skirt of his. He's soft on a girl he sees at the Queen of Hearts. Where *is* Spicer, Pinkie?'

'He's dead. Colleoni's men killed him.'

'God,' Cubitt said. He shut the knife and spat the apple out. 'I said we ought to lay off Brewer. What are we going to do?'

'Come up here,' the Boy said. 'Where's Dallow?'

'He's out.'

The Boy led the way into the bed-sitting-room and turned on the single globe. He thought of Colleoni's room in the Cosmopolitan. But you had to begin somewhere. He said, 'You've been eating on my bed again.'

'It wasn't me, Pinkie. It was Dallow. Why, Pinkie, they've cut *you* up.'

Again the Boy lied. 'I gave them as good.' But lying was a weakness. He wasn't used to lying. He said, 'We needn't get worked up about Spicer. He was milky. It's a good thing he's dead. The girl at Snow's saw him leave the ticket. Well, when he's buried, no one's going to identify him. We might even have him cremated.'

'You don't think the bogies—'

'I'm not afraid of the bogies. It's others who are nosing round.'

'They can't get over what the doctors said.'

'You know we killed him and the doctors knew he died natural. Work it out for yourself. I can't.' He sat down on the bed and swept off Dallow's crumbs. 'We're safer without Spicer.'

'Maybe you know best, Pinkie. But what made Colleoni—'

'He was scared, I suppose, that we'd let Tate have it on the course. I want Mr Prewitt fetched. I want him to fix me something. He's the only lawyer we can trust round here—if we can trust him.'

'What's the trouble, Pinkie? Anything serious?'

The Boy leant his head back against the brass bedpost. 'Maybe I'll have to get married after all.'

Cubitt suddenly bellowed with laughter, his large mouth wide, his teeth carious. Behind his head the blind was half-drawn down, shutting out the night sky, leaving the chimney-pots black and phallic, smoking palely up into the moonlit air. The Boy was silent, watching Cubitt, listening to his laughter as if it were the world's contempt.

When Cubitt stopped he said, 'Go on. Ring Mr Prewitt up. He's got to come round here,' staring past Cubitt at the acorn gently tapping on the pane at the end of the blind cord, at the chimneys and the early summer night.

'He won't come here.'

'He's got to come. I can't go out like *this*.' He touched the marks on his neck where the razors had cut him. 'I've got to get things fixed.'

'You dog, you,' Cubitt said. 'You're a young one at the game.' The game: and the Boy's mind turned with curiosity and loathing to the small cheap ready-for-anyone face, the bottles catching the moonlight on the bin, and the word 'burn', 'burn' repeated. What did people mean by 'the game'? He knew everything in theory, nothing in practice; he was only old with the knowledge of other people's lusts, those of strangers who wrote their desires on the walls in public lavatories. He knew the moves, he'd never played the game, 'Maybe,' he said, 'it won't come to that. But fetch Mr Prewitt. He knows.'

Mr Prewitt knew. You were certain of that at the first sight of him. He was a stranger to no wangle, twist, contradictory clause, ambiguous word. His yellow shaven middle-aged face was deeply lined with legal decisions. He carried a brown leather portfolio and wore striped trousers which seemed a little too new for the rest of him. He came into the room with hollow joviality, a dockside manner: he had long pointed polished shoes which caught the light. Everything about him, from his breeziness to his morning coat, was brand new, except himself and that had aged in many law courts, with many victories more damaging than defeats. He had acquired the habit of not listening: innumerable rebukes from the bench had taught him that. He was deprecating, discreet, sympathetic and as tough as leather.

The Boy nodded to him without getting up, sitting on the bed. 'Evening, Mr Prewitt,' and Mr Prewitt smiled sympathetically, put his portfolio on the floor, and sat down on the hard chair by the dressing-table. 'It's a lovely night,' he said. 'O dear, O dear, you've been in the wars.' The sympathy didn't belong; it could be peeled off his eyes like an auction ticket from an ancient flint instrument.

'It's not *that* I want to see you about,' the Boy said. 'You needn't be scared. I just want information.'

'No trouble, I hope?' Mr Prewitt asked.

'I want to avoid trouble. If I wanted to get married, what'd I do?'

'Wait a few years,' Mr Prewitt said promptly, as if he were calling a hand in cards.

'Next week,' the Boy said.

'The trouble is,' Mr Prewitt thoughtfully remarked, 'you're under age.'

'That's why I've called *you* in.'

'There are cases,' Mr Prewitt said, 'of people who give their ages wrong. I'm not suggesting it, mind you. What age is the girl?'

'Sixteen.'

'You're sure of that? Because if she was under sixteen you could be married in Canterbury Cathedral by the Archbishop himself, and it wouldn't be legal.'

'That's all right,' the Boy said. 'But if we give our ages wrong, are we married all right—legally?'

'Hard and fast.'

'The police wouldn't be able to call the girl—'

'In evidence against you? Not without her consent. Of course you'd have committed a misdemeanour. You could be sent to prison. And then—there are other difficulties.' Mr Prewitt leant back against the washstand, his grey neat legal hair brushing the ewer and eyed the Boy.

'You know I pay,' the Boy said.

'First,' Mr Prewitt said, 'you've got to remember it takes time.'

'It mustn't take long.'

'Do you want to be married in a church?'

'Of course I don't,' the Boy said. 'This won't be a real marriage.'

'Real enough.'

'Not real like when the priest says it.'

'Your religious feelings do you credit,' Mr Prewitt said. 'This I take it then will be a civil marriage. You could get a licence—fifteen days' residence—you qualify for that—and one day's notice. As far as that's concerned you could be married the day after tomorrow—in your own district. Then comes the next difficulty. A marriage of a minor's not easy.'

'Go on. I'll pay.'

'It's no good just saying you're twenty-one. No one would believe you. But if you said you were eighteen you could be married provided you had your parents' or your guardian's consent. Are your parents alive?'

'No.'

'Who's your guardian?'

'I don't know what you mean.'

Mr Prewitt said thoughtfully, 'We might arrange a guardian. It's risky though. It might be better if you'd lost touch. He'd gone to South Africa and left you. We might make quite a good thing out of that,' Mr Prewitt added softly. 'Flung on the world at an early age you've bravely made your own way.' His eyes shifted from bedball to bedball. 'We'd ask for the discretion of the registrar.'

'I never knew it was all that difficult,' the Boy said. 'Maybe I can manage some other way.'

'Given time,' Mr Prewitt said, 'anything can be managed.' He showed his tartar-coated teeth in a fatherly smile. 'Give the word, my boy, and I'll see you married. Trust me.' He stood up, his striped trousers were like a wedding guest's, hired for the day at Moss's; when he crossed the room, yellowly smiling, he might have been about to kiss the bride. 'If you'll let me have a guinea now for the consultation, there are one or two little purchases—for the spouse . . .'

'Are *you* married?' the Boy asked with sudden eagerness. It had never occurred to him that Prewitt . . . He gazed at the smile, the yellow teeth, the lined and wasted and unreliable face as if *there* possibly he might learn . . .

'It's my silver wedding next year,' Mr Prewitt said. Twenty-five years at the game. Cubitt put his head in at the door and said, 'I'm going out for a turn.' He grinned. 'How's the marriage?'

'Progressing,' Mr Prewitt said, 'progressing,' patting the portfolio as if it had been the plump cheek of a promising infant. 'We shall see our young friend spliced yet.'

Just till it all blows over, the Boy thought, leaning back on the grey pillow, resting one shoe on the mauve eiderdown: not a real marriage, just something to keep her mouth shut for a time. 'So long,' Cubitt said, giggling at the bed end. Rose, the small devoted cockney face, the sweet taste of human skin, emotion in the dark room by the bin of harvest Burgundy: lying on the bed he wanted to protest 'not yet' and 'not with her'. If it had to come some time, if he had to follow everyone else into the brutish game, let it be when he was old, with nothing else to gain, and with someone

other men could envy him. Not someone immature, simple, as ignorant as himself.

'You've only to give the word,' Mr Prewitt said. 'We'll fix it together.' Cubitt had gone. The Boy said, 'You'll find a nicker on the
washstand.'

'I don't see one,' Mr Prewitt said anxiously, shifting a tooth-
brush.

'In the soap-dish—under the cover.'

Dallow put his head into the room. 'Evening,' he said to Mr
Prewitt. He said to the Boy, 'What's up with Spicer?'

'It was Colleoni. They got him on the course,' the Boy said.
'They nearly got me too,' and he raised his bandaged hand to his
scarred neck.

'But Spicer's in his room now. I heard him.'

'*Heard*?' the Boy said. 'You're imagining things.' He was afraid
for the second time that day: a dim globe lit the passage and the
stairs: the walls were unevenly splashed with walnut paint. He felt
the skin of his face contract as if something repulsive had touched
him. He wanted to ask whether you could do more than hear this
Spicer, if he was sensible to the sight and the touch. He stood up:
it had to be faced whatever it was: passed Dallow without another
word. The door of Spicer's room swung in a draught to and fro.
He couldn't see inside. It was a tiny room; they had all had tiny
rooms but Kite, and he had inherited that. That was why his room
was the common room for them all. In Spicer's there would be
space for no one but himself—and Spicer. He could hear little
creaking leathery movements as the door swung. The words
'Dona nobis pacem' came again to mind; for the second time he
felt a faint nostalgia, as if for something he had lost or forgotten
or rejected.

He walked down the passage and into Spicer's room. His first
feeling when he saw Spicer bent and tightening the straps of his
suitcase was relief—that it was undoubtedly the living Spicer,
whom you could touch and scare and command. A long stripe of
sticking-plaster lined Spicer's cheek. The Boy watched it from the
doorway with a rising cruelty: he wanted to tear it away and see
the skin break. Spicer looked up, put down the suitcase, shifted
uneasily towards the wall. He said, 'I thought—I was afraid—

Colleoni had got you.' His fear gave away his knowledge. The Boy said nothing, watching him from the door. As if he were apologizing for being alive at all Spicer explained, 'I got away . . .' His words wilted out like a line of seaweed, along the edge of the Boy's silence, indifference and purpose.

Down the passage came the voice of Mr Prewitt, 'In the soap-dish. He said it was in the soap-dish,' and the clatter of china noisily moved about.

2

'I'm going to work on that kid every hour of the day until I get something.' She rose formidably and moved across the restaurant, like a warship going into action, a warship on the right side in a war to end wars, the signal flags proclaiming that every man would do his duty. Her big breasts, which had never suckled a child of her own, felt a merciless compassion. Rose fled at the sight of her, but Ida moved relentlessly towards the service door. Everything now was in train, she had begun to ask the questions she had wanted to ask when she had read about the inquest in Henekey's, and she was getting the answers. And Fred too had done his part, had tipped the right horse, so that now she had funds as well as friends: an infinite capacity for corruption: two hundred pounds.

'Good evening, Rose,' she said, standing in the kitchen door-way, blocking it. Rose put down a tray and turned with all the fear, obstinacy, incomprehension of a wild animal who will not recognize kindness.

'You again,' she said. 'I'm busy. I can't talk to you.'

'But the manageress, dear, has given me leave.'

'We can't talk here.'

'Where can we talk?'

'In my room if you'll let me out.'

Rose went ahead up the stairs behind the restaurant to the little linoleumed landing. 'They do you well here, don't they?' Ida said. 'I once lived in at a public, that was before I met Tom—Tom's my husband,' she patiently, sweetly, implacably explained to Rose's back. 'They didn't do you so well there. Flowers on the landing,' she exclaimed with pleasure at the withered bunch on a deal table, pulling at the petals, when a door slammed. Rose had shut her out, and as she gently knocked she heard an obstinate whisper, 'Go away. I don't want to talk to you.'

'It's serious. Very serious.' The stout which Ida had been drinking returned a little: she put her hand up to her mouth and said mechanically, 'Pardon,' belching towards the closed door.

'I can't help you. I don't know anything.'

'Let me in, dear, and I'll explain. I can't shout things on the landing.'

'Why should you care about *me*?'

'I don't want the Innocent to suffer.'

'As if you knew,' the soft voice accused her, 'who was innocent.'

'Open the door, dear.' She began, but only a little, to lose her patience: her patience was almost as deep as her good will. She felt the handle and pushed; she knew that waitresses were not allowed keys, but a chair had been wedged under the handle. She said with irritation, 'You won't escape me this way.' She put her weight against the door and the chair creaked and shifted, the door opened a crack.

'I'm going to make you listen,' Ida said. When you were lifesaving you must never hesitate, so they taught you, to stun the one you rescued. She put her hand in and detached the chair, then went in through the open door. Three iron bedsteads, a chest of drawers, two chairs and a couple of cheap mirrors: she took it all in and Rose against the wall as far as she could get, watching the door with terror through her innocent and experienced eyes, as if there was nothing which mightn't come through.

'Don't be silly now,' Ida said. 'I'm your friend. I only want to save you from that boy. You're crazy about him, aren't you? But don't you understand—he's wicked.' She sat down on the bed and went gently and mercilessly on.

Rose whispered, 'You don't know a thing.'

'I've got my evidence.'

'I don't mean *that*,' the child said.

'He doesn't care for you,' Ida said. 'Listen, I'm human. You can take my word I've loved a boy or two in my time. Why, it's natural. It's like breathing. Only you don't want to get all worked up about it. There's not one who's worth it—leave alone *him*. He's wicked. I'm not a Puritan, mind. I've done a thing or two in my time—that's *natural*. Why,' she said, extending towards the child her plump and patronizing paw, 'it's in my hand: the girdle of Venus. But I've always been on the side of Right. You're young. You'll have plenty of boys before you've finished. You'll have plenty of fun—if you don't let them get a grip on you. It's natural. Like breathing. Don't take away the notion I'm against Love. I should say not. Me. Ida Arnold. They'd laugh.' The stout came back up her throat again and she put a hand before her mouth. 'Pardon, dear. You see we can get along all right when we are together. I've never had a child of my own and somehow I've taken to you. You're a sweet little thing.' She suddenly barked, 'Come away from that wall and act sensible. He doesn't love you.'

'I don't care,' the childish voice stubbornly murmured.

'What do you mean, you don't care.'

'I love *him*.'

'You're acting morbid,' Ida said. 'If I was your mother I'd give you a good hiding. What'd your father and mother say if they knew?'

'*They* wouldn't care.'

'And how do you think it will all end?'

'I don't know.'

'You're young. That's what it is,' Ida said, 'romantic. I was like you once. You'll grow out of it. All you need is a bit of experience.' The Nelson Place eyes stared back at her without understanding. Driven to her hole the small animal peered out at the bright and breezy world; in the hole were murder, copulation, extreme poverty, fidelity and the love and fear of God, but the small animal had not the knowledge to deny that only in the glare and open world outside was something which people called experience.

The Boy looked down at the body, spread-eagled like Prometheus, at the bottom of Frank's stairs. 'Good God,' Mr Prewitt said, 'how did it happen?'

The Boy said, 'These stairs have needed mending a long while. I've told Frank about it, but you can't make the bastard spend money.' He put his bound hand on the rail and pushed until it gave. The rotten wood lay across Spicer's body, a walnut-stained eagle couched over the kidneys.

'But that happened *after* he fell,' Mr Prewitt protested; his legal voice was tremulous.

'You've got it wrong,' the Boy said. 'You were here in the passage and you saw him lean his suitcase against the rail. He shouldn't have done that. The case was too heavy.'

'My God, you can't mix me up in this,' Mr Prewitt said. 'I saw nothing. I was looking in the soap-dish, I was with Dallow.'

'You both saw it,' the Boy said. 'That's fine. It's a good thing we have a respectable lawyer like you on the spot. Your word will do the trick.'

'I'll deny it,' Mr Prewitt said. 'I'm getting out of here. I'll swear I was never in the house.'

'Stay where you are,' the Boy said. 'We don't want another accident. Dallow, go and telephone for the police—and a doctor, it looks well.'

'You can keep me here,' Mr Prewitt said, 'but you can't make me say—'

'I only want you to say what you want to say. But it wouldn't look good, would it, if I was taken up for killing Spicer, and you were here—looking in the soap-dish. It would be enough to ruin some lawyers.'

Mr Prewitt stared over the broken gap at the turn of the stairs where the body lay. He said slowly, 'You'd better lift that body and put the wood under it. The police would have a lot to ask if they found it that way.' He went back into the bedroom and sat down on the bed and put his head in his hands. 'I've got a headache,' he said, 'I ought to be at home.' Nobody paid him any attention. Spicer's door rattled in the draught. 'I've got a splitting headache,' Mr Prewitt said.

Dallow came lugging the suitcase down the passage: the cord of Spicer's pyjamas squeezed out of it like tooth-paste. 'Where was he going?' Dallow asked.

'The "Blue Anchor", Union Street, Nottingham,' the Boy said. 'We'd better wire them. They might want to send flowers.'

'Be careful about finger-prints,' Mr Prewitt implored them from the washstand without raising his aching head, but the Boy's steps on the stairs made him look up. 'Where are you going?' he asked sharply. The Boy stared up at him from the turn in the stairs. 'Out,' he said.

'You can't go now,' Mr Prewitt said.

'I wasn't here,' the Boy said. 'It was just you and Dallow. You were waiting for me to come in.'

'You'll be seen.'

'That's your risk,' the Boy said. 'I've got things to do.'

'Don't tell me,' Mr Prewitt cried hastily and checked himself. 'Don't tell me,' he repeated in a low voice, 'what things . . .'

'We'll have to fix that marriage,' the Boy said sombrely. He gazed at Mr Prewitt for a moment—the spouse, twenty-five years at the game—with the air of someone who wanted to ask a question, almost as if he were prepared to accept advice from a man so much older, as if he expected a little human wisdom from the old shady legal mind.

'It had better be soon,' the Boy went softly and sadly on. He still watched Mr Prewitt's face for some reflection of the wisdom the game must have given him in twenty-five years, but saw only a frightened face, boarded up like a store when a riot is on. He went on down the stairs, dropping into the dark well where Spicer's body had fallen. He had made his decision; he had only to move towards his aim; he could feel his blood pumped from the heart and moving indifferently back along the arteries like trains on the inner circle. Every station was one nearer safety, and then one farther away, until the bend was turned and safety again approached, like Notting Hill, and afterwards receded. The middle-aged whore on Hove front never troubled to look round as he came up behind her: like electric trains moving on the same track there was no collision. They both had the same end in view, if you could talk of an end in connection with that circle. Outside the Norfolk bar two smart scarlet racing models lay along the kerb like twin beds. The Boy was not conscious of them, but their image passed automatically into his brain, released his secretion of envy.

Snow's was nearly empty. He sat down at the table where once Spicer had sat, but he was not served by Rose. A strange girl came to take his order. He said awkwardly, 'Isn't Rose here?'

'She's busy.'

'Could I see her?'

'She's talking to someone up in her room. You can't go there. You'll have to wait.'

The Boy put half a crown on the table. 'Where is it?'

The girl hesitated. 'The manageress would bawl Hell.'

'Where's the manageress?'

'She's out.'

The Boy put another half-crown on the table.

'Through the service door,' the girl said, 'and straight up the stairs. There's a woman with her though—'

He heard the woman's voice before he reached the top of the stairs. She was saying, 'I only want to speak to you for your own good,' but he had to strain to catch Rose's reply.

'Let me be, why don't you let me be?'

'It's the business of anyone who thinks right.'

The Boy could see into the room now from the head of the stairs, though the broad back, the large loose dress, the square hips of the woman nearly blocked his view of Rose who stood back against the wall in an attitude of sullen defiance. Small and bony in the black cotton dress and the white apron, her eyes stained but tearless, startled and determined, she carried her courage with a kind of comic inadequacy, like the little man in the bowler put up by the management to challenge the strong man at a fair. She said, 'You'd better let me be.'

It was Nelson Place and Manor Street which stood there in the servant's bedroom, and for a moment he felt no antagonism but a faint nostalgia. He was aware that she belonged to his life, like a room or a chair: she was something which completed him. He thought: She's got more guts than Spicer. What was most evil in him needed her: it couldn't get along without goodness. He said softly, 'What are you worrying my girl about?' and the claim he made was curiously sweet to his ears, like a refinement of cruelty. After all, though he had aimed higher than Rose, he had this comfort: she couldn't have gone lower than himself. He stood there, with a smirk on his face, when the woman turned. 'Between the stirrup and the ground'—he had learnt the fallacy of that comfort: if he had attached to himself some bright brassy skirt, like the ones he'd seen at the Cosmopolitan, his triumph after all wouldn't have been so great. He smirked at the pair of them, nostalgia driven out by a surge of sad sensuality. She was good, he'd discovered that, and he was damned: they were made for each other.

'You leave her alone,' the woman said. 'I know all about you.' It was as if she were in a strange country: the typical Englishwoman abroad. She hadn't even got a phrase book. She was as far from either of them as she was from Hell—or Heaven. Good or evil lived in the same country, spoke the same language, came together like old friends, feeling the same completion, touching hands beside the iron bedstead. 'You want to do what's Right, Rose?' she implored.

Rose whispered again, 'You let us be.'

'You're a Good Girl, Rose. You don't want anything to do with *him*.'

'You don't know a thing.'

There was nothing she could do at the moment but threaten from the door. 'I haven't finished with you yet. I've got friends.'

The Boy watched her go with amazement. He said, 'Who the hell is she?'

'I don't know,' Rose said.

'I never seen her before.' A memory pricked him and passed: it would return. 'What did she want?'

'I don't know.'

'You're a good girl, Rose,' the Boy said, pressing his fingers round the sharp wrist.

She shook her head. 'I'm bad.' She implored him, 'I want to be bad if she's good and you—'

'You'll never be anything but good,' the Boy said. 'There's some wouldn't like you for that, but I don't care.'

'I'll do anything for you. Tell me what to do. I don't want to be like her.'

'It's not what you do,' the Boy said, 'it's what you think.' He boasted. 'It's in the blood. Perhaps when they christened me, the holy water didn't take. I never howled the devil out.'

'Is *she* good?'

'She?' The Boy laughed. 'She's just nothing.'

'We can't stay here,' Rose said. 'I wish we could.' She looked round her at a badly foxed steel engraving of Van Tromp's victory, the three black bedsteads, the two mirrors, the single chest of drawers, the pale mauve knots of flowers on the wallpaper, as if she were safer here than she could ever be in the squally summer night outside. 'It's a nice room.' She wanted to share it with him until it became a home for both of them.

'How'd you like to leave this place?'

'Snow's. Oh no, it's a good place. I wouldn't want to be anywhere else than Snow's.'

'I mean marry me?'

'We aren't old enough.'

'It could be managed. There are ways.' He dropped her wrist and put on a careless air. 'If you wanted. I don't mind.'

'Oh,' she said. 'I want it. But they'll never let us.'

He explained airily, 'It couldn't be in church, not at first. There'd be difficulties. Are you afraid?'

'I'm not afraid,' she said. 'But will they let us?'

'My lawyer'll manage somehow.'

'You got a lawyer?'

'Of course I have.'

'It sounds somehow—grand—and old.'

'A man can't get along without a lawyer.'

She said, 'It's not where I always thought it would be.'

'Where what would be?'

'Someone asking me to marry him. I thought—in the pictures or maybe at night on the front. But this is best,' she said, looking from Van Tromp's victory to the two looking-glasses. She came away from the wall and lifted her face to him. He knew what was expected of him; he regarded her unmade-up mouth with faint nausea. Saturday night, eleven o'clock, the primeval exercise. He pressed his hard puritanical mouth on hers and tasted again the sweetish smell of the human skin. He would have preferred the taste of Coty powder or Kissproof Lipstick or any chemical compound. He shut his eyes and when he opened them again it was to see her waiting like a blind girl, for further alms. It shocked him that she had been unable to detect his repulsion. She said, 'You know what that means?'

'What means?'

'It means I'll never let you down, never, never, never.'

She belonged to him like a room or a chair: the Boy fetched up a smile for the blind lost face, uneasily, with obscure shame.

PART FIVE

Everything went well: the inquest never even got on to the newspaper posters: no questions asked. The Boy walked back with Dallow, he should have felt triumphant. He said, 'I wouldn't trust Cubitt if Cubitt knew.'

'Cubitt won't know. Prewitt is scared to say a thing—and you know I don't talk, Pinkie.'

'I've got a feeling we're being followed, Dallow.'

Dallow looked behind. 'No one. I know every bogy in Brighton.'

'No woman?'

'No. Who are you thinking of?'

'I don't know.'

The blind band came up the kerb, scraping the sides of their shoes along the edge, feeling their way in the brilliant light, sweating a little. The Boy walked up the side of the road to meet them. The music they played was plaintive, pitying, something out of a hymn book about burdens: it was like a voice prophesying sorrow at the moment of victory. The Boy met the leader and pushed him out of the way, swearing at him softly, and the whole band hearing their leader move shifted uneasily a foot into the roadway and stood there stranded till the Boy was safely by, like barques becalmed on a huge and landless Atlantic. Then they edged back feeling for the landfall of the pavement.

'What's up with you, Pinkie?' Dallow said. 'They're blind.'

'Why should I get out of my way for a beggar?' but he hadn't realized they were blind, he was shocked by his own action. It was as if he were being driven too far down a road he only wanted to travel a certain distance. He stood and leant on the rail of the front while the mid-week crowd passed and the hard sun flattened.

'What's on your mind, Pinkie?'

'To think of all this trouble over Hale. He deserved what he got, but if I'd known how it would go maybe I'd have let him live. Maybe he wasn't worth killing. A dirty little journalist who played in with Colleoni and got Kite killed. Why should anyone bother about him?' He looked suddenly over his shoulder. 'Have I seen that geezer before?'

'He's only a visitor.'

'I thought I'd seen his tie.'

'Hundreds in the shops. If you were a drinking man I'd say what you needed was a pick-up. Why, Pinkie, everything's going fine. No questions asked.'

'There were only two people could hang us, Spicer and the girl. I've killed Spicer and I'm marrying the girl. Seems to me I'm doing everything.'

'Well, we'll be safe now.'

'Oh yes, *you*'ll be safe. It's me who runs all the risk. *You* know I killed Spicer. Prewitt knows. It only wants Cubitt and I'll need a massacre to put me right this time.'

'You oughtn't to talk that way to me, Pinkie. You've been all bottled up since Kite died. What you want's a bit of fun.'

'I liked Kite,' the Boy said. He stared straight out towards France, an unknown land. At his back beyond the Cosmopolitan, Old Steyne, the Lewes Road, stood the downs, villages, cattle round the dewponds, another unknown land. This was his territory, the populous foreshore, a few thousand acres of houses, a narrow peninsula of electrified track running to London, two or three railway stations with their buffets and buns. It had been Kite's territory, it had been good enough for Kite, and when Kite had died in the waiting-room at St Pancras, it had been as if a father had died, leaving him an inheritance it was his duty never to leave for strange acres. He had inherited even the mannerisms, the bitten thumb nail, the soft drinks. The sun slid off the sea and like a cuttle fish shot into the sky the stain of agonies and endurances.

'Break out, Pinkie. Relax. Give yourself a chance. Come out with me and Cubitt to the Queen of Hearts and celebrate.'

'You know I never touch a drink.'

'You'll have to on your wedding day. Whoever heard of a dry wedding?'

An old man went stooping down the shore, very slowly, turning the stones, picking among the dry seaweed for cigarette ends, scraps of food. The gulls which had stood like candles down the beach rose and cried under the promenade. The old man found a boot and stowed it in his sack and a gull dropped from the parade and swept through the iron nave of the Palace Pier, white and purposeful in the obscurity: half-vulture and half-dove. In the end one always had to learn.

'All right. I'll come,' the Boy said.

'It's the best road-house this side of London,' Dallow encouraged him.

They drove out in the old Morris into the country. 'I like a blow in the country,' Dallow said. It was between lighting-up time and the real dark when the lamps of cars burn in the grey visibility as faintly and unnecessarily as the night lights in nurseries. The advertisements trailed along the arterial road: bungalows and a broken farm, short chalky grass where a hoarding had been pulled down, a windmill offering tea and lemonade, the great ruined sails gaping.

'Poor old Spicer would have liked this ride,' Cubitt said. The Boy sat beside Dallow who drove and Cubitt sat in the dicky. The Boy could see him in the driving mirror bouncing gently up and down on the defective springs.

The Queen of Hearts was floodlit behind the petrol pumps: a Tudor barn converted, a vestige of a farmyard left in the arrangement of the restaurant and bars: a swimming pool where the paddock had been. 'We ought to 'ave brought some girls with us,' Dallow said. 'You can't pick 'em up in this gaff. It's real class.'

'Come in the bar,' Cubitt said and led the way. He stopped on the threshold and nodded towards the girl who sat and drank alone at the long steel bar under the old rafters. 'We better say something, Pinkie. You know the kind of thing—he was a real good old pal, we sympathize with what you feel.'

'What are you clapping about?'

'That's Spicer's girl,' Cubitt said.

The Boy stood in the doorway and took her reluctantly in: hair fair as silver, wide vacuous brow, trim little buttocks shaped by the high seat, alone with her glass and her grief.

'How's things, Sylvie?' Cubitt said.

'Awful.'

'Terrible, wasn't it? He was a good pal. One of the best.'

'You were there, weren't you?' she said to Dallow.

'Frank ought to 'ave mended that stair,' Dallow said. 'Meet Pinkie, Sylvie, the best one in our mob.'

'Were you there, too?'

'He wasn't there,' Dallow said.

'Have another drink?' the Boy said.

Sylvie drained her glass. 'I don't mind if I do. A Sidecar.'

'Two Scotch, a Sidecar, a grape-fruit squash.'

'Why,' Sylvie said, 'don't you drink?'

'No.'

'I bet you don't go with girls either.'

'You got him, Sylvie,' Cubitt said, 'first shot.'

'I admire a man like that,' Sylvie said. 'I think it's wonderful to be fit. Spicie always said you'd break out one day—and then—oh gosh, how wonderful.' She put down her glass, miscalculated, upset the cocktail. She said, 'I'm not drunk. I'm upset about poor Spicie.'

'Go on, Pinkie,' Dallow said, 'have a drink. It'll jerk you up.' He explained to Sylvie, 'He's upset too.' In the dance hall the band was playing, 'Love me tonight, And forget in daylight, All our delight . . .'

'Have a drink,' Sylvie said. 'I've been awful upset. You can see I've been crying. Aren't my eyes awful . . . Why, I hardly dared show myself. I can see why people go into monasteries.' The music beat on the Boy's resistance: he watched with a kind of horror and curiosity Spicer's girl friend; she knew the game. He shook his head, speechless in his scared pride. He knew what he was good at: he was the top: there was no limit to his ambition: nothing must lay him open to the mockery of people more experienced than he. To be compared with Spicer and found wanting . . . his eyes shifted miserably and the music wailed its tidings—'Forget in daylight'—about the game of which they all knew so much more than he did.

'Spicie said he didn't think you'd ever had a girl,' Sylvie said.

'There was plenty Spicer didn't know.'

'You're awful young to be so famous.'

'You and me had better go away," Cubitt said to Dallow. 'Seems we're not wanted. Come an' lamp the bathing belles.' They moved heavily out of sight. 'Dallie just knows when I like a boy,' Sylvie said.

'Who's Dallie?'

'Your friend, Mr Dallow, silly. Do you dance—why, I don't even know your proper name?' He watched her with scared lust. She had belonged to Spicer: her voice had wailed up the telephone wires making assignations: he had received letters in mauve envelopes, addressed to him: even Spicer had had something to be proud of, to show to friends—'my girl'. He remembered some flowers which had come to Frank's labelled 'Broken-hearted'. He was fascinated by her infidelity. She belonged to nobody—unlike a table or a chair. He said slowly, putting his arm round her to take her glass and pressing her breast clumsily, 'I'm going to be married in a day or two.' It was as if he were staking a claim to his share of infidelity: he wasn't to be beaten by experience. He lifted her glass and drank it. The sweetness dripped down his throat, his first alcohol touched the palate like a bad smell: this was what people called pleasure—this and the game. He put his hand on her thigh with a kind of horror: Rose and he: forty-eight hours after Prewitt had arranged things: alone in God knows what apartment— what then, what then? He knew the traditional actions as a man may know the principles of gunnery in chalk on a blackboard, but to translate the knowledge to action, to the smashed village and the ravaged woman, one needed help from the nerves. His own were frozen with repulsion: to be touched, to give oneself away, to lay oneself open—he had held intimacy back as long as he could at the end of a razor blade.

He said, 'Come on. Let's dance.'

They circulated slowly in the dance hall. To be beaten by experience was bad enough, but to be beaten by greenness and innocence, by a girl who carried plates at Snow's, by a little bitch of sixteen years . . .

'Spicie thought a lot of you,' Sylvie said.

'Come out to the cars,' the Boy said.

'I couldn't, not with Spicie dead only yesterday.'

They stood and clapped and then the dance began again. The shaker clacked in the bar, and the leaves of one small tree were pressed against the window beyond the big drum and the saxophone.

'I like the country. It makes me feel romantic. Do you like the country?'

'No.'

'This is *real* country. I saw a hen just now. They use their own eggs in the gin slings.'

'Come out to the cars.'

'I feel that way, too. O gosh, wouldn't it be fine? But I can't, not with poor Spicie . . .'

'You sent flowers, didn't you, you been crying . . .'

'My eyes are awful.'

'What more can you do?'

'It broke my heart. Poor Spicie going off like that.'

'I know. I saw your wreath.'

'It does seem awful, doesn't it? Dancing with you like this and him . . .'

'Come to the cars.'

'Poor Spicie,' but she led the way, and he noticed with uneasiness how she ran—literally ran—across the lit corner of what had once been a farmyard towards the dark car-park and the game. He thought with sickness, 'In three minutes I shall know.'

'Which is your car?' Sylvie asked.

'That Morris.'

'No good to us,' Sylvie said. She darted down the line of cars. 'This Ford.' She pulled the door open, said, 'Oh, pardon me,' and shut it, scrambled into the back of the next car in the line and waited for him. 'Oh,' her voice softly and passionately pronounced from the dim interior, 'I love a Lancia.' He stood in the doorway and the darkness peeled away between him and the fair and vacuous face. Her skirt drawn up above her knees she waited for him with luxurious docility.

He was conscious for a moment of his enormous ambitions under the shadow of the hideous and commonplace act: the suite at the

Cosmopolitan, the gold cigar-lighter, chairs stamped with crowns for a foreigner called Eugeen. Hale dropped out of sight, like a stone thrown over a cliff; he was at the beginning of a long polished parquet walk, there were busts of great men and the sound of cheering, Mr Colleoni bowed like a shopwalker, stepping backwards, an army of razors was at his back: a conqueror. Hooves drummed along the straight and a loud-speaker announced the winner: music was playing. His breast ached with the effort to enclose the whole world.

'You've got the doings, haven't you?' Sylvie asked.

With fear and horror he thought: next move, what is it?

'Quick,' Sylvie said, 'before they find us here.'

The parquet floor rolled up like a carpet. The moonlight touched a Woolworth ring and a plump knee. He said in a painful and bitter rage, 'Wait there. I'll get Cubitt for you,' and turned his back on the Lancia and walked back towards the bar. Laughter from the bathing-pool deflected him. He stood in the doorway with the taste of the alcohol on his tongue watching a thin girl in a red rubber cap giggle under the flood lighting. His mind tracked inevitably back and forth to Sylvie like a model engine electrically driven. Fear and curiosity ate at the proud future, he was aware of nausea and retched. Marry, he thought, hell, no; I'd rather hang.

A man in a bathing-slip came running down the highboard, jumped and somersaulted in the pearly brilliant light, struck the dark water; the two bathers swam together, stroke by stroke, towards the shallows, turned and came back, side by side, smooth and unhurried, playing a private game, happy and at ease.

The Boy stood and watched them, and as they came down the pool a second time he saw in the floodlit water his own image shiver at their stroke, the narrow shoulders and the hollow breast, and he felt the brown pointed shoes slip on the splashed and shining tiles.

Cubitt and Dallow chattered all the way back, a little lit; the Boy stared ahead into the bright core of the darkness. He said suddenly with fury, 'You can laugh.'

'Well, you didn't do so bad,' Cubitt said.

'You can laugh. You think you're safe. But I'm tired of the lot of you. I've a good mind to clear out.'

'Take a long honeymoon,' Cubitt said and grinned, and an owl cried with painful hunger swooping low over a filling station, into the headlights and out again, on furry and predatory wings.

'I'm not going to marry,' the Boy said.

'I knew a geezer once,' Cubitt said, 'was so scared he killed himself. They had to send back the wedding presents.'

'I'm not going to marry.'

'People often feel that way.'

'Nothing's going to make me marry.'

'You've got to marry,' Dallow said. A woman stared from a window of Charlie's Pull-in Café waiting for someone: she didn't look at the car going by, waiting.

'Have a drink,' Cubitt said; he was more drunk than Dallow. 'I brought a flask away. You can't say you don't drink now: we saw you, Dallow and me.'

The Boy said to Dallow, 'I won't marry. Why should I marry?'

'It was your doing,' Dallow said.

'What was his doing?' Cubitt said. Dallow didn't reply, laying his friendly and oppressive hand on the Boy's knee. The Boy took a squint at the stupid devoted face and felt anger at the way another's loyalty could hamper and drive. Dallow was the only man he trusted, and he hated him as if he were his mentor. He said weakly, 'Nothing will make me marry,' watching the long parade of posters going by in the submarine light: Guinness is Good for You, Try a Worthington, Keep that Schoolgirl Complexion: a long series of adjurations, people telling you things: Own Your Own Home, Bennett's for Wedding Rings.

And at Frank's they told him, 'Your girl's here.' He went up the stairs to his room in hopeless rebellion; he would go in and say—I've changed my mind. I can't marry you. Or perhaps—the lawyers say it can't be managed after all. The banisters were still broken and he looked down the long drop to where Spicer's body had lain. Cubitt and Dallow were standing on the exact spot laughing at something: the sharp edge of a broken banister scratched his hand. He put it to his mouth and went in. He thought: I've got to be calm, I've got to keep my wits about me, but he felt his integrity stained by the taste of the spirit at the bar. You could lose vice as easily as you lost virtue, going out of you from a touch.

He took a look at her. She was scared when he said softly, 'What are you doing here?' She had on the hat he disliked and she made a snatch at it as soon as he looked. 'At this time of night,' he said in a shocked way, thinking there was a quarrel to be picked there if he went about it in the right way.

'You've seen this?' Rose implored him. She had the local paper; he hadn't bothered to read it, but there on the front page was the picture of Spicer striding in terror under the iron arches. Rose said, 'It says here—it happened—'

'On the landing,' the boy said. 'I was always telling Frank to mend those banisters.'

'But you said they got him on the course. And he was the one who—'

He faced her with spurious firmness: 'Gave you the ticket? So you said. Maybe he knew Hale. He knew a lot of geezers I didn't. What of it?' He repeated his question before her dumb stare with confidence: 'What of it?' His mind, he knew, could contemplate any treachery, but she was a good kid, she was bounded by her goodness; there were things she couldn't imagine, and he thought he saw her imagination wilting now in the vast desert of dread.

'I thought,' she said, 'I thought . . .' looking beyond him to the shattered banister on the landing.

'What did you think?'

His fingers curled with passionate hatred round the small bottle in his pocket.

'I don't know. I didn't sleep last night. I had such dreams.'

'What dreams?'

She looked at him with horror, 'I dreamed you were dead.'

He laughed, 'I'm young and spry,' thinking with nausea of the car-park and the invitation in the Lancia.

'You aren't going to stay here, are you?'

'Why not?'

'I'd have thought—' she said, her eyes back again in their gaze at the banisters. She said, 'I'm scared.'

'You've no cause to be,' he said, tickling the vitriol bottle.

'I'm scared for you. Oh,' she said, 'I know I'm no account. I know you've got a lawyer and a car and friends, but this place—' she stumbled hopelessly in an attempt to convey the sense she had of the territory in which he moved: a place of accidents and unexplained events, the stranger with a card, the fight on the course, the headlong fall. A kind of boldness and brazenness came into her face, so that he felt again the faintest stirring of sensuality: 'You've got to come away from here. You've got to marry me like you said.'

'It can't be done after all. I've seen my lawyer. We're too young.'

'I don't mind about that. It's not a *real* marriage, anyway. A registrar doesn't make any difference.'

'You go back where you came from,' he said harshly. 'You little tart.'

'I can't,' she said. 'I'm sacked.'

'What for?' It was as if the handcuffs were meeting. He suspected her.

'I was rude to a customer.'

'Why? What customer?'

'Can't you guess?' she said and went passionately on. 'Who is she, anyway? Interfering . . . pestering . . . *you* must know.'

'I don't know her from Adam,' the Boy said.

She put all her fake experience—drawn from the twopenny library—into the question: 'Is she jealous? Is she someone . . . you know what I mean?' and ready there, masked behind the ingenuous question like the guns in a Q ship, was possessiveness. She was his like a table or a chair, but a table owned you, too—by your finger-prints.

He laughed uneasily. 'What, she? She's old enough to be my mother.'

'Then what does she want?'

'I wish I knew.'

'Do you think,' she said, 'I ought to take this—' she held out the paper to him—'to the police?'

The ingenuousness—or the shrewdness—of the question shocked him. Could one ever be safe with someone who realized so little how she had got mixed up in things? He said, 'You got to mind your step,' and thought with dull and tired distaste (it had been the hell of a day): I shall have to marry her after all. He managed a smile: those muscles were beginning to work. He said, 'Listen. You don't need to think about those things. I'm going to marry you. There are ways of getting round the law.'

'Why bother about the law?'

'I don't want any loose talk. Only marriage' he said with feigned anger, 'will do for me. We got to be married properly.'

'We won't be that whatever we do. The father up at St John's—he says—'

'You don't want to listen too much to priests,' he said. 'They don't know the world like I do. Ideas change, the world moves on . . .' His words stumbled before her carved devotion. That face said as clearly as words that ideas never changed, the world never moved: it lay there always, the ravaged and disputed territory between the two eternities. They faced each other as it were from opposing territories, but like troops at Christmas time they fraternized. He said, 'It's the same to you, anyway—and I want to be married—legally.'

'If you want to . . .' she said and made a small gesture of complete assent.

'Maybe,' he said, 'we could work it this way. If your father wrote a letter . . .'

'He can't write.'

'Well, he could make his mark, couldn't he, if I got a letter written . . . I don't know how these things work. Maybe he could come to the magistrate's. Mr Prewitt could see about that.'

'Mr Prewitt?' she asked quickly. 'Wasn't he the one—the one at the inquest who was here . . .'

'What of it?'

'Nothing,' she said. 'I just thought . . .' but he could see the thoughts going on and on, out of the room to the banisters and the drop, out of that day altogether . . . Somebody's turned on the radio down below: some jest of Cubitt's perhaps to represent the right romantic atmosphere. It wailed up the stairs past the telephone and into the room: somebody's band from somebody's hotel, the end of a day's programme. It switched her thoughts away and he wondered for how long it would be necessary for him to sidetrack her mind with the romantic gesture or the loving act: how many weeks and months—his mind wouldn't admit the possibility of years. Some day he would be free again. He put out his hands towards her as if she were the detective with the cuffs and said, 'Tomorrow we'll see about things: see your father: why,' the muscles of his mouth faltered at the thought, 'it only takes a couple of days to get married in.'

3

He was scared, walking alone back towards the territory he had left—oh, years ago. The pale sea curdled on the shingle and the green tower of the Metropole looked like a dug-up coin verdigrised with age-old mould. The gulls swooped up to the top promenade, screaming and twisting in the sunlight, and a well-known popular author displayed his plump too famous face in the window of the Royal Albion, staring out to sea. It was so clear a day you looked for France.

The Boy crossed over towards Old Steyne walking slowly. The streets narrowed uphill above the Steyne: the shabby secret behind the bright corsage, the deformed breast. Every step was a retreat. He thought he had escaped for ever by the whole length of the parade, and now extreme poverty took him back: a shop where a shingle could be had for two shillings in the same building as a coffin-maker's who worked in oak, elm or lead: no window-dressing but one child's coffin dusty with disuse and the list of hairdressing prices. The Salvation Amy Citadel marked with its battlements the very border of his home. He began to fear recognition and feel an obscure shame as if it were his native streets which had the right to forgive and not he to reproach them with the dreary and dingy past. Past the Albert Hostel ('Good Accommodation for Travellers') and there he was, on the top of the hill, in the thick of the bombardment—a flapping gutter, cracked windows, an iron bedstead in a front garden the size of a tabletop. Half Paradise Piece had been torn up as if by bomb bursts; the children played about the steep slope of rubble; a piece of fireplace showed houses had once been there, and a municipal notice announced new flats on a post stuck in the torn gravel and asphalt facing the little dingy damaged row, all that was left of Paradise Piece. His home was gone: a flat place among the rubble may have marked its hearth; the room at the bend of the stairs where the Saturday night exercise had taken place was now just air. He wondered with horror whether it all had to be built again for him; it looked better as air.

He had sent Rose back the night before and now draggingly he rejoined her. It was no good rebelling any more; he had to marry her: he had to be safe. The children were scouting among the rubble with pistols from Woolworth's; a group of girls surlily watched. A child with its leg in an iron brace limped blindly into him; he pushed it off; someone said in a high treble, 'Stick 'em up.' They took his mind back and he hated them for it; it was like the dreadful appeal of innocence, but *there* was not innocence; you had to go back a long way further before you got innocence; innocence was a slobbering mouth, a toothless gum pulling at the teats; perhaps not even that; innocence was the ugly cry of birth.

He found the house in Nelson Place, but before he had time to knock the door opened. Rose had spied him through the broken glass. She said, 'Oh, how glad I am . . . I thought perhaps . . .' In the awful little passage which stank like a lavatory she ran quickly and passionately on, 'It was awful last night . . . you see I've been sending them money . . . they don't understand everyone loses a job some time or another.'

'I'll settle them,' the Boy said. 'Where are they?'

'You got to be careful,' Rose said. 'They get moods.'

'Where are they?'

But there wasn't really much choice of direction: there was only one door and a staircase matted with old newspapers. On the bottom steps between the mud marks stared up the tawny child face of Violet Crow violated and buried under the West Pier in 1936. He opened the door and there beside the black kitchen stove with cold dead charcoal on the floor sat the parents. They had a mood on: they watched him with silent and haughty indifference: a small thin elderly man, his face marked deeply with the hieroglyphics of pain and patience and suspicion: the woman middle-aged, stupid, vindictive. The dishes hadn't been washed and the stove hadn't been lit.

'They got a mood,' Rose said aloud to him. 'They wouldn't let me do a thing. Not even light the fire. I like a clean house, honest I do. Ours wouldn't be like this.'

'Look here, Mr—' the Boy said.

'Wilson,' Rose said.

'Wilson. I want to marry Rose. It seems as she's so young I got to get your permission.'

They wouldn't answer him. They treasured their mood as if it was a bright piece of china only they possessed: something they could show to neighbours as 'mine'.

'It's no use,' Rose said, 'when they got a mood.'

A cat watched them from a wooden box.

'Yes or no,' the Boy said.

'It's no good,' Rose said, 'not when they've got a mood.'

'Answer a plain question,' the Boy said. 'Do I marry Rose or don't I?'

'Come back tomorrow,' Rose said. 'They won't have a mood then.'

'I'm not going to wait on them,' he said. 'They oughter be proud—'

The man suddenly got up and kicked the dead coke furiously across the floor. 'You get out of here,' he said. 'We don't want any truck with you,' he went on, 'never, never, never,' and for a moment in the sunk lost eyes there was a kind of fidelity which reminded the Boy dreadfully of Rose.

'Quiet, father,' the woman said, 'don't talk to them,' treasuring her mood.

'I've come to do business,' the Boy said, 'If you don't want 'to do business—' He looked round the battered and hopeless room. 'I thought maybe ten pounds would be of use to you,' and he saw swimming up through the blind vindictive silence incredulity, avarice, suspicion. 'We don't want—' the man began again and then gave out like a gramophone. He began to think: you could see the thoughts bob up one after another.

'We don't want your money,' the woman said. They each had their own kind of fidelity.

Rose said, 'Never mind what they say. I won't stay here.'

'Stop a moment. Stop a moment,' the man said. 'You be quiet, mother.' He said to the Boy, 'We couldn't let Rose go not for ten nicker—not to a stranger. How do we know you'd treat her right?'

'I'll give you twelve,' the Boy said.

'It's not a question of money,' the man said. 'I like the look of you. We wouldn't want to stand in the way of Rose bettering herself—but you're too young.'

'Fifteen's my limit,' the Boy said, 'take it or leave it.'

'You can't do anything without we say yes,' the man said.

The Boy moved a little away from Rose, 'I'm not all that keen.'

'Make it guineas.'

'You've had my offer.' He looked with horror round the room: nobody could say he hadn't done right to get away from this, to commit any crime . . . When the man opened his mouth he heard his father speaking, that figure in the corner was his mother: he bargained for his sister and felt no desire . . . He turned to Rose, 'I'm off,' and felt the faintest twinge of pity for goodness which couldn't murder to escape. They said that saints had got—what was the phrase?—'heroic virtues', heroic patience, heroic endurance, but there was nothing he could see that was heroic in the bony face, protuberant eyes, pallid anxiety, while they bluffed each other and her life was confused in the financial game. 'Well,' he said, 'I'll be seeing you,' and made for the door. At the door he looked back: they were like a family party. Impatiently and contemptuously he gave in to them, 'All right. Guineas. I'll be sending my lawyer,' and as he passed into the evil passage Rose was behind him panting her gratitude.

He played the game to the last card, fetching up a grin and a compliment, 'I'd do more for you.'

'You were wonderful,' she said, loving him among the lavatory smells, but her praise was poison: it marked her possession of him: it led straight to what she expected from him, the horrifying act of a desire he didn't feel. She followed him out into the fresh air of Nelson Place. The children played among the ruins of Paradise Piece, and a wind blew from the sea across the site of his home. A dim desire for annihilation stretched in him: the vast superiority of vacancy.

She said, as she had said once before, 'I always wondered how it'd be.' Her mind moved obscurely among the events of the afternoon, brought out the unexpected discovery. 'I've never known a mood go so quick. They must have liked you.'

4

Ida Arnold bit an éclair and the cream spurted between the large front teeth. She laughed a little thickly in the Pompadour Boudoir and said, 'I haven't had as much money to spend since I left Tom.' She took another bite and a wedge of cream settled on the plump tongue. 'I owe it to Fred too. If he hadn't tipped me Black Boy . . .'

'Why not give everything up,' Mr Corkery said, 'and just have a bit of fun. It's dangerous.'

'Oh, yes it's dangerous,' she admitted, but no real sense of danger could lodge behind those large vivacious eyes. Nothing could ever make her believe that one day she too, like Fred, would be where the worms . . . Her mind couldn't take that track; she could go only a short way before the points automatically shifted and set her vibrating down the accustomed line, the season ticket line marked by desirable residence and advertisements of cruises and small fenced boskages for rural love. She said, eyeing her éclair, 'I never give in. They didn't know what a packet of trouble they were stirring up.'

'Leave it to the police.'

'Oh no. I know what's right. You can't tell me. Who's that, do you think?'

An elderly man in glacé shoes, with a white slip to his waistcoat and a jewelled pin, came padding across the Boudoir. 'Distinguay,' Ida Arnold said.

A secretary trotted a little way behind him, reading out from a list. 'Bananas, oranges, grapes, peaches . . .'

'Hothouse?'

'Hothouse.'

'Who's that?' Ida Arnold repeated.

'That was all, Mr Colleoni?' the secretary asked.

'What flowers?' Mr Colleoni demanded. 'And could you get any nectarines?'

'No, Mr Colleoni.'

'My dear wife,' Mr Colleoni said, his voice dwindling out of their hearing. They could catch only the word 'passion'. Ida Arnold swivelled her eyes round the elegant furnishing of the Pompadour Boudoir. They picked out like a searchlight a cushion, a couch, the thin clerkly mouth of the man opposite her. She said, 'We could have a fine time here,' watching his mouth.

'Expensive,' Mr Corkery said nervously; a too sensitive hand stroked his thin shanks.

'Black Boy will stand it. And we can't have—you know—fun at the Belvedere. Strait-laced.'

'You wouldn't mind a bit of fun here?' Mr Corkery asked. He blinked. You couldn't tell from his expression whether he desired or dreaded her assent.

'Why should I? It doesn't do anyone any harm that I know of. It's human nature.' She bit at her éclair and repeated the familiar password. 'It's only fun after all.' Fun to be on the right side, fun to be human . . .

'You go and get my bag,' she said, 'while I book a room. After all—I owe you something. You've worked . . .'

Mr Corkery flushed a little. 'Half and half,' he said.

She grinned at him. 'It's on Black Boy. I pay my debts.'

'A man likes—' Mr Corkery said weakly.

'Trust me, I know what a man likes.' The éclair and the deep couch and the gaudy furnishings were like an aphrodisiac in her tea. She was shaken by a Bacchic and a bawdy mood. In every word either of them uttered she detected the one meaning. Mr Corkery blushed, plunged deeper in his embarrassment. 'A man can't help feeling,' and was shaken by her immense glee.

'You're telling me,' she said, 'you're telling me.'

While Mr Corkery was gone she made her preparations for carnival, the taste of the sweet cake between her teeth. The idea of Fred Hale dodged backwards like a figure on a platform when the train goes out. He belonged to somewhere left behind; the waving hand only contributes to the excitement of the new experience.

The new—and yet the immeasurably old. She gazed round the big padded pleasure dome of a bedroom with bloodshot and experienced eyes: the long mirror and the wardrobe and the enormous bed. She settled frankly down on it while the clerk waited. 'It springs,' she said, 'it springs,' and sat there for quite a long while after he'd gone planning the evening's campaign. If somebody had said to her then 'Fred Hale', she would hardly have recognized the name: there was another interest: for the next hour let the police have him.

Then she got up slowly and began to undress. She never believed in wearing much: it wasn't any time at all before she was exposed in the long mirror: a body firm and bulky: a proper handful. She stood on a deep soft rug, surrounded by gilt frames and red velvet hangings, and a dozen common and popular phrases bloomed in her mind—'A Night of Love', 'You Only Live Once', and the rest. She bore the same relation to passion as a peepshow. She sucked the chocolate between her teeth and smiled, her plump toes working in the rug, waiting for Mr Corkery—just a great big blossoming surprise.

Outside the window the sea ebbed, scraping the shingle, exposing a boot, a piece of rusty iron, and the old man stooped, searching between the stones. The sun dropped behind the Hove houses and dusk came, the shadow of Mr Corkery lengthened, coming slowly up from the Belvedere carrying the suitcases, saving on taxis. A gull swooped screaming down to a dead crab beaten and broken against the iron foundation of the pier. It was the time of near-darkness and of the evening mist from the Channel and of love.

5

The Boy closed the door behind him and turned to face the expectant and amused faces.

'Well,' Cubitt said, 'is it all fixed up?'

'Of course it is,' the Boy said, 'when I want a thing—' his voice wavered out unconvincingly. There were half a dozen bottles on his washstand: his room smelt of stale beer.

'Want a thing,' Cubitt said. 'That's good.' He opened another bottle and in the warm stuffy room the froth rose quickly and splashed on the marble top.

'What do you think you're doing?' the Boy said.

'Celebrating,' Cubitt said. 'You're a Roman, aren't you? A betrothal, that's what Romans call it.'

The Boy watched them: Cubitt a little drunk, Dallow preoccupied, two lean hungry faces he hardly knew—hangers-on at the fringes of the great racket who smiled when you smiled and frowned when you frowned. But now they smiled when Cubitt smiled, and suddenly he saw the long way he had slipped since that afternoon on the pier when he arranged the alibi, gave the orders, did what they hadn't got the nerve to do themselves.

Frank's wife Judy put her head in at the door. She was wearing a dressing-gown. Her Titian hair was brown at the roots. 'Good luck, Pinkie,' she said, blinking mascara'd lashes. She had been washing her bra: the little piece of pink silk dripped on the linoleum. Nobody offered her a drink. 'Work, work, work,' she moued at them, going on down the passage to the hot water-pipes.

A long way . . . and yet he hadn't made a single false step: if he hadn't gone to Snow's and spoken to the girl, they'd all be in the dock by now. If he hadn't killed Spicer . . . Not a single false step, but every step conditioned by a pressure he couldn't even place: a woman asking questions, messages on the telephone scaring Spicer. He thought: when I've married the girl, will it stop then? Where else can it drive me, and with a twitch of the mouth, he wondered—what worse—?

'When's the happy day?' Cubitt asked and they all smiled obediently except Dallow.

The Boy's brain began to work again. He moved slowly towards the washstand. He said, 'Haven't you got a glass for me? Don't I do any celebrating?'

He saw Dallow astonished, Cubitt thrown off his mark, the hangers-on doubtful who to follow, and he grinned at them, the one with brains.

'Why, Pinkie . . .' Cubitt said.

'I'm not a drinking man and I'm not a marrying man,' the Boy said. 'So *you* think. But I'm liking one, so why shouldn't I like the other. Give me a glass.'

'Liking,' Cubitt said and grinned uneasily, 'you *liking* . . .'

'Haven't you seen her?' the Boy said.

'Why, me and Dallow just lamped her. On the stairs. But it was too dark . . .'

'She's a lovely,' the Boy said, 'she's wasted in a kip. And intelligent. Don't make any mistake. Of course I didn't see any cause to *marry* her, but as it is—' somebody handed him a glass: he took a long draught: the bitter and bubbly fluid revolted him—so this was what they liked—he tightened the muscles of his mouth to hide his revulsion: 'as it is,' he said, 'I'm glad,' and eyed with hidden disgust the pale inch of liquid in the glass before he drained it down.

Dallow watched in silence and the Boy felt more anger against his friend than against his enemy. Like Spicer he knew too much, but what he knew was far more deadly than what Spicer had known. Spicer had known only the kind of thing which brought you to the dock, but Dallow knew what your mirror and your bedsheets knew: the secret fear and the humiliation. He said with hidden fury, 'What's getting you, Dallow?'

The stupid and broken face was hopelessly at a loss.

'Jealous?' the Boy began to boast. 'You've cause when you've

seen her. She not one of your dyed totsies. She's got class. I'm marrying her for your sake, but I'm laying her for my own.' He turned
fiendishly on Dallow. 'What's on *your* mind?'

'Well,' Dallow, said, 'it's the one you met on the pier, isn't it? I
didn't think she was all that good.'

'You,' the Boy said, 'you don't know anything. You're ignorant.
You don't know class when you see it.'

'A duchess,' Cubitt said and laughed.

An extraordinary indignation jerked in the Boy's brain and fingers. It was almost as if someone he loved had been insulted. 'Be
careful, Cubitt,' he said.

'Don't mind him,' Dallow said. 'We didn't know you'd
fallen . . .'

'We got some presents for you, Pinkie,' Cubitt said, 'furniture
for the home,' and indicated two little obscene objects beside the
beer on the washstand—the Brighton stationers were full of them—
a tiny doll's commode in the shape of a radio set labelled 'The
smallest A.1 two-valve receiving set in the world', and a mustard-
pot shaped like a lavatory seat with the legend, 'For me and my girl'.
It was like a return of all the horror he had ever felt, the hideous
loneliness of his innocence. He struck at Cubitt's face and Cubitt
dodged, laughing. The two hangers-on slipped out of the room.
They hadn't any taste for rough houses. The Boy heard them laugh
on the stairs. Cubitt said, 'You'll need 'em in the home. A bed's
not the only furniture.' He mocked and backed at the same time.

The Boy said, 'By God, I'll treat you like I treated Spicer.'

No meaning reached Cubitt at once. There was a long time lag.
He began to laugh and then saw Dallow's startled face and *heard*.
'What's that?' he said.

'He's crazy,' Dallow intervened.

'You think yourself smart,' the Boy said. 'So did Spicer.'

'It was the banister,' Cubitt said. 'You weren't here. What are
you getting at?'

'Of course he wasn't here,' Dallow said.

'You think you know things.' All the Boy's hatred was in the
word 'know' and his repulsion: he knew—like Prewitt knew after
twenty-five years at the game. 'You don't know everything.' He
tried to inject himself with pride, but all the time his eyes went

back to the humiliation. 'The smallest A.1 . . .' You could know everything there was in the world and yet if you were ignorant of that one dirty scramble you knew nothing.

'What's he getting at?' Cubitt asked.

'You don't need to listen to him,' Dallow said.

'I mean this,' the Boy said. 'Spicer was milky and I'm the only one in this mob knows how to act.'

'You act too much,' Cubitt said. 'Do you mean—it wasn't the banisters?' The question scared himself: he didn't want an answer. He made uneasily for the door, keeping his eye on the Boy.

Dallow said, 'Of course it was the banisters. I was there, wasn't I?'

'I don't know,' Cubitt said, 'I don't know,' making for the door. 'Brighton's not big enough for him. I'm through.'

'Go on,' the Boy said. 'Clear out. Clear out and starve.'

'I won't starve,' Cubitt said. 'There's others in this town . . .'

When the door closed the Boy turned on Dallow. 'Go on,' he said, 'you go too. You think you can get on without me, but I've only got to whistle . . .'

'You don't need to talk to me like that,' Dallow said. 'I'm not leaving you. I don't fancy making friends with Crab again so soon.'

But the Boy paid him no attention. He said again, 'I've only got to whistle . . .' He boasted, 'They'll come tumbling back.' He went over to the brass bed and lay down; he had had a long day. He said, 'Get me Prewitt on the blower. Tell him there's no difficulty at *her* end. Let him fix things quick.'

'The day after tomorrow if he can?' Dallow asked.

'Yes,' the Boy said. He heard the door close and lay with twitching cheek staring at the ceiling. He thought, it's not my fault they get me angry so I want to do things: if people would leave me in peace . . . His imagination wilted at the word. He tried in a half-hearted way to picture 'peace'—his eyes closed and behind the lids he saw a grey darkness going on and on without end, a country of which he hadn't seen as much as a picture postcard, a place far stranger than the Grand Canyon and the Taj Mahal. He opened them again and immediately poison moved in the veins, for there on the washstand were Cubitt's purchases. He was like a child with haemophilia: every contact drew blood.

6

A bell rang muffled in the Cosmopolitan corridor; through the wall against which the bed-end stood Ida Arnold could hear a voice talking on and on: somebody reading a report, perhaps in a conference room or dictating to a dictaphone. Phil lay asleep on the bed in his pants, his mouth a little open showing one yellow tooth and a gob of metal filling. Fun . . . human nature . . . does no one any harm . . . Regular as clockwork the old excuses came back into the alert, sad and dissatisfied brain—nothing ever matched the deep excitement of the regular desire. Men always failed you when it came to the act. She might just as well have been to the pictures.

But it did no one any harm, it was just human nature, no one could call her really bad—a bit free-and-easy perhaps, a bit Bohemian. It wasn't as if she got anything out of it, as if like some people she sucked a man dry and cast him aside like a throw-off—threw him aside like a cast-off glove. She knew what was right and what was wrong. God didn't mind a bit of human nature—what he minded—and her brain switched away from Phil in pants to her mission, to doing good, to seeing that the evil suffered . . .

She sat up in bed and put her arms round her large naked knees and felt excitement stirring again in the disappointed body. Poor old Fred—the name no longer conveyed any sense of grief or pathos. She couldn't remember anything much about him now but a monocle and a yellow waistcoat and that belonged to poor old Charlie Moyne. The hunt was what mattered. It was like life coming back after a sickness.

Phil opened an eye—yellow with the sexual effort—and watched her apprehensively. She said, 'Awake, Phil?'

'It must be nearly time for dinner,' Phil said. He gave a nervous smile. 'A penny for your thoughts, Ida.'

'I was just thinking,' Ida said, 'that what we really need now is one of Pinkie's men. Somebody scared or angry. They must get scared some time. We've only got to wait.'

She got out of the bed, opened her suitcase and began to lay out the clothes she thought were suitable for dinner in the Cosmopolitan. In the pink, reading-lamp, love-lamp light spangles glittered. She stretched her arms; she no longer felt desire or disappointment: her brain was clear. It was almost dark along the beach; the edge of sea was like a line of writing in whitewash: big sprawling letters. They meant nothing at this distance. A shadow stooped with infinite patience and disinterred some relic from the shingle.

PART SIX

I

When Cubitt got outside the front door the hangers-on had already vanished. The street was empty. He felt in a dumb, bitter and uncomprehending way like a man who has destroyed his home without having prepared another. The mist was coming up from the sea, and he hadn't got his coat. He was as angry as a child: he wouldn't go back for it: it would be like admitting he was wrong. The only thing to be done now was to drink a strong whisky at the Crown.

At the saloon bar they made way for him with respect. In the mirror marked Booth's Gin he could see his own reflection—the short flaming hair, the blunt and open face, broad shoulders. He stared like Narcissus into his pool and felt better; he wasn't the sort of man to take things lying down; he was valuable. 'Have a whisky?' somebody said. It was the greengrocer's assistant from the corner shop. Cubitt laid a heavy paw across his shoulder, accepting, patronizing: the man who had done a thing or two in his time chummy with the pale ignorant fellow who dreamed from his commercial distance of a man's life. The relationship pleased Cubitt. He had two more whiskies at the grocer's expense.

'Got a tip, Mr Cubitt?'

'I've got other things to think of beside tips,' Cubitt said darkly, adding a splash.

'We were having an argument in here about Gay Parrot for the two-thirty. Seemed to me . . .'

Gay Parrot . . . the name didn't mean a thing to Cubitt: the drink warmed him: the mist was in his brain: he leant forward towards the mirror and saw 'Booth's Gin . . . Booth's Gin', haloed above his head. He was involved in high politics: men had been killed: poor old Spicer. Allegiances shifted like heavy balances in his brain: he felt as important as a Prime Minister making treaties.

'There'll be more killing before we're through,' he mysteriously pronounced. He had his wits about him: he wasn't giving anything away; but there was no harm in letting these poor sodden creatures a little way into the secrets of living. He pushed his glass forward and said, 'A drink all round,' but when he looked to either side they'd gone; a face took a backward look through the pane of the saloon door, vanished; they couldn't stand the company of a Man.

'Never mind,' he said, 'never mind,' and drank down his whisky and left. The next thing, of course, was to see Colleoni. He'd say to him, 'Here I am, Mr Colleoni. I'm through with Kite's mob. I won't work under a boy like that. Give me a Man's job and I'll do it.' The mist got at his bones: he shivered involuntarily: a grey goose . . . He thought: if only Dallow too . . . and suddenly loneliness took away his confidence; all the heat of the drink seeped out of him, and the mist like seven devils went in. Suppose Colleoni simply wasn't interested. He came down on to the front and saw through the thin fog the high lights of the Cosmopolitan: it was cocktail time.

Cubitt sat down chilled in a glass shelter and stared out towards the sea. The tide was low and the mist hid it: it was just a sliding and a sibilation. He lit a cigarette: the match warmed for a moment the cupped hands. He offered the packet to an elderly gentleman wrapped in a heavy overcoat who shared the shelter. 'I don't smoke,' the old gentleman said sharply and began to cough: a steady hack, hack, hack towards the invisible sea.

'A cold night,' Cubitt said. The old gentleman swivelled his eyes on him like opera glasses and went on coughing: hack, hack, hack: the vocal chords dry as straw. Somewhere out at sea a violin began to play: it was like a sea beast mourning and stretching towards the shore. Cubitt thought of Spicer who'd liked a good tune. Poor old Spicer. The mist blew in, heavy compact drifts of it like ectoplasm. Cubitt had been to a séance once in Brighton: he had wanted to get in touch with his mother, dead twenty years ago. It had come over him quite suddenly—the old girl might have a word for him. She had: she was on the seventh plane where all was very beautiful: her voice had sounded a little boozed, but that wasn't really unnatural. The boys had laughed at him about it, particularly old Spicer. Well, Spicer wouldn't laugh now. He could be summoned himself any time to ring a bell and shake a tambourine. It was a lucky thing he liked music.

Cubitt got up and strolled to the turnpike of the West Pier, which straddled into the mist and vanished towards the violin. He walked up towards the Concert Hall, passing nobody. It wasn't a night for courting couples to sit out. Whatever people there were upon the pier were gathered every one inside the Concert Hall. Cubitt turned round it on the outside looking in: a man in evening dress fiddling to a few rows of people in overcoats, islanded fifty yards out to sea in the middle of the mist. Somewhere in the Channel a boat blew its siren and another answered, and another, like dogs at night waking each other.

Go to Colleoni and say . . . it was all quite easy; the old man ought to be grateful . . . Cubitt looked back towards the shore and saw above the mist the high lights of the Cosmopolitan, and they daunted him. He wasn't used to that sort of company. He went down the iron companionway to the gents and drained the whisky out of him into the movement under the piles and came up on to the deck lonelier than ever. He took a penny out of his pocket and slipped it into an automatic machine: a robot face behind which an electric bulb revolved, iron hands for Cubitt to grip. A little blue card shot out at him: 'Your Character Delineated.' Cubitt read: 'You are mainly influenced by your surroundings and inclined to be capricious and changeful. Your affections are more intense than enduring. You have a free, easy, and genial nature. You make the best of whatever you undertake. A share of the good things of life can always be yours. Your lack of initiative is counter-balanced by your good common sense, and you will succeed where others fail.'

He dragged slowly on past the automatic machines, delaying the moment when there would be nothing for him to do but go to the Cosmopolitan. 'Your lack of initiative . . .' Two leaden football teams waited behind glass for a penny to release them: an old witch with the stuffing coming out of her claw offered to tell his fortune. 'A Love Letter' made him pause. The boards were damp with mist, the long deck was empty, the violin ground on. He felt the need of a deep sentimental affection, orange blossoms and a cuddle in a corner. His great paw yearned for a sticky hand. Somebody who wouldn't mind his jokes, who would laugh with him at the two-valve receiving set. He hadn't meant any harm. The cold reached his stomach, and a little stale whisky returned into his throat. He almost felt inclined to go back to Frank's. But then he remembered Spicer. The boy was mad, killing mad, it wasn't safe. Loneliness dragged him down the solitary boards. He took out his last copper and thrust it in. A little pink card came out with a printed stamp: a girl's head, long hair, the legend 'True Love'. It was addressed to 'My Dear Pet, Spooner's Nook, With Cupid's Love', and there was a picture of a young man in evening dress kneeling on the floor, kissing the hand of a girl carrying a big fur. Up in a corner two hearts were transfixed by an arrow just above Reg. No. 745812. Cubitt thought: it's clever. It's cheap for a penny. He looked quickly over his shoulder: not a soul: and turned it quickly and began to read. The letter was addressed from Cupid's Wings, Amor Lane. 'My dear little girl. So you have discarded me for the Squire's son. You little know how you have ruined my life in breaking faith with me, you have crushed the very soul out of me, as the butterfly on the wheel; but with it all I do not wish anything but your happiness.'

Cubitt grinned uneasily. He was deeply moved. That was what always happened if you took up with anything but a buer; they gave you the air. Grand Renunciations, Tragedies, Beauty moved in Cubitt's brain. If it was a buer of course you took a razor to her, carved her face, but this love printed here was class. He read on: it was literature: it was the way he'd like to write himself. 'After all, when I think of your wondrous, winsome beauty, and culture, I feel what a fool I must have been to dream that you ever really loved me.' Unworthy. Emotion pricked behind his eyelids and he shivered in the mist with cold and beauty. 'But remember, dearest, always, that I love you, and if ever you want a friend just return the little token of love I gave you and I will be your servant and slave. Yours broken-heartedly, John.' It was his own name: an omen.

He moved again past the lighted concert hall and down the deserted deck. Loved and Lost. Tragic griefs flamed under his carrot hair. What can a man do but drink? He got another whisky just opposite the pier head and moved on, planting his feet rather too firmly, towards the Cosmopolitan—plank, plank, plank along the pavement as if he were wearing iron weights under his shoes, like a statue might move, half-flesh, half-stone.

'I want to speak to Mr Colleoni.' He said it defiantly. The plush and gilding smoothed away his confidence. He waited uneasily beside the desk while a pageboy searched through the lounges and boudoirs for Mr Colleoni. The clerk turned over the leaves of a big book and then consulted a *Who's Who*. Across the deep carpet the page returned and Crab followed him, sidling and triumphant with his black hair smelling of pomade.

'I said Mr Colleoni,' Cubitt said to the clerk, but the clerk took no notice, wetting his finger, skimming through *Who's Who*.

'You wanted to see Mr Colleoni,' Crab said.

'That's right.'

'You can't. He's occupied.'

'Occupied,' Cubitt said. 'That's a fine word to use. Occupied.'

'Why, if it isn't Cubitt,' Crab said. 'I suppose you want a job.' He looked round in a busy preoccupied way and said to the clerk, 'Isn't that Lord Feversham over there?'

'Yes, sir,' the clerk said.

'I've often seen him at Doncaster,' Crab said, squinting at a nail on his left hand. He swept round on Cubitt. 'Follow me, my man. We can't talk here,' and before Cubitt could reply he was sidling off at a great rate between the gilt chairs.

'It's like this,' Cubitt said, 'Pinkie—'

Half-way across the lounge Crab paused and bowed and moving on became suddenly confidential. 'A fine woman.' He flickered like an early movie. He had picked up between Doncaster and London a hundred different manners; travelling first-class after a successful meeting he had learnt how Lord Feversham spoke to a porter: he had seen old Digby scrutinize a woman.

'Who is she?' Cubitt asked.

But Crab took no notice of the question. 'We can talk here.' It was the Pompadour Boudoir. Through the gilt and glass door beyond the boule tables you could see little signboards pointing down a network of passages—tasteful little chinoiserie signboards with a Tuileries air: 'Ladies'. 'Gentlemen'. 'Ladies' Hairdressing'. 'Gentlemen's Hairdressing.'

'It's Mr Colleoni I want to talk to,' Cubitt said. He breathed whisky over the marquetry, but he was daunted and despairing. He resisted with difficulty the temptation to say 'sir'. Crab had moved on since Kite's day, almost out of sight. He was part of the great racket now—with Lord Feversham and the fine woman. He had grown up.

'Mr Colleoni hasn't time to see everyone,' Crab said. 'He's a busy man.' He took one of Mr Colleoni's cigars out of his pocket and put it in his mouth: he didn't offer one to Cubitt. Cubitt with uncertain hand offered him a match. 'Never mind, never mind,' Crab said, fumbling in his double-breasted waistcoat. He fetched out a gold lighter and flourished it at his cigar. 'What do you want, Cubitt?' he asked.

'I thought maybe,' Cubitt said, but his words wilted among the gilt chairs. 'You know how it is,' he said, staring desperately around. 'What about a drink?'

Crab took him quickly up. 'I wouldn't mind one—just for old time's sake.' He rang for a waiter.

'Old times,' Cubitt said.

'Take a seat,' Crab said, waving a possessive hand at the gilt chairs. Cubitt sat gingerly down. The chairs were small and hard. He saw a waiter watching them and flushed. 'What's yours?' he asked.

'A sherry,' Crab said. 'Dry.'

'Scotch and splash for me,' Cubitt said. He sat waiting for his drink, his hands between his knees, silent, his head lowered. He took furtive glances. This was where Pinkie had come to see Colleoni—he had nerve all right.

'They do you pretty well here,' Crab said. 'Of course Mr Colleoni likes nothing but the best.' He took his drink and watched Cubitt pay. 'He likes things smart. Why, he's worth fifty thousand nicker if he's worth a penny. If you ask me what I think,' Crab said, leaning back, puffing at the cigar, watching Cubitt through remote and supercilious eyes, 'he'll go in for politics one day. The Conservatives think a lot of him—he's got contacts.'

'Pinkie—' Cubitt began and Crab laughed. 'Take my advice,'

Crab said. 'Get out of that mob while there's time. There's no future . . .' He looked obliquely over Cubitt's head and said, 'See
that man going to the gents. That's Mais. The brewer. He's worth
a hundred thousand nicker.'

'I was wondering,' Cubitt said, 'if Mr Colleoni . . .'

'Not a chance,' Crab said. 'Why, ask yourself—what good
would you be to Mr Colleoni?'

Cubitt's humility gave way to a dull anger. 'I was good enough
for Kite.'

Crab laughed. 'Excuse me,' he said, 'but Kite . . .' He shook his
ash out on to the carpet and said, 'Take my advice. Get out. Mr
Colleoni's going to clean up this track. He likes things done properly. No violence. The police have great confidence in Mr
Colleoni.' He looked at his watch. 'Well, well, I must be going.
I've got a date at the Hippodrome.' He put his hand with patronage on Cubitt's arm. 'There,' he said. 'I'll put in a word for you—
for old times' sake. It won't be any good, but I'll do that much.
Give my regards to Pinkie and the boys.' He passed—a whiff of
pomade and Havana, bowing slightly to a woman at the door, an
old man with a monocle on a black ribbon. 'Who the hell—' the
old man said.

Cubitt drained his drink and followed. An enormous depression bowed his carrot head, a sense of ill-treatment moved
through the whisky fumes—somebody some time had got to pay
for something. All that he saw fed the flame: he came out into the
entrance hall: a pageboy with a salver infuriated him. Everybody
was watching him, waiting for him to go, but he had as much
right there as Crab. He glanced round him, and there alone at a
little table with a glass of port was the woman Crab knew. He
watched her with covetous envy and she smiled at him—'I think
of your wondrous, winsome beauty and culture.' A sense of the
immeasurable sadness of injustice took the place of anger. He
wanted to confide, to lay down burdens . . . he belched once . . . 'I
will be your loving slave.' The great body turned like a door, the
heavy feet altered direction and padded towards a table where Ida
Arnold sat.

'I couldn't help hearing,' she said, 'when you went across just
now that you knew Pinkie.'

He realized with immense pleasure when she spoke that she wasn't class. It seemed to him like the meeting of two fellow countrymen a long way from home. He said, 'You a friend of Pinkie's?' and felt the whisky in his legs. He asked, 'Mind if I sit down?'

'Tired?'

'That's it,' he said, 'tired.' He sat down with his eyes on her large friendly bosom. He remembered the lines on his character. 'You have a free, easy and genial nature.' By God, he had. He only needed to be treated right.

'Have a drink?'

'No, no,' he said with woolly gallantry, 'it's on me,' but when the drinks came he realized he was out of cash. He had meant to borrow from one of the boys—but then the quarrel . . . He watched Ida Arnold pay with a five-pound note.

'Know Mr Colleoni?' he asked.

'I wouldn't call it *know*,' she said.

'Crab said you were a fine woman. He's right.'

'Oh—Crab,' she said vaguely, as if she didn't recognize the name.

'You oughter steer clear though,' Cubitt said. 'You've no call to get mixed up in things.' He stared into his glass as into a deep darkness: outside innocence, winsome beauty and culture—unworthy, a tear gathered behind the bloodshot eyeball.

'You a friend of Pinkie's?' Ida Arnold asked.

'Christ, no,' Cubitt said and took some more whisky.

A vague memory of the Bible, where it lay in the cupboard next the Board, the Warwick Deeping, *The Good Companions*, stirred in Ida Arnold's memory. 'I've seen you with him.' she lied: a courtyard, a sewing wench beside the fire, the cock crowing.

'I'm no friend of Pinkie's.'

'It's not safe being friends with Pinkie,' Ida Arnold said. Cubitt stared into his glass like a diviner into his soul, reading the dooms of strangers. 'Fred was a friend of Pinkie's,' she said.

'What do you know about Fred?'

'People talk,' Ida Arnold said. 'People talk all the time.'

'You're right,' Cubitt said. The stained eyeballs lifted: they gazed at comfort, understanding. He wasn't good enough for Colleoni: he had broken with Pinkie. Behind her head through the window of the lounge darkness and retreating sea. 'Christ,' he said, 'you're right.' He had an enormous urge to confession, but the facts were confused. He only knew that these were the times when a man needed a woman's understanding. 'I've never held with it,' he told her. 'Carving's different.'

'Of course, carving's different,' Ida Arnold smoothly and deftly agreed.

'And Kite—that was an accident. They only meant to carve him. Colleoni's no fool. Somebody slipped. There wasn't any cause for bad feeling.'

'Have another drink?'

'It oughter be on me,' Cubitt said. 'But I'm cleaned out. Till I see the boys.'

'It was fine of you—breaking with Pinkie like that. It needed courage after what happened to Fred.'

'Oh, he can't scare me. No broken banisters . . .'

'What do you mean—broken banisters?'

'I wanted to be friendly,' Cubitt said. 'A joke's a joke. When a man's getting married, he oughter take a joke.'

'Married? Who married?'

'Pinkie, of course.'

'Not to the little girl at Snow's?'

'Of course.'

'The little fool,' Ida Arnold said with sharp anger. 'Oh, the little fool.'

'He's not a fool,' Cubitt said. 'He knows what's good for him. If she chose to say a thing or two—'

'You mean, say it wasn't Fred left the ticket?'

'Poor old Spicer,' Cubitt said, watching the bubbles rise in the whisky. A question floated up, 'How did you . . .' but broke in the doped brain. 'I want air,' he said, 'stuffy in here. What say you and I . . . ?'

'Just wait awhile,' Ida Arnold said. 'I'm expecting a friend. I'd like you and him to be acquainted.'

'This central heating,' Cubitt said, 'it's not healthy. You go out and catch a chill and the next you know . . .'

'When's the wedding?'

'Whose wedding?'

'Pinkie's.'

'I'm no friend of Pinkie's.'

'You didn't hold with Fred's death, did you?' Ida Arnold softly persisted.

'You understand a man.'

'Carving would have been different.'

Cubitt suddenly, furiously, broke out, 'I can't see a piece of Brighton rock without . . .' He belched and said with tears in his voice, 'Carving's different.'

'The doctors said it was natural causes. He had a weak heart.'

'Come outside,' Cubitt said, 'I got to get some air.'

'Just wait a bit. What do you mean—Brighton rock?'

He stared inertly back at her. He said, 'I got to get some air. Even if it kills me. This central heating . . .' he complained. 'I'm liable to colds.'

'Just wait two minutes.' She put her hand on his arm, feeling an intense excitement, the edge of discovery above the horizon, and was aware herself for the first time of the warm close air welling up round them from hidden gratings, driving them into the open. She said, 'I'll come out with you. We'll take a walk . . .' He watched her with nodding head, with an immense indifference as if he had lost grip on his thought as you loose a dog's lead and it has disappeared, too far to be followed, in what wood . . . He was astonished when she said, 'I'll give you—twenty pounds.' What had he said that was worth that money? She smiled enticingly at him. 'Just let me put on a bit of powder and have a wash.' He didn't respond, he was scared, but she couldn't wait for a reply: she dived for the stairs—no time for the lift. A wash: they were the words she had used to Fred. She ran upstairs, people were coming down, changed, to dinner. She hammered on her door and Phil Corkery let her in. 'Quick,' she said, 'I want a witness.' He was dressed, thank goodness, and she raced him down, but immediately she got into the hall she saw that Cubitt had gone. She ran out on to the steps of the Cosmopolitan, but he wasn't in sight.

'Well,' Mr Corkery said.

'Gone, Never mind,' Ida Arnold said. 'I know now all right. It wasn't suicide. They murdered him.' She said slowly over to herself: '. . . Brighton rock . . .' The clue would have seemed hopeless to many women, but Ida Arnold had been trained by the Board. Queerer things than that had spidered out under her fingers and Old Crowe's: with complete confidence her mind began to work.

The night air stirred Mr Corkery's thin yellow hair. It may have occurred to him that on an evening like this—after the actions of love—romance was required by any woman. He touched her elbow timidly, 'What a night,' he said. 'I never dreamed—what a night,' but words drained out as she switched towards him her large thoughtful eyes, uncomprehending, full of other ideas. She said slowly, 'The little fool . . . to marry him . . . why, there's no knowing what he'll do.' A kind of righteous mirth moved her to add with excitement, 'We got to save her, Phil.'

2

At the bottom of the steps the Boy waited. The big municipal
building lay over him like a shadow—departments for births and
deaths, for motor licences, for rates and taxes, somewhere in
some long corridor the room for marriages. He looked at his
watch and said to Mr Prewitt, 'God damn her. She's late.'

Mr Prewitt said, 'It's the privilege of a bride.'

Bride and groom: the mare and the stallion which served her:
like a file on metal or the touch of velvet to a sore hand. The Boy
said, 'Me and Dallow—we'll walk and meet her.'

Mr Prewitt called after him. 'Suppose she comes another way.
Suppose you miss her . . . I'll wait here.'

They turned to the left out of the official street. 'This ain't the
way,' Dallow said.

'There's no call on us to wait on her,' the Boy said.

'You can't get out of it now.'

'Who wants to? I can take a bit of exercise, can't I?' He stopped
and stared into a small newsagent's window—two-valve receiving
sets, the grossness everywhere.

'Seen Cubitt?' he asked, staring in.

'No,' Dallow said. 'None of the boys either.'

The daily and the local papers, a poster packed with news:
Scene at Council Meeting. Woman Found Drowned at Black
Rock. Collision in Clarence Street: a Wild West magazine, a copy
of *Film Fun*; behind the inkpots and the fountain pens and the paper plates for picnics and the little gross toys, the works of well-
known sexologists. The Boy stared in.

'I know how you feel,' Dallow said. 'I was married once myself.
It kind of gets you in the stomach. Nerves. Why,' Dallow said, 'I

even went and got one of those books, but it didn't tell me anything I didn't know. Except about flowers. The pistils of flowers.
You wouldn't believe the funny things that go on among flowers.'

The Boy turned and opened his mouth to speak, but the teeth
snapped to again. He watched Dallow with pleading and horror.
If Kite had been there, he thought, he could have spoken—but if
Kite had been there, he would have had no need to speak . . . he
would never have got mixed up.

'These bees . . .' Dallow began to explain and stopped. 'What is
it, Pinkie? You don't look too good.'

'I know the rules all right,' the Boy said.

'What rules?'

'You can't teach me the rules,' the Boy went on with gusty
anger. 'I watched 'em every Saturday night, didn't I? Bouncing
and ploughing.' His eyes flinched as if he were watching some
horror. He said in a low voice, 'When I was a kid, I swore I'd be a
priest.'

'A priest? You a priest? That's good,' Dallow said. He laughed
without conviction, uneasily shifted his foot so that it trod in a
dog's ordure.

'What's wrong with being a priest?' the Boy asked. 'They know
what's what. They keep away—' his whole mouth and jaw loosened: he might have been going to weep: he beat out wildly with
his hands towards the window: Woman Found Drowned, two-
valve, *Married Passion,* the horror—'from this.'

'What's wrong with a bit of fun?' Dallow took him up, scraping
his shoe against the pavement edge. The word 'fun' shook the Boy
like malaria. He said, 'You wouldn't have known Annie Collins,
would you?'

'Never heard of her.'

'She went to the same school I did,' the Boy said. He took a
look down the grey street and then the glass before *Married Passion* reflected again his young and hopeless face. 'She put her head
on the line.' he said, 'up by the Hassocks. She had to wait ten
minutes for the seven-five. Fog made it late from Victoria. Cut off
her head. She was fifteen. She was going to have a baby and she
knew what it was like. She'd had one two years before, and they
could 'ave pinned it on twelve boys.'

'It does happen,' Dallow said. 'It's the luck of the game.'

'I've read love stories,' the Boy said. He had never been so vocal before, staring in at the paper plates with frilly edges and the two-valve receiving set: the daintiness and the grossness. 'Frank's wife reads them. You know the sort. Lady Angeline turned her starry eyes towards Sir Mark. They make me sick. Sicker than the other kind'—Dallow watched with astonishment this sudden horrified gift of tongues—'the kind you buy under the counter. Spicer used to get them. About girls being beaten. Full of shame to expose herself thus before the boys she stooped . . . It's all the same thing,' he said, turning his poisoned eyes away from the window, from point to point of the long shabby street: a smell of fish, the sawdusted pavement below the carcasses. 'It's fun. It's the game.'

'The world's got to go on,' Dallow said uneasily.

'Why?'

'You don't need to ask me,' Dallow said. 'You know best. You're a Roman aren't you? You believe . . .'

'Credo in unum Satanum,' the Boy said.

'I don't know Latin. I only know . . .'

'Come on,' the Boy said. 'Let's have it. Dallow's creed.'

'The world's all right if you don't go too far.'

'Is that all?'

'It's time for you to be at the registrar's. Hear the clock? It's striking two now.' A peal of bells stopped their cracked chime and struck—one, two—

The Boy's whole face loosened again: he put his hand on Dallow's arm. 'You're a good sort, Dallow. You know a lot. Tell me—' his hand fell away. He looked beyond Dallow down the street. He said hopelessly, 'Here she is. What's she doing in *this* street?'

'She's not hurrying either,' Dallow commented, watching the thin figure slowly approach. At that distance she didn't even look her age. He said, 'It was clever of Prewitt to get the licence at all considering.'

'Parents' consent,' the Boy said dully. 'Best for morality.' He watched the girl as if she were a stranger he had got to meet. 'And then you see there was a stroke of luck. I wasn't registered. Not anywhere they could find. They added a year or two. No parents. No guardian. It was a touching story old Prewitt spun.'

She had tricked herself up for the wedding, discarded the hat he hadn't liked: a new mackintosh, a touch of powder and cheap lipstick. She looked like one of the small gaudy statues in an ugly church: a paper crown wouldn't have looked odd on her or a painted heart: you could pray to her but you couldn't expect an answer.

'Where've you been?' the Boy said. 'Don't you know you're late?'

They didn't even touch hands. An awful formality fell between them.

'I'm sorry, Pinkie. You see'—she brought the fact out with shame, as if she were admitting conversation with his enemy—'I went to the church.'

'What for?' he said.

'I don't know, Pinkie. I got confused. I thought I'd go to confession.'

He grinned at her. 'Confession? That's rich.'

'You see I wanted—I thought—'

'For Christ's sake what?'

'I wanted to be in a state of grace when I married you.' She took no notice at all of Dallow. The theological term lay oddly and pedantically on her tongue. They were two Romans together in the grey street. They understood each other. She used terms common to heaven and hell.

'And did you?' the Boy said.

'No. I went and rang the bell and asked for Father James. But then I remembered. It wasn't any good confessing. I went away,' she said with a mixture of fear and pride. 'We're going to do a mortal sin.'

The Boy said, with bitter and unhappy relish, 'It'll be no good going to confession ever again—as long as we're both alive.' He had graduated in pain: first the school dividers had been left behind, next the razor. He had a sense now that the murders of Hale and Spicer were trivial acts, a boy's game, and he had put away childish things. Murder had only led up to this—this corruption. He was filled with awe at his own powers. 'We'd better be moving,' he said and touched her arm with next to tenderness. As once before he had a sense of needing her.

Mr Prewitt greeted them with official mirth. All his jokes seemed to be spoken in court, with an ulterior motive, to catch a magistrate's ear. In the great institutional hall from which the corridors led off to deaths and births there was a smell of disinfectant. The walls were tiled like a public lavatory. Somebody had dropped a rose. Mr Prewitt quoted promptly, inaccurately, 'Roses, roses all the way, and never a sprig of yew.' A soft hollow hand guided the Boy by the elbow: 'No, no, not that way. That's taxes. That comes later.' He led them up great stone stairs. A clerk passed them carrying printed forms. 'And what is the little lady thinking?' Mr Prewitt said. She didn't answer him.

Only the bride and groom were allowed to mount the sanctuary steps, to kneel down within the sanctuary rails with the priest and the Host.

'Parents coming?' Mr Prewitt asked. She shook heir head. 'The great thing is,' Mr Prewitt said, 'it's over quickly. Just sign the names along the dotted line. Sit down here. We've got to wait our turn, you know.'

They sat down. A mop leant in a corner against the tiled wall. The footsteps of a clerk squealed on the icy paving down another passage. Presently a big brown door opened: they saw a row of clerks inside who didn't look up: a man and wife came out into the corridor. A woman followed them and took the mop. The man—he was middle-aged—said 'thank you', gave her sixpence. He said, 'We'll catch the three-fifteen after all.' On the woman's face there was a look of faint astonishment, bewilderment, nothing so definite as disappointment. She wore a brown straw and carried an attaché case. She was middle-aged too. She might have been thinking, 'Is that all there is to it—after all these years?' They went down the big stairs walking a little apart, like strangers in a store.

'Our turn,' Mr Prewitt said, rising briskly. He led the way through the room where the clerks worked. Nobody bothered to look up. Nibs wrote smooth numerals and ran on. In a small inner room with green washed walls like a clinic's the registrar waited: a table, three or four chairs against the wall. It wasn't what she thought a marriage would be like—for a moment she was daunted by the cold poverty of a state-made ceremony.

'Good morning,' the registrar said. 'If the witnesses will just sit down—would you two'—he beckoned them to the table and stared at them with gold-rimmed and glassy importance: it was as if he considered himself on the fringe of the priestly office. The Boy's heart beat: he was sickened by the reality of the moment. He wore a look of sullenness and of stupidity.

'You're both very young,' the registrar said.

'It's fixed,' the Boy said. 'You don't have to talk about it. It's fixed.'

The registrar gave him a glance of intense dislike; he said, 'Repeat after me,' and then ran too quickly on, 'I do solemnly declare that I know not of any lawful impediment,' so that the Boy couldn't follow him. The registrar said sharply, 'It's quite simple. You've only to repeat after me . . .'

'Go slower,' the Boy said. He wanted to lay his hand on speed and brake it down, but it ran on: it was no time at all, a matter of seconds, before he was repeating the formula 'my lawful wedded wife.' He tried to make it careless, he kept his eyes off Rose, but the words were weighted with shame.

'No ring?' the registrar asked sharply.

'We don't need any ring,' the Boy said. 'This isn't a church,' feeling he could never now rid his memory of the cold green room and the glassy face. He heard Rose repeating by his side: 'I call upon these persons here present to witness . . .' and then the word 'husband', and he looked sharply up at her. If there had been any complacency in her face then he would have struck it. But there was only surprise as if she were reading a book and had come to the last page too soon.

The registrar said, 'You sign here. The charge is seven and six-pence.' He wore an air of official unconcern while Mr Prewitt fumbled.

'These persons,' the Boy said and laughed brokenly. 'That's you, Prewitt and Dallow.' He took the pen and the Government nib scratched into the page, gathering fur; in the old days, it occurred to him, you signed covenants like this in your blood. He stood back and watched Rose awkwardly sign—his temporal safety in return for two immortalities of pain. He had no doubt whatever that this was mortal sin, and he was filled with a kind of gloomy hilarity and pride. He saw himself now as a full grown man for whom the angels wept.

'These persons,' he repeated, ignoring the registrar altogether. 'Come and have a drink.'

'Well,' Mr Prewitt said, 'that's a surprise from you.'

'Oh, Dallow will tell you,' the Boy said. 'I'm a drinking man these days.' He looked across at Rose. 'There's nothing I'm not now,' he said. He took her by the elbow and led the way out to the tiled passage and the big stairs: the mop was gone and somebody had picked up the flower. A couple rose as they came out: the market was firm. He said, 'That was a wedding. Can you beat it? We're'—he meant to say 'husband and wife', but his mind flinched from the defining phrase. 'We got to celebrate,' he said, and like an old relation you can always trust for the tactless word his brain beat on—'celebrate what?' and he thought of the girl sprawling in the Lancia and the long night coming down.

They went to the pub round the corner. It was nearly closing time, and he stood them pints of bitter and Rose took a port. She hadn't spoken since the registrar had given her the words to say. Mr Prewitt took a quick look round and parked his portfolio. With his dark striped trousers he might really have been at a wedding. 'Here's to the bride,' he said with a jocularity which petered unobtrusively out. It was as if he had tried to crack a joke with a magistrate and scented a rebuff: the old face recomposed itself quickly on serious lines. He said reverently, 'To your happiness, my dear.'

She didn't answer; she was looking at her own face in a glass marked Extra Stout: in the new setting with a foreground of beer handles, it was a strange face. It seemed to carry an enormous weight of responsibility.

'A penny for your thoughts,' Dallow said to her. The Boy put the glass of bitter to his mouth and tasted for the second time—the nausea of other people's pleasures stuck in his throat. He watched her sourly as she gazed wordlessly back at his companions; and again he was sensible of how she completed him. *He* knew her thoughts: they beat unregarded in his own nerves. He said with triumphant venom, 'I can tell you what she's thinking of. Not much of a wedding, she's thinking. She's thinking—it's not what I pictured. That's right, isn't it?'

She nodded, holding the glass of port as if she hadn't learned the way to drink.

'With my body I thee worship,' he began to quote at her, 'with all my worldly goods . . . and then,' he said, turning to Prewitt, 'I give her a gold piece.'

'Time, gentlemen,' the barman said, swilling not quite empty glasses into the lead trough, mopping with a yeasty cloth.

'We're up in the sanctuary, do you see, with the priest . . .'

'Drink up, gentlemen.'

Mr Prewitt said uneasily, 'One wedding's as good as another in the eyes of the law.' He nodded encouragingly at the girl who watched them all with famished immature eyes. 'You're married all right. Trust me.'

'Married?' the Boy said. 'Do you call that married?' He screwed up the beery spittle on his tongue.

'Easy on,' Dallow said. 'Give the girl a chance. You don't need to go too far.'

'Come along, gentlemen, empty your glasses.'

'Married!' the Boy repeated. 'Ask her.' The two men drank up in a shocked furtive way and Mr Prewitt said, 'Well, I'll be getting on.' The Boy regarded them with contempt; they didn't understand a thing, and again he was touched by the sense of communion between himself and Rose—she too knew that this evening meant nothing at all, that there hadn't been a wedding. He said with rough kindness, 'Come on. We'll be going,' and raised a hand to put it on her arm—then saw the double image in the mirror (Extra Stout) and let it fall: a married couple the image winked at him.

'Where?' Rose asked.

Where? he hadn't thought of that—you had to take them somewhere—the honeymoon, the weekend at the sea, the present from Margate on the mantelpiece his mother'd had; from one sea to another, a change of pier.

'I'll be seeing you,' Dallow said. He paused a moment at the door, met the Boy's eye, the question, the appeal, understood nothing, and sloped away cheerily waving after Mr Prewitt, leaving them alone.

It was as if they'd never been alone before in spite of the barman drying the glasses: not really alone in the room at Snow's, nor above the sea at Peacehaven—not alone as they were now.

'We'd better be off,' Rose said.

They stood on the pavement and heard the door of the 'Crown' closed and locked behind them—a bolt grind into place; they felt as if they were shut out from an Eden of ignorance. On this side there was nothing to look forward to but experience.

'Are we going to Frank's?' the girl asked. It was one of those moments of sudden silence that falls on the busiest afternoon: not a tram bell, not a cry of steam from the terminus: a flock of birds shot up together into the air above Old Steyne and hovered there as if a crime had been committed on the ground. He thought with nostalgia of the room at Frank's—he knew exactly where to put his hand for money in the soap-dish; everything was familiar; nothing strange there; it shared his bitter virginity.

'No,' he said and again, as noise came back, the clang and crash of afternoon, 'No.'

'Where?'

He smiled with hopeless malice—where did you bring a swell blonde to if not to the Cosmopolitan, coming down by Pullman at the weekend, driving over the downs in a scarlet roadster? Expensive scent and furs, sailing like a new-painted pinnace into the restaurant, something to swank about in return for the nocturnal act. He absorbed Rose's shabbiness like a penance in a long look. 'We'll take a suite,' he said, 'at the Cosmopolitan.'

'No, but where—really?'

'You heard me—the Cosmopolitan.' He flared up. 'Don't you think I'm good enough?'

'You are,' she said, 'but I'm not.'

'We're going there,' he said. 'I can afford it. It's the right place. There was a woman called—Eugeen used to go there. That's why they have crowns on the chairs.'

'Who was she?'

'A foreign polony.'

'Have you been there, then?'

'Of course I've been there.'

Suddenly she put her hands together in an excited gesture. 'I dreamed,' she said and then looked sharply up to see if he was only mocking after all.

He said airily, 'The car's being repaired. We'll walk and send them round for my bag. Where's yours?'

'My what?'

'Your bag.'

'It was so broken, dirty . . .'

Never mind,' he said with desperate swagger, 'we'll buy you another. Where's your things?'

'Things . . .'

'Christ, how dumb you are,' he said. 'I mean . . .' but the thought of the night ahead froze his tongue. He drove on down the pavement, the afternoon waning on his face.

She said, 'There was nothing . . . nothing I could marry you in only this. I asked them for a little money. They wouldn't give it me. They'd a right. It was theirs.'

They walked a foot apart along the pavement. Her words scratched tentatively at the barrier like a bird's claws on a window pane. He could feel her all the time trying to get at him: even her humility seemed to him a trap. The crude quick ceremony was a claim on him. *She* didn't know the reason; she thought—God save the mark—he wanted her. He said roughly, 'You needn't think there's going to be a honeymoon. That nonsense. I'm busy. I've got things to do. I've got . . .' He stopped and turned to her with a kind of scared appeal—let this make no difference, 'I got to be away a lot.'

'I'll wait,' she said. He could already see the patience of the poor and the long-married working up under her skin like a second personality, a modest and shameless figure behind a transparency.

They came out on to the front and evening stood back a pace; the sea dazzled the eyes; she watched it with pleasure as if it was a different sea. He said, 'What did your Dad say today?'

'He didn't say a thing. He'd got a mood.'

'And the old woman?'

'She had a mood too.'

'They took the money all right.'

They came to a halt on the front opposite the Cosmopolitan and under its enormous bulk moved a few inches closer. He remembered the pageboy calling a name and Colleoni's gold cigarette case . . . He said slowly and carefully, shutting uneasiness out, 'Well, we oughter be comfortable there.' He put a hand up to his withered tie, straightened his jacket and set unconvincingly his narrow shoulders. 'Come on.' She followed a pace behind, across the road, up the wide steps. Two old ladies sat on the terrace in wicker chairs in the sun, wrapped round and round with veils. They had an absolute air of security: when they spoke they didn't look at each other, just quietly dropped their remarks into the understanding air. 'Now Willie . . .' 'I always like Willie,' The Boy made an unnecessary noise coming up the steps.

He walked across the deep pile to the reception desk, Rose just behind him. There was nobody there. He waited furiously—it was a personal insult. A page called 'Mr Pinecoffin. Mr Pinecoffin' across the lounge. The Boy waited. A telephone rang. When the entrance door swung again they could hear one of the old ladies say, 'It was a great blow to Basil.' Then a man in a black coat appeared and said, 'Can I do anything for you?'

The Boy said furiously: 'I've been waiting here . . .'

'You could have touched the bell,' the clerk said coldly and opened a large register.

'I want a room,' the Boy said. 'A double room.'

The clerk stared past him at Rose, then turned a page. 'We haven't a room free,' he said.

'I don't mind what I pay,' the Boy said. 'I'll take a suite.'

'There's nothing vacant,' the clerk said without looking up.

The pageboy, returning with a salver, paused and watched. The Boy said in a low furious voice, 'You can't keep me out of here. My money's as good as anybody else's . . .'

'No doubt,' the clerk said, 'but there happens to be no room free.' He turned his back and picked up a jar of Stickphast.

'Come on,' the Boy said to Rose, 'this kip stinks.' He strode back down the steps, past the old ladies; tears of humiliation pricked behind his eyes. He had an insane impulse to shout out to them all that they couldn't treat him like that, that he was a killer, he could kill men and not be caught. He wanted to boast. He could afford that place as well as anyone: he had a car, a lawyer, two hundred pounds in the bank . . .

Rose said, 'If I'd had a ring . . .'

He said furiously, 'A ring . . . what sort of a ring? We aren't married. Don't forget that. We aren't married.' But outside on the pavement he restrained himself with immense difficulty and remembered bitterly that he still had a part to play—they couldn't make a wife give evidence, but nothing could prevent a wife except— love, lust he thought with sour horror, and turning back to her he unconvincingly apologized, 'They get me angry,' he said. 'You see I'd promised you—'

'I don't care,' she said. Suddenly with wide astonished eyes she made the foolhardy claim, 'Nothing can spoil today.'

'We got to find somewhere,' he said.

'I don't mind where—Frank's?'

'Not tonight,' he said. 'I don't want any of the boys around tonight.'

'We'll think of a place,' she said. 'It's not dark yet.'

These were the hours—when the races were not on, when there was no one to see on business—that he spent stretched on the bed at Frank's. He'd eat a packet of chocolate or a sausage roll, watch the sun shift from the chimney-pots, fall asleep and wake and eat again and sleep with the dark coming in through the window. Then the boys would return with the evening papers and life would start again. Now he was at a loss; he didn't know how to spend so much time when he wasn't alone.

'One day,' she said, 'let's go into the country like we did that time . . .' Staring out to sea she planned ahead . . . he could see the years advancing before her eyes like the line of the tide.

'Anything you say,' he said.

'Let's go on the pier,' she said. 'I haven't been since we went that night—you remember?'

'Nor've I,' he lied quickly and smoothly, thinking of Spicer and the dark and the lightning on the sea—the beginning of something of which he couldn't see the end. They went through the turnstile; there were a lot of people about: a row of anglers watched their floats in the thick green swell: the water moved under their feet.

'Do you know that girl?' Rose asked. The Boy turned his head apathetically. 'Where?' he said. 'I don't know any girls in this place.'

'There,' Rose said. 'I bet she's talking about you.'

The fat stupid spotty face swam back into his memory, nuzzled the glass like some monstrous fish in the Aquarium—dangerous— a sting-ray from another ocean. Fred had spoken to her and he had come up to them upon the front: she'd given evidence—he couldn't remember what she had said—nothing important. Now she watched him, nudged her pasty girl friend, spoke of him, told he didn't know what lies. Christ! he thought, had he got to massacre a world?

'*She* knows you,' Rose said.

'I've never seen her,' he lied, walking on.

Rose said, 'It's wonderful being with you. Everyone knows you. I never thought I'd marry someone famous.'

Who next he thought, who next? An angler drew back across their path to make his cast, whirling his line, dropped it far out; the float was caught in the cream of a wave and drove a line's length towards the shore. It was cold on the sunless side of the pier; on one side of the glass division it was day: on the other evening advanced. 'Let's cross over,' he said. He began to think again of Spicer's girl: why had he left her in the car? God damn it, after all, she knew the game.

Rose stopped him. 'Look,' she said, 'won't you give me one of those? As a souvenir. They don't cost much,' she said, 'only sixpence.' It was a small glass box like a telephone cabinet. 'Make a record of your own voice,' the legend ran.

'Come on,' he said. 'Don't be soft. What's the good of that?'

For the second time he came up against her sudden irresponsible resentment. She was soft, she was dumb, she was sentimental— and then suddenly she was dangerous. About a hat, about a gramophone record. 'All right,' she said, 'go away. You've never given me a thing. Not even today you haven't. If you don't want me why don't you go away? Why don't you leave me alone?' People turned and looked at them—at his acid and angry face, at her hopeless resentment. 'What do you want me for?' she cried at him.

'For Christ's sake . . .' he said.

'I'd rather drown,' she began, but he interrupted her, 'You can have your record.' He smiled nervously. 'I just thought you were crazy,' he said. 'What do you want to hear me on a record for? Aren't you going to hear me every day?' He squeezed her arm. 'You're a good kid. I don't grudge you things. You can have anything you say.' He thought: she's got me where she wants . . . how long? 'You didn't mean those things now, did you?' he wheedled her. His face crinkled in the effort of amiability like an old man's.

'Something came over me,' she said, avoiding his eyes with an expression he couldn't read, obscure and despairing.

He felt relieved, but reluctant. He didn't like the idea of putting anything on a record: it reminded him of finger-prints. 'Do you really,' he said, 'want me to get one of those things? We haven't got a gramophone anyway. You won't be able to hear it. What's the good?'

'I don't want a gramophone,' she said. 'I just want to have it there. Perhaps one day you might be away somewhere and I could borrow a gramophone. And you'd speak,' she said with a sudden intensity that scared him.

'What do you want me to say?'

'Just anything,' she said. 'Say something to me. Say Rose and—something.'

He went into the box and closed the door. There was a slot for his sixpence: a mouthpiece: an instruction, 'Speak clearly and close to the instrument'. The scientific paraphernalia made him nervous. He looked over his shoulder and there outside she was watching him, without a smile. He saw her as a stranger: a shabby child from Nelson Place, and he was shaken by an appalling resentment. He put in a sixpence, and, speaking in a low voice for fear it might carry beyond the box, he gave his message up to be graven on vulcanite: 'God damn you, you little bitch, why can't you go back home for ever and let me be?' He heard the needle scratch and the record whirr: then a click and silence.

Carrying the black disc he came out to her. 'Here,' he said, 'take it. I put something on it—loving.'

She took it from him carefully, carried it like something to be defended from the crowd. Even on the sunny side of the pier it was getting cold, and the cold fell between them like an unanswerable statement—you'd better be getting home now. He had the sense of playing truant from his proper work—he should be at school, but he hadn't learned his lesson. They passed through the turnstile, and he watched her out of the corner of an eye to see what she expected now. If she had shown any excitement he would have slapped her face. But she hugged the record as chilled as he.

'Well,' he said, 'we got to go somewhere.'

She pointed down the steps to the covered walk under the pier. 'Let's go there,' she said, 'it's sheltered there.'

The Boy looked sharply round at her; it was as if deliberately she had offered him an ordeal. For a moment he hesitated: then he grinned at her. 'All right,' he said, 'we'll go *there*.' He was moved by a kind of sensuality: the coupling of good and evil.

In the trees of the Old Steyne the fairy lights were switched on—it was too early, their pale colours didn't show in the last of the day. The long tunnel under the parade was the noisiest, lowest, cheapest section of Brighton's amusements. Children rushed past them in paper sailor-caps marked 'I'm no Angel'; a ghost train rattled by carrying courting couples into a squealing and shrieking darkness. All the way along the landward side of the tunnel were the amusements; on the other little shops: Magpie Ices, Photoweigh, Shellfish, Rocko. The shelves rose to the ceiling: little doors let you in to the obscurity behind, and on the sea side there were no doors at all, no windows, nothing but shelf after shelf from the pebbles to the roof: a breakwater of Brighton rock facing the sea. The lights were always on in the tunnel; the air was warm and thick and poisoned with human breath.

'Well,' the Boy said, 'what's it to be—winkles or Brighton rock?' He watched her as if something important really depended on her answer.

'I'd like a stick of Brighton rock,' she said.

Again he grinned: only the devil, he thought, could have made her answer that. She was good, but he'd got her like you got God in the Eucharist—in the guts. God couldn't escape the evil mouth which chose to eat its own damnation. He padded across to a doorway and looked in. 'Miss,' he said. 'Miss. Two sticks of rock.' He looked around the little pink barred cell as if he owned it; his memory owned it, it was stamped with footmarks, a particular patch of floor had eternal importance: if the cash register had been moved he'd have noticed it. 'What's that?' he asked and nodded at a box, the only unfamiliar object there.

'It's broken rock,' she said, 'going cheap.'

'From the maker's?'

'No. It got broken. Some clumsy fools—' she complained. 'I wish I knew who . . .'

He took the sticks and turned: he knew what he would see—nothing: the promenade was shut out behind the rows of Brighton rock. He had a momentary sense of his own immense cleverness. 'Goodnight,' he said, stooped in the little doorway and went out. If only one could boast of one's cleverness, relieve the enormous pressure of pride . . .

They stood side by side sucking their sticks of rock: a woman bustled them to one side. 'Out of the way, you children.' Their glances met: a married couple.

'Where now?' he asked uneasily.

'Perhaps we ought to find—somewhere,' she said.

'There's not all that hurry.' His voice caught a little with anxiety. 'It's early yet. Like a movie?' He wheedled her again. 'I've never took you to a movie.'

But the sense of power left him. Again her passionate assent—'You're good to me'—repelled him.

Slumped grimly in the three and sixpenny seat, in the half-dark, he asked himself crudely and bitterly what she was hoping for: beside the screen an illuminated clock marked the hour. It was a romantic film: magnificent features, thighs shot with studied care, esoteric beds shaped like winged coracles. A man was killed, but that didn't matter. What mattered was the game. The two main characters made their stately progress towards the bed-sheets: 'I loved you that first time in Santa Monica . . .' A song under a window, a girl in a nightdress and the clock beside the screen moving on. He whispered suddenly, furiously, to Rose, 'Like cats.' It was the commonest game under the sun—why be scared at what the dogs did in the streets? The music moaned—'I know in my heart you're divine'. He whispered, 'Maybe we'd better go to Frank's after all,' thinking: we won't be alone there: something may happen:

maybe the boys will have drinks: maybe they'll celebrate—there won't be any bed for anyone tonight. The actor with a lick of black hair across a white waste of face said, 'You're mine. All mine.' He sang again under the restless stars in a wash of incredible moonshine, and suddenly, inexplicably, the Boy began to weep. He shut his eyes to hold in his tears, but the music went on—it was like a vision of release to an imprisoned man. He felt constriction and saw—hopelessly out of reach—a limitless freedom: no fear, no hatred, no envy. It was as if he were dead and were remembering the effect of a good confession, the words of absolution: but being dead it was a memory only—he couldn't experience contrition—the ribs of his body were like steel bands which held him down to eternal unrepentance. He said at last, 'Let's go. We'd better go.'

It was quite dark now: the coloured lights were on all down the Hove front. They walked slowly past Snow's, past the Cosmopolitan. An aeroplane flying low burred out to sea, a red light vanishing. In one of the glass shelters an old man struck a match to light his pipe and showed a man and girl cramped in the corner. A wail of music came off the sea. They turned up through Norfolk Square towards Montpellier Road: a blonde with Garbo cheeks paused to powder on the steps up to the Norfolk bar. A bell tolled somewhere for someone dead and a gramophone in a basement played a hymn. 'Maybe,' the Boy said, 'after tonight we'll find some place to go.'

He had his latchkey but he rang the bell. He wanted people, talk . . . but no one answered. He rang again. It was one of those old bells you have to pull: it jangled on the end of its wire: the kind of bell that knows from long experience of dust and spiders and untenanted rooms how to convey that a house is empty. 'They can't 'ave all gone out,' he said, slipped in his latchkey.

A globe had been left burning in the hall. He saw at once the note stuck under the telephone—'Two's company,' he recognized the drab and sprawling hand of Frank's wife. 'We gone out to celebrate the wedding. Lock your door. Have a good time.' He crumpled the paper up and dropped it on the linoleum. 'Come on,' he said, 'upstairs.' At the top he put his hand on the new banister rail and said, 'You see. We got it mended.' A smell of cabbages and

cooking and burnt cloth hung about the dark passage. He nodded—
'That was old Spicer's room. Do you believe in ghosts?'

'I don't know.'

He pushed open his own door and switched on the naked dusty
light. 'There,' he said, 'take it or leave it,' and drew aside to expose the big brass bed, the washstand and chipped ewer, the var-
nished wardrobe with its cheap glass front.

'It's better than a hotel,' she said, 'it's more like home.'

They stood in the middle of the room as if they didn't know
what their next move should be. She said, 'Tomorrow I'll tidy up
a bit.'

He banged the door to. 'You won't touch a thing,' he said. 'It's
my home, do you hear? I won't have you coming in, changing
things . . .' He watched her with fear—to come into your own
room, your cave, and find a strange thing there . . . 'Why don't
you take off your hat?' he said. 'You're staying, aren't you?' She
took off her hat, her mackintosh—this was the ritual of mortal
sin: this, he thought, was what people damned each other for . . .
The bell in the hall clanged. He paid it no attention. 'It's Saturday
night,' he said with a bitter taste on his tongue, 'it's time for bed.'

'Who is it?' she asked, and the bell jangled again—its unmistakable message to whoever was outside that the house was no
longer empty. She came across the room to him, her face was
white. 'Is it the police?' she said.

'Why should it be the police? Some friend of Frank's.' But the
suggestion startled him. He stood and waited for the clang. It didn't
come again. 'Well,' he said, 'we can't stand here all night. We better get to bed.' He felt an appalling emptiness as if he hadn't fed
for days. He tried to pretend, taking off his jacket and hanging it
over a chair back, that everything was as usual. When he turned
she hadn't moved: a thin and half-grown child she trembled between the washstand and the bed. 'Why,' he mocked her with a
dry mouth, 'you're scared.' It was as if he had gone back four
years and was taunting a schoolfellow into some offence.

'Aren't you scared?' Rose said.

'Me,' He laughed at her unconvincingly and advanced: an em-
bryo of sensuality—he was mocked by the memory of a gown, a
back, 'I loved you that first time in Santa Monica . . .' Shaken by

a kind of rage, he took her by the shoulders. He had escaped from Nelson Place to this: he pushed her against the bed. 'It's mortal sin,' he said, getting what savour there was out of innocence, trying to taste God in the mouth: a brass bedball, her dumb, frightened and acquiescent eyes—he blotted everything out in a sad brutal now-or-never embrace: a cry of pain and then the jangling of the bell beginning all over again. 'Christ,' he said, 'can't they let a man alone?' He opened his eyes on the grey room to see what he had done: it seemed to him more like death than when Hale and Spicer had died.

Rose said, 'Don't go. Pinkie, don't go.'

He had an odd sense of triumph: he had graduated in the last human shame—it wasn't so difficult after all. He had exposed himself and nobody had laughed. He didn't need Mr Prewitt or Spicer, only—a faint feeling of tenderness woke for his partner in the act. He put out a hand and pinched the lobe of her ear. The bell clanged in the empty hall. An enormous weight seemed to have lifted. He could face anyone now. He said, 'I'd better see what the bugger wants.'

'Don't go. I'm scared, Pinkie.'

But he had a sense that he would never be scared again. Running down from the track he had been afraid, afraid of pain and more afraid of damnation—of the sudden and unshriven death. Now it was as if he was damned already and there was nothing more to fear ever again. The ugly bell clattered, the long wire humming in the hall, and the bare globe burnt above the bed—the girl, the washstand, the sooty window, the blank shape of a chimney, a voice whispered, 'I love you, Pinkie.' This was hell then; it wasn't anything to worry about: it was just his own familiar room. He said, 'I'll be back. Don't worry. I'll be back.'

At the head of the stairs he put his hand on the new unpainted wood of the mended banister. He pushed it gently and saw how firm it was. He wanted to crow at his own cleverness. The bell shook below him. He looked down: it was a long drop, but you couldn't really be certain that a man from that height would be killed. The thought had never occurred to him before, but men sometimes lived for hours with broken backs, and he knew an old man who went about to this day with a cracked skull which clicked in cold weather when he sneezed. He had a sense of being befriended. The bell jangled: it knew he was at home. He went on down the stairs, his toes catching in the worn linoleum—he was too good for this place. He felt an invincible energy—he hadn't lost vitality upstairs, he'd gained. it. What he had lost was a fear. He hadn't an idea who stood outside the door, but he was seized by a sense of wicked amusement. He put up his hand to the old bell and held it silent: he could feel the pull at the wire. An odd tug of war went on with the stranger down the length of the hall, and the Boy won. The pull ceased and a hand beat at the door. The Boy released the bell and moved softly towards the door, but immediately behind his back the bell began to clap again, cracked and hollow and urgent. A ball of paper—'Lock your door. Have a good time'—scuffled at his toes.

He swung the door boldly open, and there was Cubitt, Cubitt hopelessly and drearily drunk. Somebody had blacked his eye and his breath was sour: drink always upset his digestion.

The Boy's sense of triumph increased: he felt an immeasurable victory. 'Well,' he said, 'what do *you* want?'

'I got my things here,' Cubitt said. 'I want to get my things.'

'Come in and get 'em then,' the Boy said.

Cubitt sidled in. He said, 'I didn't think I'd see you . . .'

'Go on,' the Boy said. 'Get your things and clear out.'

'Where's Dallow?'

The Boy didn't answer.

'Frank?'

Cubitt cleared his throat: his sour breath reached the Boy. 'Look here, Pinkie,' he said, 'you and me—why shouldn't we be friends? Like we always was.'

'*We* were never friends,' the Boy said.

Cubitt took no notice. He got his back to the telephone and watched the Boy with his drunken and cautious eyes. 'You an' me,' he said, the sour phlegm rising in his throat and thickening every word, 'you an' me can't get on separate. Why,' he said, 'we're kind of brothers. We're tied together.'

The Boy watched him, standing against the opposite wall.

'You an' me—it's what I said. We can't get on separate,' Cubitt repeated.

'I suppose,' the Boy said, 'Colleoni wouldn't touch you—not with a stick, but I'm not taking his leavings, Cubitt.'

Cubitt began to weep a little. It was a stage he always reached: the Boy could measure his glasses by his tears: they squeezed reluctantly out, two tears like drops of spirits oozed out of the yellow eyeballs. 'You've no cause to take on like that,' he said, 'Pinkie.'

'You better get your things.'

'Where's Dallow?'

'He's out,' the Boy said. 'They're all out.' The spirit of cruel mischief moved again. 'We're quite alone, Cubitt,' he said. He glanced down the hall at the new patch of linoleum over the place where Spicer had fallen. But it didn't work: the stage of tears was transitory—what came after was sullenness, anger . . .

Cubitt said, 'You can't treat me like dirt.'

'That how Colleoni treated you?'

'I came here to be friendly,' Cubitt said. 'You can't afford not to be friendly.'

'I can afford more than you'd think,' the Boy said.

Cubitt took him quickly up. 'Lend me five nicker.'

The Boy shook his head. He was shaken by sudden impatience and pride: he was worth more than this—this squabble on worn linoleum under the bare and dusty globe with Cubitt. 'For Christ's sake,' he said, 'get your things and clear out.'

'I've got things I could tell about you . . .'

'Nothing.'

'Fred . . .'

'You'd hang,' the Boy said. He grinned. 'But not me. I'm too young to hang.'

'There's Spicer too.'

'Spicer fell down there.'

'I heard you . . .'

'You heard me? Who's going to believe that?'

'Dallow heard.'

'Dallow's all right,' the Boy said. 'I can trust Dallow. Why, Cubitt,' he went quietly on, 'if you were dangerous, I'd do something about you. But thank your lucky stars you aren't dangerous.' He turned his back on Cubitt and mounted the stairs. He could hear Cubitt behind him—panting; he had no wind.

'I didn't come here to give hard words. Lend me a couple of nicker, Pinkie. I'm broke.'

The Boy didn't answer—'For the sake of old times'—turned off at the bend of the stairs to his own room.

Cubitt said, 'Wait a moment and I'll tell you a thing or two, you bloody little geezer. There's someone'll give me money—twenty nicker. You—why you—I'll tell you what you are.'

The Boy stopped in front of his door. 'Go on,' he said, 'tell me.'

Cubitt struggled to speak. He hadn't got the right words. He flung his rage and resentment away in phrases light as paper. 'You're mean' he said, 'you're yellow. You're so yellow you'd kill your best friend to save your own skin. Why'—he laughed thickly—'you're scared of a girl. Sylvie told me'—but that accusation had come too late. He had graduated now in knowledge of the last human weakness. He listened with amusement, with a kind of infernal pride. The picture Cubitt drew had got nothing to do with him: it was like the pictures men drew of Christ, the image of their own sentimentality. Cubitt couldn't know. He was like a professor describing to a stranger some place he had only read about in books: statistics of imports and exports, tonnage and mineral resources and if the budget balanced, when all the time it was a country the stranger *knew* from thirsting in the desert and being shot at in the foothills. Mean . . . yellow . . . scared: he laughed gently with derision. It was as if he had outsoared the shadow of any night Cubitt could be aware of. He opened his door, went in, closed it and locked it.

Rose sat on the bed with dangling feet like a child in a classroom waiting for a teacher in order to say her lesson. Outside the door Cubitt swore and hacked with his foot, rattled the handle and moved off. She said with immense relief—she was used to drunken men, 'Oh, then it's not the police.'

'Why should it be the police?'

'I don't know,' she said, 'I thought maybe—'

'Maybe what?'

He could only just catch her answer. 'Kolley Kibber.'

For a moment he was amazed. Then he laughed softly with infinite contempt and superiority at a world which used words like innocence. 'Why,' he said, 'that's rich. You knew all along. You guessed. And I thought you were so green you hadn't lost the eggshell. And there you were'—he built her up in the mind's eye that day at Peacehaven, among the harvest wines at Snow's—'there you were, knowing.'

She didn't deny it: sitting there with her hands locked between her knees she accepted everything. 'It's rich,' he said. 'Why, when you come to think of it—you're as bad as me.' He came across the room and added with a kind of respect, 'There's not a pin to choose between us.'

She looked up with childish devoted eyes and swore solemnly, 'Not a pin.'

He felt desire move again, like nausea in the belly. 'What a wedding night,' he said, 'did you think a wedding night would be like this?' . . . the piece of gold in the palm, the kneeling in the sanctuary, the blessing . . . footsteps in the passage, Cubitt pounded on the door, pounded and lurched away, the stairs creaked, a door slammed. She made her vow again, holding him in her arms, in the attitude of mortal sin, 'Nothing to choose.'

The Boy lay on his back—in his shirt-sleeves—and dreamed. He was in an asphalt playground: one plane tree withered: a cracked bell clanged and the children came out to him. He was new: he knew no one: he was sick with fear—they came towards him with a purpose. Then he felt a cautious hand on his sleeve and in a mirror hanging on the tree he saw the reflection of himself and Kite behind—middle-aged, cheery, bleeding from the mouth. 'Such tits,' Kite said and put a razor in his hand. He knew then what to do: they only needed to be taught once that he would stop at nothing, that there were no rules.

He flung out his arm in a motion of attack, made some indistinguishable comment and turned upon his side. A piece of blanket fell across his mouth; he breathed with difficulty. He was upon the pier and he could see the piles breaking—a black cloud came racing up across the Channel and the sea rose: the whole pier lurched and settled lower. He tried to scream: no death was so bad as drowning. The deck of the pier lay at a steep angle like that of a liner on the point of its deadly dive; he scrambled up the polished slope away from the sea and slipped again, down and down into his bed in Nelson Place. He lay still thinking. 'What a dream!' and then heard the stealthy movement of his parents in the other bed. It was Saturday night. His father panted like a man at the end of a race and his mother made a horrifying sound of pleasurable pain. He was filled with hatred, disgust, loneliness: he was completely abandoned: he had no share in their thoughts—for the space of a few minutes he was dead, he was like a soul in purgatory watching the shameless act of a beloved person.

Then quite suddenly he opened his eyes, it was as if the nightmare couldn't go further. It was black night, he could see nothing and for a few seconds he believed he was back in Nelson Place. Then a clock struck three, clashing close by like the lid of a dustbin in the backyard, and he remembered with immense relief that he was alone. He got out of bed in his half drowse (his mouth was clotted and evil-tasting) and felt his way to the washstand. He took up his tooth-mug, poured out a glass of water and heard a voice say, 'Pinkie? What is it, Pinkie?' He dropped the glass and as the water spilt across his feet he bitterly remembered.

He said cautiously into the dark, 'It's all right. Go to sleep.' He no longer had a sense of triumph or superiority. He looked back on a few hours ago as if he had been drunk then or dreaming—he had been momentarily exhilarated by the strangeness of his experience. Now there would be nothing strange ever again—he was awake. You had to treat these things with common sense—she knew. The darkness thinned before his wakeful and calculating gaze—he could see the outline of the bedknobs and a chair. He had won a move and lost a move: they couldn't *make* her give evidence, but she knew . . . She loved him whatever that meant but love was not an eternal thing like hatred and disgust. They saw a better face, a smarter suit . . . The truth came home to him with horror that he had got to keep her love for a lifetime; he would never be able to discard her. If he climbed he had to take Nelson Place with him like a visible scar; the registry office marriage was as irrevocable as a sacrament. Only death could ever set him free.

He was taken by a craving for air, walked softly to the door. In the passage he could see nothing: it was full of the low sound of breathing—from the room he had left, from Dallow's room. He felt like a blind man watched by people he couldn't see. He felt his way to the stairhead and on down to the hall, step by step, creakingly. He put out his hand and touched the telephone, then with his arm outstretched made for the door. In the street the lamps were out, but the darkness no longer enclosed between four walls seemed to thin out across the vast expanse of a city. He could see basement railings, a cat moving, and, reflected on the dark sky, the phosphorescent glow of the sea. It was a strange world: he had never been alone in it before. He had a deceptive sense of freedom as he walked softly down towards the Channel.

The lights were on in Montpellier Road. Nobody was about, and an empty milk bottle stood outside a gramophone shop; far down were the illuminated clock tower and the public lavatories. The air was fresh like country air. He could imagine he had escaped. He put his hands for warmth into his trouser-pockets and felt a scrap of paper which should not have been there. He drew it out—a scrap torn from a notebook—big, unformed, stranger's writing. He held it up into the grey light and read—with difficulty. 'I love you, Pinkie. I don't care what you do. I love you for ever. You've been good to me. Wherever you go, I'll go too.' She must have written it while he talked to Cubitt and slipped it into his pocket while he slept. He crumpled it in his fist, a dustbin stood outside a fishmonger's—then he held his hand. An obscure sense told him you never knew—it might prove useful one day.

He heard a whisper, looked sharply round, and thrust the paper back. In an alley between two shops, an old woman sat upon the ground; he could just see the rotting and discoloured face: it was like the sight of damnation. Then he heard the whisper, 'Blessed art thou among women,' saw the grey fingers fumbling at the beads. This was not one of the damned: he watched with horrified fascination: this was one of the saved.

PART SEVEN

I

It did not seem in the least strange to Rose that she should wake alone—she was a stranger in the country of mortal sin, and she assumed that everything was customary. He was, she supposed, about his business. No alarm-clock dinned her to get up but the morning light woke her, pouring through the uncurtained glass. Once she heard footsteps in the passage, and once a voice called 'Judy' imperatively. She lay there wondering what a wife had to do—or rather a mistress.

But she didn't lie long—that was frightening, the unusual passivity. It wasn't like life at all—to have nothing to do. Suppose they assumed she knew—about the stove to be lit, the table to be laid, the debris to be cleared away. A clock struck seven; it was an unfamiliar clock (all her life she had lived in hearing of the same one till now), and the strikes seemed to fall more slowly and more sweetly through the early summer air than any she had ever heard before. She felt happy and scared: seven o'clock was a terribly late hour. She scrambled out and was about to mutter her quick 'Our Fathers' and 'Hail Marys' while she dressed, when she remembered again . . . What was the good of praying now? She'd finished with all that: she had chosen her side: if they damned him they'd got to damn her, too.

In the ewer there was only an inch of water with a grey heavy surface, and when she lifted the lid of the soap-box she found three pound notes wrapped round two half-crowns. She put the lid back: that was just another custom you had to get used to. She took a look round the room, opened a wardrobe and found a tin of biscuits and a pair of boots; some crumbs crunched under her tread. The gramophone record caught her attention on the chair where she'd lain it and she stowed it in the cupboard for greater safety. Then she opened the door: not a sound or sign of life: looked over the banisters, the new wood squeaked under her pressure. Somewhere down below must be the kitchen, the living room, the places where she had to work. She went cautiously down—seven o'clock—what furious faces—in the hall a ball of paper scuffled under her feet. She smoothed it out and read a pencilled message: 'Lock your door. Have a good time.' She didn't understand it: it might as well have been in code—she assumed it must have something to do with this foreign world where you sinned on a bed and people lost their lives suddenly and strange men hacked at your door and cursed you in the night.

She found the basement stairs; they were dark where they dropped under the hall, but she didn't know where to find a switch. Once she nearly tripped and held the wall close with beating heart, remembering the evidence at the inquest, how Spicer had fallen. His death gave the house a feeling of importance: she had never been on the scene of a recent death. At the bottom of the stairs she opened the first door she came to, cautiously, expecting a curse: it was the kitchen all right, but it was empty. It wasn't like either of the kitchens she knew: the one at Snow's clean, polished, busy: the one at home which was just the room where you sat, where people cooked and ate and had moods and warmed themselves on bitter nights and dozed in chairs. This was like the kitchen in a house for sale: the stove was full of cold coke: on the window-sill there were two empty sardine tins: a dirty saucer lay under the table for a cat which wasn't there: a cupboard stood open full of empties.

She went and raked at the dead coke; the stove was cold to the touch: there hadn't been a fire alight there for hours or days. The thought struck her that she'd been deserted: perhaps this was what happened in *this* world, the sudden flight, leaving everything behind, your empty bottles and your girl and the message in code on a scrap of paper. When the door opened she expected a policeman.

It was Dallow in pyjama trousers. He looked in, said, 'Where's Judy?' then seemed to notice her. He said, 'You're up early.'

'Early?' She couldn't understand what he meant.

'I thought it was Judy routing around. You remember me. I'm Dallow.'

She said, 'I thought maybe I'd better light the stove.'

'What for?'

'Breakfast.'

He said, 'If that polony's gone and forgotten—' He went to a dresser and pulled open a drawer. 'Why,' he said, 'what's got you? You don't want a stove. There's plenty here.' Inside the drawer were stacks of tins: sardines, herrings . . . She said, 'But tea.'

He looked at her oddly. 'Anyone'd think you wanted work. No one here wants any tea. Why take the trouble? There's beer in the cupboard, and Pinkie drinks the milk out of the bottle.' He padded back to the door. 'Help yourself, kid, if you're hungry. Pinkie want anything?'

'He's gone out.'

'Christ's sake, what's come over this house?' He stopped in the doorway and took another look at her as she stood with helpless hands near the dead stove. He said, 'You don't *want* to work, do you?'

'No,' she said doubtfully.

He was puzzled. 'I wouldn't want to stop you,' he said. 'You're Pinkie's girl. You go ahead and light that stove if you want. I'll shut up Judy if she barks, but Christ knows where you'll find the coke. Why, that stove's not been lit since March.'

'I don't want to put anyone out,' Rose said. 'I came down . . . I thought . . . I'd *got* to light it.'

'You don't need to do a stroke,' Dallow said. 'You take it from me, this is Liberty Hall.' He said, 'You've not seen a bitch with red hair routing around, have you?'

'I haven't seen a soul.'

'Well,' Dallow said, 'I'll be seeing you.' She was alone again in the cold kitchen. Needn't do a stroke . . . Liberty Hall . . . She leant against the whitewashed wall and saw an old flypaper dangling above the dresser; somebody a long time ago had set a mousetrap by a hole, but the bait had been stolen and the trap had snapped on nothing at all. It was a lie when people said that sleeping with a man made no difference: you emerged from pain to this—freedom, liberty, strangeness. A stifled exhilaration moved in her breast, a kind of pride. She opened the kitchen door boldly and there at the head of the basement stairs was Dallow and the red-haired bitch, the woman he'd called Judy. They stood with lips glued together in an attitude of angry passion: they might have been inflicting on each other the greatest injury of which they were either of them capable. The woman wore a mauve dressing-gown with a dusty bunch of paper poppies, the relic of an old November. As they fought mouth to mouth the sweet-toned clock sounded the half-hour. Rose watched them from the foot of the stairs. She had lived years in a night. She knew all about this now.

The woman saw her and took her mouth from Dallow's. 'Well,' she said, 'who's here?'

'It's Pinkie's girl,' Dallow said.

'You're up early. Hungry?'

'No. I just thought—maybe I ought to light the fire.'

'We don't use that fire often,' the woman said. 'Life's too short.' She had little pimples round her mouth and an air of ardent sociability. She stroked her carrot hair and coming down the stairs to Rose fastened a mouth wet and prehensile like a sea anemone upon her cheek. She smelt faintly, stalely, of Californian Poppy. 'Well, dear,' she said, 'you're one of us now,' and she seemed to present to Rose in a generous gesture the half-naked man, the bare dark stairs, the barren kitchen. She whispered softly so that Dallow couldn't hear, 'You won't tell anyone you saw us, dear, will you? Frank gets worked up, an' it don't mean anything, not anything at all.'

Rose dumbly shook her head: this foreign land absorbed her too quickly—no sooner were you past the customs than the naturalization papers were signed, you were conscripted . . .

'There's a duck,' the woman said. 'Any friend of Pinkie's is a friend of all of us. You'll be meeting the boys before long.'

'I doubt it,' said Dallow from the top of the stairs.

'You mean—'

'We got to talk to Pinkie serious.'

'Did you have Cubitt here last night?' the woman asked.

'I don't know,' Rose said. 'I don't know who anyone is. Someone rang the bell and swore a lot and kicked the door.'

'That was Cubitt,' the woman gently explained.

'We got to talk to Pinkie serious. It's not safe,' Dallow said.

'Well, dear, I'd better be getting back to Frank.' She paused on a step just above Rose. 'If you ever want a dress cleaned, dear, you couldn't do better than give it to Frank. Though I say it who shouldn't. There's no one like Frank for getting out grease marks. An' he hardly charges a thing to lodgers.' She bent down and laid a freckled finger on Rose's shoulder. 'It could do with a sponge now.'

'But I haven't got anything to wear, only this.'

'Oh well, dear, in that case . . .' She bent and whispered confidentially, 'Make your hubby buy you one,' then gathered the faded dressing-gown around her and loped up the stairs. Rose could see a dead white leg, like something which has lived underground, covered with russet hairs, a dingy slipper flapped a loose heel. It seemed to her that everyone was very kind: there seemed to be a companionship in mortal sin.

Pride swelled in her breast as she came up from the basement. She was accepted. She had experienced as much as any woman. Back in the bedroom she sat on the bed and waited and heard the clock strike eight. She wasn't hungry; she was sensible of an immense freedom—no time-table to keep, no work which had got to be done. You suffered a little pain and then came out on the other side to this amazing liberty. There was only one thing she wanted now—to let others see her happiness. She could walk into Snow's now like any other customer, rap the table with a spoon and demand service. She could boast . . . It was a fantasy, but sitting on the bed while time drifted by it became an idea, something she was really able to do. In less than half an hour they would be opening for breakfast. If she had the money . . . She brooded with her eyes on the soap-dish. She thought: after all we are married—in a way; he's given me nothing but that record; he wouldn't grudge me half a crown. She stood up and listened, then walked softly over to the washstand. With her fingers on the lid of the soap-dish she waited—somebody was coming down the passage: it wasn't Judy and it wasn't Dallow—perhaps it was the man they called Frank. The footsteps passed; she lifted the lid and unwrapped the half-crown. She had stolen biscuits, she had never stolen money before. She expected to feel shame, but it didn't come—only again the odd swell of pride. She was like a child in a new school who finds she can pick up the esoteric games and passwords in the cement playground, at once, by instinct.

In the world outside it was Sunday—she'd forgotten that: the church bells reminded her, shaking over Brighton. Freedom again in the early sun, freedom from the silent prayers at the altar, from the awful demands made on you at the sanctuary rail. She had joined the other side now for ever. The half-crown was like a medal for services rendered. People coming back from seven-thirty Mass, people on the way to eight-thirty Matins—she watched them in their dark clothes like a spy. She didn't envy them and she didn't despise them: they had their salvation and she had Pinkie and damnation.

At Snow's the blinds had just gone up; a girl she knew called Maisie was laying a few tables—the only girl she cared about, a new girl like herself and not much older. She watched her from the pavement—and Doris, the senior waitress with her habitual sneer, doing nothing at all except flick a duster where Maisie had already been. Rose clutched the half-crown closer; well, she had only got to go in, sit down, tell Doris to fetch her a cup of coffee and a roll, tip her a couple of coppers—she could patronize the whole lot of them. She was married. She was a woman. She was happy. What would they feel like when they saw her coming through the door?

And she didn't go in. That was the trouble. How would she feel, flaunting her freedom? Then through the pane she caught Maisie's eye; she stood there with a duster staring back, bony, immature, like her own image in a mirror. And *she* stood now where Pinkie had stood—outside, looking in. This was what the priests meant by one flesh. And just as she days ago had motioned, Maisie motioned—a slant of the eyes, an imperceptible nod towards the side door. There was no reason at all why she shouldn't go in at the front, but she obeyed Maisie. It was like doing something you'd done before.

The door opened and Maisie was there. 'Rose, what's wrong?' She ought to have had wounds to show: she felt guilty at having only happiness. 'I thought I'd come,' she said, 'and see you. I'm married.'

'Married?'

'Kind of.'

'Oh, Rose, what's it like?'

'Lovely.'

'You got rooms?'

'Yes.'

'What do you do all day?'

'Nothing at all. Just lie about.'

The childish face in front of her took on the wrinkled expression of grief. 'God, Rosie, you're lucky. Where did you meet him?'

'Here.'

A hand bonier than her own seized her by the wrist: 'Oh, Rosie, ain't he got a friend?'

She said lightly, 'He's not got friends.'

'Maisie,' a voice called shrilly from the café, 'Maisie.' Tears lay ready in the eyes: in Maisie's eyes not Rose's: she hadn't meant to hurt her friend. An impulse of pity made her say, 'It's not all that good, Maisie.' She tried to destroy the appearance of her own happiness. 'Sometimes he's bad to me. Oh, I can tell you,' she urged, 'it's not all roses.'

But 'not roses,' she thought as she turned back to the parade, 'if it's not all roses, what is it?' And mechanically, walking back towards Frank's without her breakfast, she began to think—what have I done to deserve to be so happy? She'd committed a sin? that was the answer: she was having her cake in this world, not in the next, and she didn't care. She was stamped with him, as his voice was stamped on the vulcanite.

A few doors from Frank's, from a shop where they sold the Sunday papers, Dallow called to her. 'Hi, kid.' She stopped. 'You got a visitor.'

'Who?'

'Your mother.'

She was stirred by a feeling of gratitude and pity: her mother hadn't been happy like this. She said, 'Give me a *News of the World*. Mum likes a Sunday paper.' In the back room somebody was playing a gramophone. She said to the man who kept the shop, 'Sometime would you let me come here—and play a record I got?'

'O' course he will,' Dallow said.

She crossed the road and rang at Frank's door. Judy opened it; she was still in her dressing-gown, but underneath she now had on her corsets. 'You got a visitor,' she said.

'I know.' Rose ran upstairs: it was the biggest triumph you could ever expect—to greet your mother for the first time in your own house—ask her to sit down on your own chair: to look at one another with an equal experience. There was nothing now, Rose felt, her mother knew about men she didn't know: that was the reward for the painful ritual upon the bed. She flung the door gladly open and there was the woman.

'What are you—?' she began, and said, 'They told me it was my mother.'

'I had to tell them something,' the woman gently explained. She said, 'Come in, dear, and shut the door behind you,' as if it were *her* room.

'I'll call Pinkie.'

'I'd like a word with your Pinkie.' You couldn't get round her; she stood there like the wall at the end of an alley scrawled with the obscene chalk messages of an enemy. She was the explanation—it seemed to Rose—of sudden harshnesses, of the nails pressing her wrist. She said, 'You'll not see Pinkie. I won't have anyone worry Pinkie.'

'He's going to have plenty to worry him soon.'

'Who are you?' Rose implored her. 'Why do you interfere with us? You're not the police.'

'I'm like everyone else. I want justice,' the woman cheerfully remarked, as if she were ordering a pound of tea. Her big prosperous carnal face hung itself with smiles. She said, 'I want to see *you're* safe.'

'I don't want any help,' Rose said.

'You ought to go home.'

Rose clenched her hands in defence of the brass bed, the ewer of dusty water: 'This is home.'

'It's no good your getting angry, dear,' the woman continued. 'I'm not going to lose my temper with you again. It's not your fault. You don't understand how things are. Why, you poor little thing, I pity you,' and she advanced across the linoleum as if she intended to take Rose in her arms.

Rose backed against the bed, 'You keep your distance.'

'Now don't get agitated, dear. It won't help. You see—I'm determined.'

'I don't know what you mean. Why can't you talk straight?'

'There's things I've got to break—gently.'

'Keep away from me. Or I'll scream.'

The woman stopped. 'Now let's talk sensible, dear. I'm here for your own good. You got to be saved. Why—' she seemed for a moment at a loss for words. She said in a hushed voice, 'Your life's in danger.'

'You go away if that's all—'

'All,' the woman was shocked. 'What do you mean, all?' Then she laughed resolutely. 'Why, dear, for a moment you had me rattled. All, indeed. It's enough, isn't it? I'm not joking now. If you don't know it, you got to know it. There's nothing he wouldn't stop at.'

'Well?' Rose said, giving nothing away.

The woman whispered softly across the few feet between them, 'He's a murderer.'

'Do you think I don't know *that*?' Rose said.

'God's sake,' the woman said, 'do you mean—'

'There's nothing *you* can tell me.'

'You crazy little fool—to marry him knowing that. I got a good mind to let you be.'

'I won't complain,' Rose said.

The woman hooked on another smile, as you hook on a wreath. 'I'm not going to lose my temper, dear. Why if I let you be, I wouldn't sleep at nights. It wouldn't be Right. Listen to me; maybe you don't know what happened. I got it all figured out. They took Fred down under the parade, into one of those little shops and strangled him—least they would have strangled him, but his heart gave out first.' She said in an awestruck voice, 'They strangled a dead man,' then added sharply, 'you aren't listening.'

'I know it all,' Rose lied. She was thinking hard—she was remembering Pinkie's warning—'Don't get mixed up.' She thought wildly and vaguely: he did his best for me; I got to help him now. She watched the woman closely; she would never forget that plump, good-natured, ageing face: it stared out at her like an idiot's from the ruins of a bombed home. She said, 'Well, if you think that's how it was, why don't you go to the police?'

'Now you're talking sense,' the woman said. 'I only want to make things clear. This is the way it is, dear. There's a certain person I've paid money to who's told me things. And there's things I've figured out for myself. But that person—he won't give evidence. For reasons. And you need a lot of evidence—seeing how the doctors made it natural death. Now if you—'

'Why don't you give it up?' Rose said. 'It's over and done, isn't it? Why not let us all be?'

'It wouldn't be right. Besides—he's dangerous. Look what happened here the other day. You don't tell *me* that was an accident.'

'You haven't thought, have you,' Rose said, 'why he did it? You don't kill a man for no reason.'

'Well, why did he?'

'I don't know.'

'Ask him.'

'I don't need to know.'

'You think he's in love with you,' the woman said, 'he's not.'

'He married me.'

'And why? because they can't make a wife give evidence. You're just a witness like that other man was. My dear,' she again tried to close the gap between them, 'I only want to save you. He'd kill *you* as soon as look at you if he thought he wasn't safe.'

With her back to the bed Rose watched her approach. She let her put her large cool pastry-making hands upon her shoulders. 'People change,' she said.

'Oh, no they don't. Look at me. I've never changed. It's like those sticks of rock: bite it all the way down, you'll still read Brighton. That's human nature.' She breathed mournfully over Rose's face—a sweet and winey breath.

'Confession . . . repentance,' Rose whispered.

'That's just religion,' the woman said. 'Believe me, it's the world we got to deal with.' She went pat pat on Rose's shoulder, her breath whistling in her throat. 'You pack a bag and come away with me. I'll look after you. You won't have any cause to fear.'

'Pinkie . . .'

'I'll look after Pinkie.'

Rose said, 'I'll do anything—anything you want . . .'

'That's the way to talk, dear.'

'If you'll let us alone.'

The woman backed away. A momentary look of fury was hung up among the wreaths discordantly. 'Obstinate,' she said. 'If I was your mother . . . a good hiding.' The bony and determined face stared back at her: all the fight there was in the world lay there—warships cleared for action and bombing fleets took flight between the set eyes and the stubborn mouth. It was like the map of a campaign marked with flags.

'Another thing,' the woman bluffed. 'They can send you to gaol. Because you know. You told me so. An accomplice, that's what you are. After the fact.'

'If they took Pinkie, do you think,' she asked with astonishment, 'I'd mind?'

'Gracious,' the woman said, 'I only came here for your sake. I wouldn't have troubled to see you first, only I don't want to let the Innocent suffer'—the aphorism came clicking out like a ticket from a slot machine. 'Why, won't you lift a finger to stop him killing you?'

'He wouldn't do me any harm.'

'You're young. You don't know things like I do.'

'There's things *you* don't know.' She brooded darkly by the bed, while the woman argued on: a God wept in a garden and cried out upon a cross; Molly Carthew went to everlasting fire.

'I know one thing you don't. I know the difference between Right and Wrong. They didn't teach you *that* at school.'

Rose didn't answer; the woman was quite right: the two words meant nothing to her. Their taste was extinguished by stronger foods—Good and Evil. The woman could tell her nothing she didn't know about these—she knew by tests as clear as mathematics that Pinkie was evil—what did it matter in that case whether he was right or wrong?

'You're crazy,' the woman said. 'I don't believe you'd lift a finger if he was killing you.'

Rose came slowly back to the outer world. She said, 'Maybe I wouldn't.'

'If I wasn't a kind woman I'd give you up. But I've got a sense of responsibility.' Her smiles hung very insecurely when she paused at the door. 'You can warn that young husband of yours,' she said, 'I'm getting warm to him. I got my plans.' She went out and closed the door, then flung it open again for a last attack. 'You be careful, dear,' she said. 'You don't want a murderer's baby,' and grinned mercilessly across the bare bedroom floor. 'You better take precautions.'

Precautions . . . Rose stood at the bed-end and pressed a hand against her body, as if under that pressure she could discover . . . *That* had never entered her mind; and the thought of what she might have let herself in for came like a sense of glory. A child . . . and that child would have a child . . . it was like raising an army of friends for Pinkie. If They damned him and her, They'd have to deal with them, too. There was no end to what the two of them had done last night upon the bed: it was an eternal act.

2

The Boy stood back in the doorway of the newspaper shop and saw Ida Arnold come out. She looked a little flushed, a little haughty sailing down the street; she paused and gave a small boy a penny. He was so surprised he dropped it, staring after her heavy careful retreat.

The Boy gave a sudden laugh, rusty and half-hearted. He thought: she's drunk . . . Dallow said, 'That was a narrow squeak.'

'What was?'

'Your mother-in-law.'

'Her . . . how did *you* know?'

'She asked for Rose.'

The Boy put down the *News of the World* upon the counter—a headline stood up—'Assault on Schoolgirl in Epping Forest'. He walked across to Frank's thinking hard, and up the stairs. Halfway he stopped: she'd dropped an artificial violet from a spray. He picked it off the stair: it smelt of Californian Poppy. Then he went in, holding the flower concealed in his palm, and Rose came across to him, welcoming. He avoided her mouth. 'Well,' he said and tried to express in his face a kind of rough and friendly jocularity, 'I hear your Mum's been visiting you,' and waited anxiously for her reply.

'Oh, yes,' Rose said doubtfully, 'she did look in.'

'Not one of her moody days?'

'No.'

He kneaded the violet furiously in his palm. 'Well, did she think it suited you—being married?'

'Oh, yes, I think she did . . . She didn't say much.'

The Boy went across to the bed and slipped on his coat. He said, 'You been out too I hear?'

'I thought I'd go and see friends.'

'What friends?'

'Oh—at Snow's.'

'You call *them* friends?' he asked with contempt. 'Well, did you see them?'

'Not really. Only one—Maisie. For a minute.'

'And then you got back here in time to catch your Mum. Don't you want to know what I've been up to?'

She stared stupidly at him: his manner scared her. 'If you like.'

'What do you mean, if I like? You aren't as dumb as that.' The wire anatomy of the flower pricked his palm. He said, 'I got to have a word with Dallow. Wait here,' and left her.

He called to Dallow, across the street, and when Dallow joined them, he said, 'Where's Judy?'

'Upstairs.'

'Frank working?'

'Yes.'

'Come down to the kitchen then.' He led the way down the stairs; in the basement dusk his feet crunched on dead coke. He sat down on the edge of the kitchen table and said, 'Have a drink.'

'Too early,' Dallow said.

'Listen,' the Boy said. An expression of pain crossed his face as if he were about to wring out an appalling confession. 'I trust you,' he said.

'Well,' Dallow, said, 'what's getting you?'

'Things aren't too good,' the Boy said. 'People are getting wise to a lot of things. Christ,' he said, 'I killed Spicer and I married the girl. Have I got to have that massacre?'

'Was Cubitt here last night?'

'He was and I sent him away. He begged—he wanted a fiver.'

'Did you give it him?'

'Of course I didn't. D'you think I'd let myself be blackmailed by a thing like him?'

'You oughter have given him something.'

'It's not him I'm worried about.'

'You ought to be.'

'Be quiet, can't you,' the Boy suddenly and shrilly squealed at him. He jerked his thumb towards the ceiling. 'It's *her* I'm worried about.' He opened his hand and said, 'God damn it I dropped that flower.'

'Flower . . . ?'

'Be quiet, can't you, and listen,' he said low and furiously. 'That wasn't her Mum.'

'Who was it?' Dallow asked.

'The buer who's been asking questions . . . the one who was with Fred in the taxi the day . . .' He put his head for a moment between his hands in an attitude of grief or desperation—but it wasn't either: it was the rush of memories. He said, 'I got a headache. I got to think clear. Rose told me it was her Mum. What's she after?'

'You don't think,' Dallow said, 'she's talked?'

'I got to find out,' the Boy said.

'I'd have trusted her,' Dallow said, 'all the way.'

'I wouldn't trust anyone that far. Not you, Dallow.'

'But if she's talking, why does she talk to *her*—why not to the police?'

'Why don't any of them talk to the police?' He stared with troubled eyes at the cold stove. He was haunted by his ignorance. 'I don't know what they're getting at.' Other people's feelings bored at his brain: he had never before felt this desire to understand. He said passionately, 'I'd like to carve the whole bloody boiling.'

'After all,' Dallow said, 'she don't know much. She only knows it wasn't Fred left the card. If you ask me she's a dumb little piece. Affectionate, I daresay, but dumb.'

'You're the dumb one, Dallow. She knows a lot. She knows I killed Fred.'

'You sure?'

'She told me so.'

'An' she married you?' Dallow said. 'I'm damned if I understand what they *want*.'

'If we don't do something quick it looks to me as if all Brighton'll know we killed Fred. All England. The whole Goddamned world.'

'What can *we* do?'

The Boy went over to the basement window crunching on the

coke: a tiny asphalt yard with an old dustbin which hadn't been used for weeks: a blocked grating, and a sour smell. He said, 'It's no good stopping now. We got to go on.' People passed overhead, invisible from the waist upwards: a shabby shoe scuffled the pavement wearing out the toecap; a bearded face stooped suddenly into sight looking for a cigarette-end. He said slowly, 'It ought to be easy to quiet her. We quieted Fred an' Spicer, an' she's only a kid . . .'

'Don't be crazy,' Dallow said. 'You can't go on like that.'

'Maybe I got to. No choice. Maybe it's always that way—you start and then you go on going on.'

'We're making a mistake,' Dallow said. 'I'd stake you a fiver she's straight. Why—you told me yourself—she's stuck on you.'

'Why did she say it was her Mum then?' He watched a woman go by: young as far as the thighs: you couldn't see further up than that. A spasm of disgust shook him. He'd given way: he had even been proud of *that*—what he could have done with Spicer's girl, Sylvie, in a Lancia. Oh, it was all right, he supposed, to take every drink once—if you could stop at that, say 'never again', not go on—going on.

'I can tell it myself,' Dallow said. 'Clear as clear. She's stuck on you all right.'

Stuck: high heels trodden over, bare legs moving out of sight. 'If she's stuck,' he said, 'it makes it easier—she'll do what I say.' A piece of newspaper blew along the street: the wind was from the sea.

Dallow said. 'Pinkie, I won't stand for any more killing.'

The Boy turned his back to the window and his mouth made a bad replica of mirth. He said, 'But suppose she killed herself?' An insane pride bobbed in his breast; he felt inspired: it was like a love of life returning to the blank heart: the empty tenement and then the seven devils worse than the first . . .

Dallow said, 'For Christ's sake, Pinkie. You're imagining things.'

'We'll soon see,' the Boy said.

He came up the stairs from the basement, looking this way and that for the scented flower of cloth and wire. He could see it nowhere. Rose's voice said, 'Pinkie,' over the new banister: she was waiting there for him anxiously on the landing. She said, 'Pinkie, I got to tell you. I wanted to keep you from worrying—but there's got to be someone I don't have to lie to. That wasn't Mum, Pinkie.'

He came slowly up, watching her closely, judging. 'Who was it?'

'It was that woman. The one who used to come to Snow's asking questions.'

'What did she want?'

'She wanted me to go away from here.'

'Why?'

'Pinkie, she *knows*.'

'Why did you say it was your Mum?'

'I told you—I didn't want you to worry.'

He was beside her, watching her. She faced him back with a worried candour, and he found that he believed her as much as he believed anyone: his restless cocky pride subsided: he felt an odd sense of peace, as if—for a while—he hadn't got to plan.

'But then,' Rose went anxiously on, 'I thought—perhaps you ought to worry.'

'That's all right,' he said and put his hand on her shoulder in an awkward embrace.

'She said something about paying money to someone. She said she was getting warm to you.'

'I don't worry,' he said and pressed her back. Then he stopped, looking over her shoulder. In the doorway of the room the flower lay. He had dropped it when he closed the door—and then—he began at once to calculate—she followed me, of course she saw the flower, she knew I *knew*. That explains everything, the confession . . . All the while he was down there below with Dallow she had been wondering what she had to do to cover her mistake. A clean breast—the phrase made him laugh—a clean tart's breast, the kind of breast Sylvie sported—cleaned up for use. He laughed again: the horror of the world lay like infection in his throat.

'What is it, Pinkie?'

'That flower,' he said.

'What flower?'

'The one *she* brought.'

'What . . . where . . . ?'

Perhaps she hadn't seen it then . . . maybe she was straight after all . . . who knows? Who, he thought, will ever know? And with a kind of sad excitement—what did it matter anyway? He had been a fool to think it made any difference; he couldn't afford to take risks. If she were straight and loved him it would be just so much easier, that was all. He repeated, 'I don't worry. I don't need to worry. I know what to do. Even if she got to know everything I know what to do.' He watched her shrewdly. He brought his hand round and pressed her breast. 'It won't hurt,' he said.

'What won't hurt, Pinkie?'

'The way I'll manage things—' he started agilely away from his dark suggestion. 'You don't want to leave me, do you?'

'Never,' Rose said.

'That's what I meant,' he said. 'You wrote it, didn't you. Trust me, I'll manage things if the worst comes to the worst—so it won't hurt either of us. You can trust me,' he went smoothly and rapidly on, while she watched him with the tricked expression of someone who has promised too much, too quickly. 'I knew,' he said, 'you'd feel like that. About us never parting. What you wrote.'

She whispered with dread. 'It's a mortal . . .'

'Just one more,' he said. 'What difference does it make? You can't be damned twice over, and we're damned already—so they say. And anyway it's only if the worst . . . if she finds out about Spicer.'

'Spicer,' Rose moaned, 'you don't mean Spicer too . . .'

'I only mean,' he said, 'if she finds out that I was here—in the house—but we don't need to worry till she does.'

'But Spicer . . .' Rose said.

'I was here,' he said, 'when it happened, that's all. I didn't even see him fall, but my solicitor . . .'

'He was here too?' Rose said.

'Oh, yes.'

'I remember now,' Rose said. 'Of course I read the paper. They couldn't believe, could they, that he'd cover up anything really wrong. A solicitor.'

'Old Prewitt,' the Boy said, 'why—' again the unused laugh came into rusty play. 'He's the Soul of Honour.' He pressed her breast again and uttered his qualified encouragement. 'Oh no, there's no cause to worry till *she* finds out. Even then you see there's *that* escape. But perhaps she never will. And if she doesn't, why,'—his fingers touched her with secret revulsion—'we'll just go on, won't we,' and he tried to make the horror sound like love, 'the way we are.'

3

But it was the Soul of Honour none the less who really worried him. If Cubitt had given that woman the idea that there was something wrong about Spicer's death as well, who could she go to now but Mr Prewitt? She wouldn't attempt anything with Dallow; but a man of law—when he was as clever as Prewitt was— was always frightened of the law. Prewitt was like a man who keeps a tame lion cub in his house. He could never be quite certain that the lion to whom he had taught so many tricks, to beg and eat out of his hand, might not one day unexpectedly mature and turn on him. Perhaps he might cut his cheek shaving—and the law would smell the blood.

In the early afternoon he couldn't wait any longer; he set out for Prewitt's house. First he told Dallow to keep an eye on the girl in case . . . More than ever yet he had the sense that he was being driven further and deeper than he'd ever meant to go. A curious and cruel pleasure touched him—he didn't really care so very much—it was being decided for him, and all he had to do was to let himself easily go. He knew what the end might be—it didn't horrify him: it was easier than life.

Mr Prewitt's house was in a street parallel to the railway, beyond the terminus: it was shaken by shunting engines; the soot settled continuously on the glass and the brass plate. From the basement window a woman with tousled hair stared suspiciously up at him—she was always there watching visitors from a hard and bitter face. She was never explained: he had always thought she was the cook, but it appeared now she was the 'spouse'—twenty-five years at the game. The door was opened by a girl with grey underground skin—an unfamiliar face. 'Where's Tilly?' the Boy said.

'She's left.'

'Tell Prewitt, Pinkie's here.'

'He's not seeing anyone,' the girl said. 'This is a Sunday, ain't it?'

'He'll see me.' The Boy walked into the hall, opened a door, sat down in a room lined with filing boxes: he knew the way. 'Go on,' he said, 'tell him. I know he's asleep. You wake him up.'

'You seem to be at home here,' the girl said.

'I am.' He knew what those filing boxes contained marked Rex *v.* Innes, Rex *v.* T. Collins—they contained just air. A train shunted and the empty boxes quivered on the shelves: the window was open only a crack, but the radio from next door came in—Radio Luxembourg.

'Shut the window,' he said. She shut it sullenly. It made no difference, the walls were so thin you could hear the neighbour move behind the shelves like a rat. He said, 'Does that music always play?'

'Unless it's a talk,' she said.

'What are you waiting for? Go and wake him.'

'He told me not to. He's got indigestion.'

Again the room vibrated and the music wailed through the wall.

'He's always got it after lunch. Go on and wake him.'

'It's a Sunday.'

'You'd better go quick.' He obscurely threatened her, and she slammed the door on him—a little plaster fell.

Under his feet in the basement someone was moving the furniture about—the spouse, he thought. A train hooted and a smother of smoke fell into the street. Over his head Mr Prewitt began to speak—there was nothing anywhere to keep out sound. Then footsteps across the ceiling and on the stairs.

Mr Prewitt's smile went on as the door opened. 'What brings our young cavalier?'

'I just wanted to see you,' the Boy said. 'See how you were getting along.' A spasm of pain drove the smile from Mr Prewitt's face, 'You ought to eat more careful,' the Boy said.

'Nothing does it any good,' Mr Prewitt said.

'You drink too much.'

'Eat, drink, for tomorrow . . .' Mr Prewitt writhed with his hand on his stomach.

'You got an ulcer?' the Boy said.

'No, no, nothing like that.'

'You ought to have your inside photographed.'

'I don't believe in the knife,' Mr Prewitt said quickly and nervously, as if it were a suggestion constantly made for which he had to have the answer on the tongue.

'Don't that music ever stop?'

'When I get tired of it,' Mr Prewitt said, 'I beat on the wall.' He took a paper-weight off his desk and struck the wall twice: the music broke into a high oscillating wail and ceased. They could hear the neighbour move furiously behind the shelves. 'How now? A rat?' Mr Prewitt quoted. The house shook as a heavy engine pulled out. 'Polonius,' Mr Prewitt explained.

'Polony? What polony?'

'No, no,' Mr Prewitt said. 'The rank intruding fool, I mean. In Hamlet.'

'Listen,' the Boy said impatiently, 'has a woman been round here asking questions?'

'What sort of questions?'

'About Spicer.'

Mr Prewitt said with sickly despair, 'Are people asking questions?' He sat down quickly and bent with indigestion. 'I've just been waiting for this.'

'There's no need to get scared,' the Boy said. 'They can't prove anything. You just stick to your story.' He sat down opposite Mr Prewitt and regarded him with grim contempt. 'You don't want to ruin yourself,' he said.

Mr Prewitt looked sharply up. 'Ruin?' he said. 'I'm ruined now.' He vibrated with the engines on his chair, and somebody in the basement slammed the floor beneath their feet. 'What-ho! old mole,' Mr Prewitt said. 'The spouse—you've never met the spouse.'

'I've seen her,' the Boy said.

'Twenty-five years. Then this.' The smoke came down outside the window like a blind. 'Has it ever occurred to you,' Mr Prewitt said, 'that you're lucky? The worst that can happen to you is you'll hang. But I can rot.'

'What's upsetting you?' the Boy said. He was confused—as if a weak man had struck him back. He wasn't used to this—the infringement of other people's lives. Confession was an act one did—or didn't do—oneself.

'When I took on your work,' Mr Prewitt said, 'I lost the only other job I had. The Bakely Trust. And now I've lost you.'

'You got everything there is of mine.'

'There won't be any more soon. Colleoni's going to take over this place from you, and he's got his lawyer. A man in London. A swell.'

'I haven't thrown my sponge in yet.' He sniffed the air tainted with gasometers and said, 'I know what's wrong with you. You're drunk.'

'On Empire burgundy,' Mr Prewitt said. 'I want to tell you things. Pinkie, I want—' the literary phrase came glibly out—'to unburden myself.'

'I don't want to hear them. I'm not interested in *your* troubles.'

'I married beneath me,' Mr Prewitt said. 'It was my tragic mistake. I was young. An affair of uncontrollable passion. I was a passionate man,' he said wriggling with indigestion. 'You should see her,' he said, 'now. My God.' He leant forward and said in a whisper—'I watch the little typists go by carrying their cases. I'm quite harmless. A man may watch. My God, how neat and trim.' He broke off, his hand vibrating on the chair arm. 'Listen to the old mole down there. She's ruined me.' His old lined face had taken a holiday—from bonhomie, from cunning, from the legal jest. It was a Sunday and it was itself. Mr Prewitt said, 'You know what Mephistopheles said to Faustus when he asked where Hell was? He said, "Why, this is Hell, nor are we out of it".' The Boy watched him with fascination and fear.

'She's cleaning in the kitchen,' Mr Prewitt said, 'but she'll be coming up later. You ought to meet her—it'd be a treat. The old hag. What a joke it would be, wouldn't it, to tell her—everything. That I'm concerned in a murder. That people are asking questions. To pull down the whole damned house like Samson.' He stretched his arms wide and contracted them in the pain of indigestion. 'You're right,' he said, 'I've got an ulcer. But I won't have the knife. I'd rather die. I'm drunk, too. On Empire burgundy. Do you see that photo there—by the door? A school group. Lancaster

College. Not one of the great schools perhaps, but you'll find it in the Public Schools Year Book. You'll see me there—cross-legged in the bottom row. In a straw hat.' He said softly, 'We had field days with Harrow. A rotten set they were. No *esprit de corps*.'

The Boy didn't so much as turn his head to look. He had never known Prewitt like this before: it was a frightening and an entrancing exhibition. A man was coming alive before his eyes: he could see the nerves set to work in the agonized flesh, thought bloom in the transparent brain.

'To think,' Mr Prewitt said, 'an old Lancaster boy—to be married to that mole in the cellarage down there and to have as only client—' he gave his mouth an expression of fastidious disgust— 'you. What would old Manders say? A great Head.'

He had the bit between his teeth: he was like a man determined to live before he died; all the insults he had swallowed from police witnesses, the criticisms of magistrates, regurgitated from his tormented stomach. There was nothing he wouldn't tell to anybody. An enormous self-importance was blossoming out of his humiliation; his wife, the Empire burgundy, the empty files and the vibration of locomotives on the line, they were the important landscape of his great drama.

'You talk too easily,' the Boy said.

'Talk?' Mr Prewitt said. 'I could shake the world. Let them put me in the dock if they like. I'll give them—revelation. I've sunk so deep I carry—' he was shaken by an enormous windy self-esteem— he hiccupped twice—'the secrets of the sewer.'

'If I'd known you drank,' the Boy said, 'I wouldn't have touched you.'

'I drink—on Sundays. It's the day of rest.' He suddenly beat his foot upon the floor and screamed furiously, 'Be quiet down there.'

'You need a holiday,' the Boy said.

'I sit here and sit here—the bell rings, but it's only the groceries—tinned salmon, she has a passion for tinned salmon. Then I ring the bell—and in comes that pasty stupid—I watch the typists going by. I could embrace their little portable machines.'

'You'd be all right,' the Boy said—nervous and shaken with the conception of another life growing in the brain—'if you took a holiday.'

'Sometimes,' Mr Prewitt said, 'I have an urge to expose myself—shamefully—in a park.'

'I'll give you money.'

'No money can heal a mind diseased. This is Hell nor are we out of it. How much could you spare?'

'Twenty nicker.'

'It would go only a little way.'

'Boulogne—why not slip across the Channel?' the Boy asked with horrified disgust, 'enjoy yourself,' watching the grubby and bitten nails, the shaky hands which were the instruments of pleasure.

'Could you spare some small sum like that, my boy? Don't let me rob you. Though, of course, "I have done the state some service".'

'You can have it tomorrow—on conditions. You got to leave by the morning boat—stay away as long as you can. Maybe I'll send you more.' It was like fastening a leech on to the flesh—he felt weakness and disgust. 'Let me know when it's finished and I'll see.'

'I'll go, Pinkie—when you say. And—you won't tell my spouse?'

'I keep *my* mouth shut.'

'Of course. I trust you, Pinkie, and you can trust me. Recuperated by this holiday I shall return—'

'Take a long one.'

'Bullying police sergeants shall recognize my renewed astuteness. Defending the outcast.'

'I'll send the money first thing. Till then you don't see anyone. You go back to bed. Your indigestion's cruel. If anyone comes round you're not in.'

'As you say, Pinkie, as you say.'

It was the best he could do. He let himself out of the house and looking down met in the basement the hard suspicious gaze of Mr Prewitt's spouse; she had a duster in her hand and she watched him like a bitter enemy from her cave, under the foundations. He crossed the road and took one more look at the villa, and there in an upper window half-concealed by the curtains stood Mr Prewitt. He wasn't watching the Boy—he was just looking out—hopelessly, for what might turn up. But it was a Sunday and there weren't any typists.

4

He said to Dallow. 'You got to watch the place. I don't trust him
a yard. I can just see him looking out there, waiting for something, and seeing *her* . . .'

'He wouldn't be such a fool.'

'He's drunk. He says he's in Hell.'

Dallow laughed. 'Hell. That's good.'

'You're a fool, Dallow.'

'I don't believe in what my eyes don't see.'

'They don't see much then,' the Boy said. He left Dallow and
went upstairs. But oh, if this was Hell, he thought, it wasn't so
bad: the old-fashioned telephone, the narrow stairs, the snug and
dusty darkness—it wasn't like Prewitt's house, comfortless,
shaken, with the old bitch in the basement. He opened the door of
his room and there, he thought, was *his* enemy—he looked round
with angry disappointment at his changed room—the position of
everything a little altered and the whole place swept and clean and
tidied. He condemned her, 'I told you not to.'

'I've only cleared up, Pinkie.'

It was her room now, not his: the wardrobe and the washstand
shifted, and the bed—of course she hadn't forgotten the bed. It
was her Hell now if it was anybody's—he disowned it. He felt
driven out, but any change must be for the worse. He watched
her, disguising his hatred, trying to read age into her face, how she
would look one day staring up from his basement. He had come
back wrapped in another person's fate—a doubled darkness.

'Don't you like it, Pinkie?'

He wasn't Prewitt: he'd got guts: he hadn't lost his fight. He
said, 'Oh, this—it's fine. It was just I wasn't expecting it.'

She misread his constraint. 'Bad news?'

'Not yet. We got to be prepared, of course. I *am* prepared.' He went to the window and stared out through a forest of wireless masts towards a cloudy peaceful Sunday sky, then back at the changed room. This was how it might look if he had gone away and other tenants . . . He watched her closely while he did his sleight of hand, passing off his idea as hers. 'I got the car all ready. We could go out into the country where no one would hear . . .' He measured her terror carefully and before she could pass the card back to him, he changed his tone. 'That's only if the worst comes to the worst.' The phrase intrigued him: he repeated it: the worst—that was the stout woman with her glassy righteous eye coming up the smoky road—to the worst—and that was drunken ruined Mr Prewitt watching from behind the curtains for just one typist. 'It won't happen,' he encouraged her.

'No,' she passionately agreed. 'It won't, it can't.' Her enormous certainty had a curious effect on him—it was as if that plan of his too were being tidied, shifted, swept until he couldn't recognize his own. He wanted to argue that it *might* happen: he discovered in himself an odd nostalgia for the darkest act of all.

She said, 'I'm so happy. It can't be so bad after all.'

'What do you mean?' he said. 'Not bad? It's mortal sin.' He glanced with furious disgust at the made bed as if he contemplated a repetition of the act there and then—to thrust the lesson home.

'I know,' she said. 'I know, but still—'

'There's only one thing worse,' he said. It was as if she were escaping him: already she was domesticating their black alliance.

'I'm happy,' she argued bewilderedly. 'You're good to me.'

'That doesn't mean a thing.'

'Listen,' she said, 'what's that?' A thin wailing came through the window.

'The kid next door.'

'Why doesn't somebody quiet it?'

'It's a Sunday. Maybe they're out,' he said. 'You want to do anything? The flickers?'

She wasn't listening to him: the unhappy continuous cry absorbed her: she wore a look of responsibility and maturity. 'Somebody ought to see what it wants,' she said.

'It's just hungry or something.'

'Maybe it's ill.' She listened with a kind of vicarious agony. 'Things happen to babies suddenly. You don't know what it mightn't be.'

'It isn't yours.'

She turned bemused eyes towards him. 'No,' she said, 'but I was thinking—it might be.' She said with passion, 'I wouldn't leave it all an afternoon.'

He said uneasily, 'They haven't either. It's stopped. What did I tell you?' But her words lodged in his brain—'It might be.' He had never thought of that. He watched her with terror and disgust as if he were watching the ugly birth itself, the rivet of another life already pinning him down, and she stood there listening—with relief and patience, as if already she had passed through years of this anxiety and knew that the relief never lasted long and that the anxiety always began again.

5

Nine o'clock in the morning: he came furiously out into the passage; the morning sun trickled in over the top of the door below, staining the telephone. He called, 'Dallow, Dallow.'

Dallow came slowly up from the basement in his shirtsleeves. He said, 'Hallo, Pinkie. You look as if you hadn't slept.'

The Boy said, 'You keeping away from me?'

'Of course I'm not, Pinkie. Only—you being married—I thought you'd want to be alone.'

'You call it,' the Boy said, 'being alone?' He came down the stairs; he carried in his hand the mauve scented envelope Judy had thrust under the door. He hadn't opened it. His eyes were bloodshot. He carried down with him the marks of a fever—the beating pulse and the hot forehead and the restless brain.

'Johnnie phoned me early,' Dallow said. 'He's been watching since yesterday. No one's been to see Prewitt. We got scared for nothing.'

The Boy paid him no attention. He said, 'I want to be alone, Dallow. Really alone.'

'You been taking on too much at your age,' Dallow said and began to laugh. 'Two nights . . .'

The Boy said, 'She's got to go before she—' He couldn't express the magnitude of his fear or its nature to anyone.

'It's not safe to quarrel,' Dallow said quickly and cautiously.

'No,' the Boy said, 'it won't ever be safe again. I know that. No divorce. Nothing at all except dying. All the same,' he put his hand on the vulcanite for coolness, 'I told you—I had a plan.'

'It was crazy. Why should that poor kid want to die?'

He said with bitterness, 'She loves me. She says she wants to be with me always. And if I don't want to live . . .'

234

'Dally,' a voice called, 'Dally.' The Boy looked sharply and guiltily round; he hadn't heard Judy moving silently above in her naked feet and her corsets. He was absorbed, trying to get the plan straight, tied up in its complexity, uncertain who it was who had to die . . . himself or her or both . . .

'What you want, Judy?' Dallow said.

'Frank's finished your coat.'

'Let it be,' Dallow said. 'I'll fetch it in a shake.'

She blew him an avaricious unsatisfied kiss and padded back to her room.

'I started something there all right,' Dallow said. 'Sometimes I wish I hadn't. I don't want trouble with poor old Frank, an' she's so careless.'

The Boy looked at Dallow broodingly, as if perhaps he knew from his long service what one did.

'Suppose,' he said, 'you had a child?'

'Oh,' Dallow said, 'I leave that to her. It's *her* funeral.' He said, 'You got a letter there from Colleoni?'

'But what does she do?'

'The usual, I suppose.'

'And if she doesn't,' the Boy persisted, 'an' she began a child?'

'There's pills.'

'They don't always work, do they?' the Boy said. He had thought he'd learned everything, but he was back now in his state of appalled ignorance.

'They never work, if you ask me,' Dallow said. 'Colleoni written?'

'If Prewitt grassed, there wouldn't be a hope, would there?' the Boy brooded.

'He won't grass. And anyway he'll be in Boulogne tonight.'

'But *if* he did . . . or say I thought he had . . . there'd be nothing to do then, would there, but kill myself. And she—she wouldn't want to live without me. If she thought . . . And all the time perhaps it wouldn't be true. They call it—don't they?—a suicide pact.'

'What's got you, Pinkie? You're not giving in?'

'I mightn't die.'

'That's murder, too.'

'They don't hang you for it.'

'You're crazy, Pinkie. Why, I wouldn't stand for a thing like that.'

He gave the Boy a shocked and friendly blow. 'You're joking, Pinkie—there's nothing wrong with the poor kid—except for liking you.' The Boy said not a thing; he had an air of removing his thoughts, like heavy bales and stacking them inside, turning the key on all the world. 'You want to lie down a bit and rest,' Dallow said uneasily.

'I want to lie down alone,' the Boy said. He went slowly upstairs. When he opened the door he knew what he would see: he looked away as if to shut out temptation from the ascetic and the poisoned brain. He heard her say: 'I was just going out for a while, Pinkie. Is there anything I can do for you?'

Anything . . . His brain staggered with the immensity of its demands. He said gently, 'Nothing,' and schooled his voice to softness. 'Come back soon. We got things to talk about.'

'Worried?'

'Not worried. I got things straight,' he gestured with deadly humour at his head, 'in the box here.'

He was aware of her fear and tension—the sharp breath and the silence and then the voice steeled for despair. 'Not bad news, Pinkie?'

He flew out at her. 'For Christ's sake go.'

He heard her coming back across the room to him, but he wouldn't look up: this was his room, his life. He felt that if he could concentrate enough, it would be possible to eliminate every sign of her . . . everything would be just the same as before . . . before he entered Snow's and felt under that cloth for a ticket which wasn't there and began the deception and shame. The whole origin of the thing was lost; he could hardly remember Hale as a person or his murder as a crime—it was all now him and her.

'If anything's happened . . . you can tell me . . . I'm not scared. There must be some way, Pinkie, not to . . .' She implored him, 'Let's talk about it first.'

He said, 'You're fussed about nothing. I want you to go all right, you can go,' he went savagely on, 'to . . .' But he stopped in time, raked up a smile, 'Go and enjoy yourself.'

'I won't be gone long, Pinkie.' He heard the door close, but he knew she was lingering in the passage—the whole house was hers now. He put his hand in his pocket and pulled out the paper—'I don't care what you do . . . wherever you go, I'll go too.' It sounded like a letter read in court and printed in the newspapers. He heard her feet upon the stairs going down.

Dallow looked in and said, 'Prewitt should be starting now. I'll feel better when he's on that boat. You don't think, do you, she'd get the police to hunt him out?'

'She hasn't got the evidence,' the Boy said. 'You're safe enough when he's out of the way.' He spoke dully as if he'd lost all interest in whether Prewitt went or stayed—it was something which concerned other people. He'd gone beyond that.

'You too,' Dallow said. 'You'll be safe.'

The Boy didn't answer.

'I told Johnnie to see he got on the boat safe and then phone us. He'll be ringing up now almost any time. We oughter have a party to celebrate, Pinkie. My God, how sunk she'll feel when she turns up there and finds him gone.' He went to the window and looked out. 'Maybe we'll have some peace then. We'll have got out of it easy. When you come to think. Hale and poor old Spicer. I wonder where he is now.' He stared sentimentally out through the thin chimney smoke and the wireless masts. 'What about you an' me—an' the girl, of course—shifting off to some new place? It's not going to be so good here now with Colleoni butting in.' He turned back into the room. 'That letter'—and the telephone began to ring. He said, 'That'll be Johnnie,' and hurried out.

It occurred to the Boy that it wasn't the sound of feet on the stairs he recognized, it was the sound of the stairs themselves—he could tell those particular stairs even under a stranger's weight: there was always a creak at the third and seventh step down. This was the place he had come to after Kite had picked him up—he had been coughing on the Palace Pier in the bitter cold, listening to the violin wailing behind the glass. Kite had given him a cup of hot coffee and brought him here—God knows why—perhaps because he was out and wasn't down, perhaps because a man like Kite needed a little sentiment like a tart who keeps a Pekinese. Kite had opened the door of No. 63 and the first thing he'd seen was Dallow embracing Judy on the stairs and the first thing he had smelt was Frank's iron in the basement. Everything had been of a piece: nothing had really changed: Kite had died, but he had prolonged Kite's existence—not touching liquor, biting his nails in the Kite way, until *she* came and altered everything.

Dallow's voice drifted up the stairs. 'Oh, I dunno. Send some pork sausages. Or a tin of beans.'

He came back into the room. 'It wasn't Johnnie,' he said. 'Just the International. We oughter be hearing from Johnnie.' He sat anxiously down on the bed and said, 'That letter from Colleoni. What does it say?'

The Boy tossed it across to him. 'Why,' Dallow said, 'you haven't opened it.' He began to read: 'Well,' he said, 'it's bad, of course. It's what I thought. And yet it's not so bad either. Not when you come to look at it.' He glanced cautiously up over the mauve notepaper at the Boy, sitting there by the washstand, thinking. 'We're played out here, that's what it comes to. He's got most of our boys and all the bookies. But he doesn't want trouble. He's a business man—he says a fight like you had the other day brings a track into—disrepute. Disrepute,' Dallow repeated thoughtfully.

'He means,' the Boy said, 'the suckers stay away.'

'Well, that's sense. He says he'll pay you three hundred nicker for the goodwill. Goodwill?'

'He means not carving his geezers.'

'It's a good offer,' Dallow said. 'It's what I was saying just now—we could clear out right away from this damned town and this phoney buer asking questions, start again on a good line—or maybe retire altogether, buy a pub, you an' me—an' the girl, of course.' He said, 'When the hell's Johnnie going to phone. It makes me nervous.'

The Boy said nothing for a while, looking at his bitten nails. Then he said, 'Of course—you know the world, Dallow. You've travelled.'

'There's not many places I don't know,' Dallow agreed, 'between here and Leicester.'

'I was born here,' the Boy said. 'I know Goodwood and Hurst Park. I've been to Newmarket. But I'd feel a stranger away from here.' He claimed with dreary pride, 'I suppose I'm real Brighton', as if his single heart contained all the cheap amusements, the Pullman cars, the unloving weekends in gaudy hotels, and the sadness after coition.

A bell rang. 'Listen,' Dallow said. 'Is that Johnnie?'

But it was only the front door. Dallow looked at his watch. 'I can't think what's keeping him,' he said. 'Prewitt oughter be on board by now.'

'Well,' the Boy said with gloom, 'we change, don't we? It's as you say. We got to see the world . . . After all I took to drink, didn't I? I can take to other things.'

'An' you got a girl,' Dallow said with hollow cheeriness. 'You're growing up, Pinkie—like your father.'

Like my father . . . The Boy was shaken again with his nocturnal Saturday disgust. He couldn't blame his father now . . . it was what you came to . . . you got mixed up, and then, he supposed, the habit grew . . . you gave yourself away weakly. You couldn't even blame the girl. It was life getting at you . . . there were the blind seconds when you thought it fine. 'We'd be safer,' he said, 'without her,' touching the loving message in the trouser-pocket.

'She's safe enough now. She's crazy about you.'

'The trouble with you is,' the Boy said, 'you don't look ahead. There's years . . . And any day she might fall for a new face or get vexed or something . . . if I don't keep her smooth . . . there's no security,' he said. The door opened and there she was back again: he bit his words short and smirked a welcome. But it wasn't hard—she took deception with such hopeless ease that he could feel a sort of tenderness for her stupidity and a companionship in her goodness—they were both doomed in their own way. Again he got the sense that she completed him.

She said, 'I hadn't got a key. I had to ring. I felt afraid soon as I'd gone out that something might be wrong. I wanted to be here, Pinkie.'

'There's nothing wrong,' he said. The telephone began to ring. 'There you see, there's Johnnie now.' He said to Dallow joylessly, 'You got your wish.'

They heard his voice at the phone shrill with suspense. 'That you, Johnnie? Yes? What was that? You don't mean . . . Oh yes, we'll see you later. Of course you'll get your money.' He came back up and at the right place the stairs creaked—his broad, brutal and innocent face bore good news like a boar's head at a feast. 'That's fine,' he said, 'fine. I was getting anxious, I don't mind telling you. But he's on the boat now an' she left the pier ten minutes ago. We got to celebrate this. By God, you're clever, Pinkie. You think of everything.'

6

Ida Arnold had had more than a couple. She sang softly to herself over the Guinness—'One night in an alley, Lord Rothschild said to me . . .' The heavy motion of the waves under the pier was like the sound of bath water; it set her going. She sat there massively alone—no harm in her for anybody in the world—minus one. The world was a good place if you didn't weaken; she was like the chariot in a triumph—behind her were all the big battalions—right's right, an eye for an eye, when you want to do a thing well, do it yourself. Phil Corkery made his way towards her—behind him through the long glass windows of the tea-room you could see the lights of Hove; green copper Metropole domes swam in the layer of last light under the heavy nocturnal clouds slumping down. The spray tossed up like fine rain against the windows. Ida Arnold stopped singing and said, 'Do you see what I see?'

Phil Corkery sat down; it wasn't like summer at all in this glass breakwater: he looked cold in his grey flannel trousers and his blazer with the old something-or-other arms on the pocket: a little pinched, all passion spent. 'It's them,' he said wearily. 'How did *you* know they'd be here?'

'I didn't,' Ida said. 'It's fate.'

'I'm tired of the sight of them.'

'But think *how* tired,' she said with cheery relish, '*they* are.' They looked across a waste of empty tables towards France, towards the Boy and Rose—and a man and woman they didn't recognize. If the party had come there to celebrate or something, she had spoiled their fun. The Guinness welled warmly up into her throat. She had an enormous sense of well-being; she belched and said, 'Pardon me,' lifting a black-gloved hand. She said, 'I suppose he's gone, too?'

'He's gone.'

'We aren't lucky with our witnesses,' she said. 'First Spicer, then the girl, then Prewitt and now Cubitt.'

'He took the first morning train—with your money.'

'Never mind,' she said. 'They're alive. They'll come back. An' I can wait—thanks to Black Boy.'

Phil Corkery looked at her askance; it was astonishing that he had ever had the nerve to send her, to send that power and purpose, postcards from seaside resorts—from Hastings a crab from whose stomach you could wind out a series of views, from Eastbourne a baby sitting upon a rock which lifted to disclose the High Street and Boots' Library and a fernery, from Bournemouth (was it?) a bottle containing photographs of the promenade, the rock garden, the new swimming pool . . . It was like offering a bun to an elephant in Africa. He was shaken by a sense of terrific force . . . When she wanted a good time nothing would stop her, and when she wanted justice . . . He said nervously, 'Don't you think, Ida, we've done enough . . .'

She said, 'I haven't finished yet,' with her eyes on the little doomed party. 'You never know. They think they're safe: they'll do something crazy now.' The Boy sat there silent beside Rose. He had a glass of drink but he hadn't tasted it; only the man and the woman chattered about this and that.

'We've done our best. It's a matter for the police or no one,' Phil said.

'You heard them that first time.' She began to sing again, 'One night in an alley . . .'

'It's not our business now.'

'Lord Rothschild said to me . . .' She broke off to set him gently right. You couldn't let a friend have wrong ideas. 'It's the business of anyone who knows the difference between right and wrong.'

'But you're so terribly certain about things, Ida. You go busting in . . . Oh, you mean well, but how do we know the reasons he may have had . . . And besides,' he accused her, 'you're only doing it because it's fun. Fred wasn't anyone you cared about.'

She switched towards him her large and lit-up eyes. 'Why,' she said, 'I don't say it hasn't been—exciting.' She felt quite sorry it was all over now. 'What's the harm in that? I like doing what's right, that's all.'

Rebellion bobbed weakly up—'And what's wrong, too, Ida.'

She smiled at him with enormous and remote tenderness. 'Oh, that. That's not wrong. That does no one any harm. That's not like murder.'

'Priests say it is.'

'Priests,' she exclaimed with scorn. 'Why, even Romans don't believe in *that*. Or that girl wouldn't be living with him now.' She said, 'You can trust me. I've seen the world. I know people,' and she turned her attention heavily back on Rose. 'You wouldn't let me leave a little girl like that—to him? She's vexing, of course, she's stupid, but she don't deserve that.'

'How do you know she doesn't *want* to be left?'

'You aren't telling me, are you, that she wants to die? Nobody wants that. Oh, no. I don't give up until she's safe. Get me another Guinness.' A long way out beyond the West Pier you could see the lights of Worthing—a sign of bad weather, and the tide rolled regularly in, a gigantic white splash in the dark against the breakwaters nearer shore. You could hear it pounding at the piles, like a boxer's fist against a punchball in training for the human jaw, and softly and just a little tipsily Ida Arnold began to recall the people she had saved: a man she had once pulled out of the sea when she was a young woman, the money to a blind beggar, and the kind word in season to the despairing schoolgirl in the Strand.

7

'Poor old Spicer too,' Dallow said, 'he got the same idea—he thought he'd have a pub somewhere some day.' He slapped Judy's thigh and said, 'What about me an' you settling in with the young people.' He said, 'I can see it now. Right out in the country. On one of those arterials with the charabancs stopping: the Great North Road: "Pull in here". I wouldn't be surprised if there wasn't more money in the long run . . .' He stopped and said to the Boy, 'What's up? Take a drink. There's nothing to worry about now.'

The Boy looked across the tea-room and the empty tables to where the woman sat. How she hung on. Like a ferret he'd seen on the Down, among the chalky holes, fastened to a hare's throat. All the same *this* hare escaped. He had no cause to fear her now. He said in a dull voice, 'The country. I don't know much about the country.'

'It's healthy,' Dallow said. 'Why, you'll live to eighty with your missus.'

'Sixty-odd years,' the Boy said, 'it's a long time.' Behind the woman's head the Brighton lamps beaded out towards Worthing. The last sunset light slid lower in the sky and the heavy indigo clouds came down over the Grand, the Metropole, the Cosmopolitan, over the towers and domes. Sixty years: it was like a prophecy—a certain future: a horror without end.

'You two,' Dallow said. 'What's got you both?'

This was the tea-room to which they had come after Fred's death—Spicer and Dallow and Cubitt. Dallow was right, of course: they were safe—Spicer dead and Prewitt out of the way and Cubitt God knows where. (They'd never get *him* into a witness box: he knew too well he'd hang—he'd played too big a part—and the prison record of 1923 lay behind him.) And Rose was his wife. As safe as they could ever be. They'd won out—finally. He had—Dallow right again—sixty years ahead. His thoughts came to pieces in his hand: Saturday nights: and then the birth, the child, habit and hate. He looked across the tables; the woman's laughter was like defeat.

He said, 'This place is stuffy. I got to have some air.' He turned slowly to Rose. 'Come for a stroll,' he said. Between the table and the door he picked the right thought out of all the pieces, and when they came out on the windy side of the pier he shouted to her, 'I got to go away from here.' He put his hand on her arm and guided her with terrible tenderness into shelter. The waves came breaking up from France, pounding under their feet. A spirit of recklessness took him: it was like the moment when he had seen Spicer bending by his suitcase, Cubitt begging for money in the passage. Through the glass panes Dallow sat with Judy by the drinks. It was like the first week of the sixty years—the contact and the sensual tremble and the stained sleep and waking not alone; in the wild and noisy darkness he had the whole future in his brain. It was like a slot machine: you put in a penny and the light goes on and the doors open and the figures move. He said with agile tenderness, 'This was where we met that night. Remember?'

'Yes,' she said and watched him with fear.

'We don't want *them* with us,' he said. 'Let's get into the car an' drive'—he watched her closely—'into the country.'

'It's cold.'

'It won't be in the car.' He dropped her arm and said, 'Of course—if you don't want to come—I'll go alone.'

'But where?'

He said with studied lightness, 'I told you. In the country.' He took a penny out of his pocket, and slammed it home in the nearest slot-machine. He pulled a handle, didn't look at what he did, and with a rattle the packets of fruit gums came dropping out—a bonus—lemon and grape-fruit and liquorice all-sorts. He said, 'I've got a lucky hand.'

'Is something wrong?' Rose said.

He said, 'You saw her, didn't you? Believe me—she's never going to leave go. I saw a ferret once—out by the track.' As he turned one of the pier lights caught his eyes: a gleam: an exhilaration. He said, 'I'm going for a ride. You stay here if you want to.'

'I'll come,' she said.

'You needn't.'

'I'll come.'

At the shooting range he paused. He was taken with a kind of wild humour. 'Got the time?' he asked the man.

'You know what the time is. I've told you before how I won't stand . . .'

'You needn't get your rag out,' the Boy said. 'Give me a gun.' He lifted it, got the sight firmly on the bull, then deliberately shifted it and fired. He thought: 'Something had agitated him, the witness said.'

'What's up with you today?' the man exclaimed. 'You only got an outer.'

He laid the rifle down. 'We need a freshener. We're going for a ride in the country. Good night.' He planted his information pedantically, as carefully as he had had them lay Fred's cards along the route—for later use. He even turned back and said, 'We're going Hastings way.'

'I don't want to know,' the man said, 'where you're going.'

The old Morris was parked near the pier. The self-starter wouldn't work: he had to turn the handle. He stood a moment looking at the old car with an expression of disgust: as if this was all you got out of a racket . . . He said, 'We'll go the way we went that day. Remember. In the bus.' Again he planted his information for the attendant to hear. 'Peacehaven. We'll get a drink.'

They swung out round by the Aquarium and ground up hill in second gear. He had one hand in his pocket feeling for the scrap of paper on which she had written her message. The hood flapped and the split discoloured glass of the windscreen confined his view. He said, 'It's going to rain like hell soon.'

'Will this hood keep it out?'

'It doesn't matter,' he said, staring ahead. 'We won't get wet.'

She didn't dare ask him what he meant—she wasn't sure, and as long as she wasn't sure she could believe that they were happy, that they were lovers taking a drive in the dark with all the trouble over. She put a hand on him and felt his instinctive withdrawal: for a moment she was shaken by an awful doubt—if this was the darkest nightmare of all, if he didn't love her, as the woman said . . . The wet windy air flapped her face through the rent. It didn't matter: she loved him: she had her responsibility. The buses passed them going downhill to the town: little bright domestic cages in which people sat with baskets and books: a child pressed her face to the glass and for a moment at a traffic light they were so close the face might have been held against her breast. 'A penny for your thoughts,' he said and caught her unawares—'Life's not so bad.'

'Don't you believe it,' he said. 'I'll tell you what it is. It's gaol, it's not knowing where to get some money. Worms and cataract, cancer. You hear 'em shrieking from the upper windows—children being born. It's dying slowly.'

It was coming now—she knew it: the dashboard light lit the bony mind-made-up fingers: the face was in darkness, but she could imagine the exhilaration, the bitter excitement, the anarchy in the eyes. A rich man's private car—Daimler or Bentley she didn't know the make—rolled smoothly past them. He said, 'What's the hurry?' He took his hand out of his pocket and laid on his knee a paper she recognized. He said, 'You mean that—don't you?' He had to repeat it—'Don't you?' She felt as if she were signing away more than her life—heaven, whatever that was, and the child in the bus, and the baby crying in the neighbour's house. 'Yes,' she said.

'We'll go and have a drink,' he said, 'and then—you'll see. I got everything settled.' He said with hideous ease, 'It won't take a minute.' He put his arm round her waist and his face was close to hers: she could see him now, considering and considering; his skin smelt of petrol: everything smelt of petrol in the little leaking outdated car. She said, 'Are you sure . . . can't we wait . . . one day?'

'What's the good? You saw her there tonight. She's hanging on. One day she'll get her evidence. What's the use?'

'Why not *then*?'

'It might be too late *then*.' He said disjointedly through the flapping hood, 'A knock and the next thing you know . . . the cuffs . . . too late . . .' He said with cunning, 'We wouldn't be together then.' He put down his foot and the needle quivered up to thirty-five—

the old car wouldn't do more than forty, but it gave an immense impression of reckless speed: the wind battered on the glass and tore through the rent. He began softly to intone—'Dona nobis pacem.'

'He won't.'

'What do you mean?'

'Give us peace.'

He thought: there'll be time enough in the years ahead sixty years—to repent of this. Go to a priest. Say: 'Father, I've committed murder twice. And there was a girl—she killed herself.' Even if death came suddenly, driving home tonight, the smash on the lamp-post—there was still 'between the stirrup and the ground'. The houses on one side ceased altogether, and the sea came back to them, beating at the undercliff drive, a darkness and deep sound. He wasn't really deceiving himself—he'd learnt the other day that when the time was short there were other things than contrition to think about. It didn't matter anyway . . . he wasn't made for peace, he couldn't believe in it. Heaven was a word: hell was something he could trust. A brain was only capable of what it could conceive, and it couldn't conceive what it had never experienced; his cells were formed of the cement school-playground, the dead fire and the dying man in the St Pancras waiting-room, his bed at Frank's and his parents' bed. An awful resentment stirred in him—why shouldn't he have had his chance like all the rest, seen his glimpse of heaven if it was only a crack between the Brighton walls . . . He turned as they went down to Rottingdean and took a long look at her as if she might be it—but the brain couldn't conceive—he saw a mouth which wanted the sexual embrace, the shape of breasts demanding a child. Oh, she was good all right, he supposed, but she wasn't good enough: he'd got her down.

Above Rottingdean the new villas began: pipe-dream architecture: up on the downs the obscure skeleton of a nursing home, winged like an aeroplane. He said, 'They won't hear us in the country.' The lights petered out along the road to Peacehaven: the chalk of a new cutting flapped like white sheets in the headlight: cars came down on them blinding them. He said, 'The battery's low.'

She had the sense that he was a thousand miles away—his thoughts had gone on beyond the act she couldn't tell where. He was wise; he was foreseeing, she thought, things she couldn't conceive—eternal punishment, the flames . . . She felt terror, the idea of pain shook her, their purpose drove up in a flurry of rain against the old stained windscreen. This road led nowhere else. It was said to be the worst act of all, the act of despair, the sin without forgiveness; sitting there in the smell of petrol she tried to realize despair, the mortal sin, but she couldn't; it didn't feel like despair. He was going to damn himself, but she was going to show them that they couldn't damn him without damning her too. There was nothing he could do, she wouldn't do: she felt capable of sharing any murder. A light lit his face and left it; a frown, a thought, a child's face. She felt responsibility move in her breasts; she wouldn't let him go into that darkness alone.

The Peacehaven streets began, running out towards the cliffs and the downs: thorn-bushes grew up round the To Let boards; streets ended in obscurity, in a pool of water and in salty grass. It was like the last effort of despairing pioneers to break new country. The country had broken them. He said, 'We'll go to the hotel and have a drink and then—I know the right place.'

The rain was coming tentatively down; it beat on the faded scarlet doors of Lureland, the poster of next week's Whist Drive and last week's Dance. They ran for it to the hotel door. In the lounge there was nobody at all—white marble statuettes and on the green dado above the panelled walls Tudor roses and lilies picked out in gold. Siphons stood about on blue-topped tables, and on the stained-glass windows medieval ships tossed on cold curling waves. Somebody had broken the hands off one of the statuettes—or perhaps it was made like that, something classical in white drapery, a symbol of victory or despair. The Boy rang a bell and a boy of his own age came out of the public bar to take his order: they were oddly alike and allusively different—narrow shoulders, thin face, they bristled like dogs at the sight of each other.

'Piker,' the Boy said.

'What of it?'

'Give us service,' the Boy said. He took a step forward and the other backed and Pinkie grinned at him. 'Bring us two double brandies,' he said, 'and quick.' He said softly, 'Who would have thought I'd find Piker here?' She watched him with amazement that he could find any distraction from their purpose. She could hear the wind on the upstair windows; where the steps curved another tombstone statuette raised its ruined limbs. He said, 'We were at the school together. I used to give him hell in the breaks.' The other returned with the brandies and brought, sidelong and scared and cautious, a whole smoky childhood with him. She felt a pang of jealousy against him because tonight she should have had all there was of Pinkie.

'You a servant?' the Boy said.

'I'm not a servant, I'm a waiter.'

'You want me to tip you?'

'I don't want your tips.'

The Boy took his brandy and drank it down; he coughed when it took him by the throat. It was like the stain of the world in his stomach. He said, 'Here's courage.' He said to Piker, 'What's the time?'

'You can read it on the clock,' Piker said, 'if you can read.'

'Haven't you any music?' the Boy said. 'God damn it, we want to celebrate.'

'There's the piano. An' the wireless.'

'Turn it on.'

The wireless was hidden behind a potted plant: a violin came wailing out, the notes shaken by atmospherics. The Boy said, 'He hates me. He hates my guts,' and turned to mock at Piker, but he'd gone. He said to Rose, 'You'd better drink that brandy.'

'I don't need it,' she said.

'Have it your own way.'

He stood by the wireless and she by the empty fireplace: three tables and three siphons and a Moorish-Tudor-God-knows-what-of-a-lamp were between them: they were gripped by an awful unreality, the need to make conversation, to say 'What a night!' or 'It's cold for the time of year.' She said, 'So he was at your school.'

'That's right.' They both looked at the clock: it was almost nine, and behind the violin the rain tapped against the seaward windows. He said awkwardly, 'We'd better be moving soon.'

She began to pray to herself, 'Holy Mary, Mother of God,' but then she stopped—she was in mortal sin: it was no good praying. Her prayers stayed here below with the siphons and statuettes: they had no wings. She waited by the fireplace in terrified pa-

tience. He said uneasily, 'We ought to write—something, so people will know.'

'It doesn't matter, does it?' she said.

'Oh yes,' he said quickly, 'it does. We got to do things right.
This is a pact. You read about them in the newspapers.'

'Do lots of people—do it?'

'It's always happening,' he said; an awful and airy confidence
momentarily possessed him: the violin faded out and the time signal pinged through the rain. A voice behind the plant gave them the
weather report—storms coming up from the Continent, a depression in the Atlantic, tomorrow's forecast. She began to listen and
then remembered that tomorrow's weather didn't matter at all.

He said, 'Like another drink—or something?' He looked round
for a Gents sign—'I just got to go—an' wash.' She noticed the
weight in his pocket—it was going to be that way. He said, 'Just
add a piece on that note while I'm gone. Here's a pencil. Say you
couldn't live without me, something like that. We got to do this
right, as it's always done.' He went out into the passage and called
to Piker and got his directions, then went up the stairs. At the statuette he turned and looked down into the panelled lounge. This
was the kind of moment one kept for memory—the wind at the
pier end, Sherry's and the men singing, lamplight on the harvest
Burgundy, the crisis as Cubitt battered at the door. He found that
he remembered it all without repulsion; he had a sense that somewhere, like a beggar outside a shuttered house, tenderness stirred,
but he was bound in a habit of hate. He turned his back and went
on up the stairs. He told himself that soon he would be free
again—they'd see the note. He hadn't known she was all that unhappy, he would say, because they'd got to part: she must have
found the gun in Dallow's room and brought it with her. They'd
test it for finger-prints, of course, and then—he stared out through
the lavatory window: invisible rollers beat under the cliff. Life
would go on. No more human contacts, other people's emotions
washing at the brain—he would be free again: nothing to think
about but himself. Myself: the word echoed hygienically on
among the porcelain basins, the taps and plugs and wastes. He
took the revolver out of his pocket and loaded it—two chambers.
In the mirror above the wash-basin he could see his hand move

round the metal death, adjusting the safety-catch. Down below the news was over and the music had begun again—it wailed upwards like a dog over a grave, and the huge darkness pressed a wet mouth against the panes. He put the revolver back and went out into the passage. That was the next move. Another statuette pointed an obscure moral with cemetery hands and a chaplet of marble flowers, and again he felt the prowling presence of pity.

8

'They've been gone a long while,' Dallow said. 'What are they up to?'

'Who cares?' Judy said. 'They want to be'—she pressed her plump lips against Dallow's cheek—'alone'—her red hair caught in his mouth—a sour taste. 'You know what love is,' she said.

'He doesn't.' He was uneasy—conversations came back to him. He said, 'He hates her guts.' He put his arm half-heartedly round Judy—it was no good spoiling a party, but he wished he knew what Pinkie had in mind. He took a long drink out of Judy's glass, and somewhere Worthing way a siren wailed. Through the window he could see a couple mooning at the pier end, and an old man got his fortune card from the witch behind glass.

'Why don't he get clear of her then?' Judy asked. Her mouth looked for his mouth down the line of his jaw. She drew herself indignantly up and said, 'Who's that polony over there? What does she want lamping us all the time? This is a free country.'

Dallow turned and looked. His brain worked very slowly, first the statement—'I never seen her,' and then the memory. 'Why,' he said, 'it's that damned buer who's been getting Pinkie rattled.' He got cumbrously to his feet and stumbled a little between the tables. 'Who are you?' he asked. 'Who are you?'

'Ida Arnold,' she said, 'for what it's worth. My friends call me Ida.'

'I'm not your friend.'

'You better be,' she said gently. 'Have a drink. Where's Pinkie gone—and Rose? You ought to 'ave brought them along. This is Phil. Introduce the lady friend.' She ran softly on, 'It's time we all got together. What's your name?'

253

'Don't you know what people get who poke their noses . . .'

'Oh, I know,' she said. 'I know all right. I was with Fred the day you finished him.'

'Talk sense,' Dallow said. 'Who the hell are you?'

'You ought to know. You followed us all the way up the front in that old Morris of yours.' She smiled quite amiably at him. He wasn't her game. 'It seems an age ago now, doesn't it?'

It was true all right—it seemed an age.

'Have a drink,' Ida said, 'you may as well. An' where's Pinkie? He didn't seem to like the look of me tonight. What were you celebrating? Not what's happened to Mr Prewitt? You won't have heard that.'

'What do you mean?' Dallow said. The wind got up against the glass and the waitresses yawned.

'You'll see it in the morning papers. I don't want to spoil your fun. And of course you'll know it sooner than that if he talks.'

'He's gone abroad.'

'He's at the police-station now,' she said with complete confidence. 'They brought him right back,' she went elaborately on. 'You ought to choose your solicitors better, men who can afford to take a holiday. They've got him for swindling. Arrested on the quay.'

He watched her uneasily. He didn't believe her—but all the same . . . 'You know an awful lot,' he said. 'Do you sleep at nights?'

'Do you?'

The big broken face had a kind of innocence about it. 'Me?' he said. 'I don't know a thing.'

'It was a waste giving him all that money. He'd have run anyway—and it didn't look good. When I got hold of Johnnie at the pier—'

He stared at her with hopeless amazement. 'You got hold of Johnnie? How the hell . . . ?'

She said simply, 'People like me.' She took a drink and said, 'His mother treated him shameful when he was a kid.'

'Whose mother?'

'Johnnie's.'

Dallow was impatient, puzzled, scared. 'What the hell,' he said, 'do you know about Johnnie's mother?'

'What he told me,' she said. She sat there completely at her ease, her big breasts ready for any secrets. She carried her air of compassion and comprehension about her like a rank cheap perfume. She said gently, 'I got nothing against you. I like to be friendly. Bring over your lady friend.'

He glanced quickly over his shoulder and back again. 'I better not,' he said. His voice fell. He too began automatically to confide. 'Truth is, she's a jealous bitch.'

'You don't say. And her old man . . .'

'Oh, her old man,' he said, 'he's all right. What Frank doesn't see, he doesn't mind.' He dropped his voice still lower. 'And he can't see much—he's blind.'

'I didn't know that,' she said.

'You wouldn't,' he said. 'Not from his pressing and ironing. He's got a wonderful hand with an iron.' He broke suddenly off. 'What the hell,' he said, 'did you mean—you didn't know *that*? What did you know?'

'There isn't much,' she said, 'I've not picked up—here and there. The neighbours always talk.' She was barnacled with pieces of popular wisdom.

'Who's talking?' It was Judy now. She'd come across to them. 'An' what 'ave they got to talk about? Why, if I chose to put my tongue round some of their doings. But I wouldn't like to,' Judy said. 'I wouldn't like to.' She looked vaguely round. 'What *has* happened to those two?'

'Perhaps I scared them,' Ida Arnold said.

'*You* scared them?' Dallow said. 'That's rich. Pinkie's not scared that easy.'

'What I want to know is,' Judy said, 'what neighbour's said what?'

Somebody was shooting at the range: when the door opened and a couple came in they could hear the shots—one, two, three. 'That'll be Pinkie,' Dallow said. 'He was always good with a gun.'

'You better go an' see,' Ida gently remarked, 'that he doesn't do something desperate—with his gun—when he gets to know.'

Dallow said, 'You jump to things. We got no cause to be afraid of Mr Prewitt.'

'You gave him money, I suppose, for something.'

'Aw,' he said, 'Johnnie's been joking.'

'Your friend Cubitt seemed to think . . .'

'Cubitt doesn't know a thing.'

'Of course,' she admitted, 'he wasn't there, was he? That time, I mean. But you . . .' she said. 'Wouldn't twenty pounds be of use to you? After all you don't want to get into trouble. . . . Let Pinkie carry his own crimes.'

'You make me sick,' he said. 'You think you know a lot and you don't know a thing.' He said to Judy, 'I'm goin' to have a drain. You want to keep your mouth shut or this polony . . .' He stretched a gesture, hopelessly—he couldn't express what she mightn't put over on you. He went uneasily out, and the wind caught him, so that he had to grab at his old greasy hat and hold it on. Going down the step to the gents was like going down into a ship's engine-room in a storm. The whole place shook a little under his feet as the swell came up against the piles and drove on to break against the beach. He thought: I oughter warn Pinkie about Prewitt if it's true. . . . He *had* things on his mind, other things besides old Spicer. He came up the ladder and looked down the dock—Pinkie wasn't to be seen. He went on past the peep machines—not in sight. It was someone else shooting at the booth.

He asked the man, 'Seen Pinkie?'

'What's the game?' the man said. 'You know I seen him. *An'* he's gone for a ride in the country—with his girl—for a freshener—Hastings way. *An'* I suppose you want to know the time too. Well,' the man said, 'I'm swearing nothing. You can pitch on someone else for your phoney alibis.'

'You're crackers,' Dallow said. He moved away. Across the noisy sea the hour began to strike in Brighton churches: he counted one, two, three, four, and stopped. He was scared—suppose it *was* true, suppose Pinkie knew, and it was that mad scheme . . . Why the hell was he taking anyone for a ride in the country at this hour, except to a roadhouse, and Pinkie didn't go to roadhouses? He said softly, 'I won't stand for it,' aloud. He was confused, he wished he hadn't drunk all that beer. She was a good kid. He remembered her in the kitchen, going to light the stove. And why not? he thought, staring gloomily out to sea; he was shaken by a sudden sentimental desire which Judy couldn't satisfy: for a paper with your breakfast and warm fires. He began to walk rapidly down the pier towards the turnstiles. There were things he wouldn't stand for.

He knew the Morris wouldn't be on the rank, but all the same he had to go and see for himself. Its absence was like a voice speaking quite plainly in his ear. 'Suppose she kills herself . . . a pact may be murder, but they don't hang you for it.' He stood there hopelessly, not knowing what to do. Beer clouded his brain: he passed a harassed hand across his face. He said to the attendant, 'You see that Morris go out?'

'Your friend and his girl took it,' the man said, hobbling between a Talbot and an Austin. One leg was gammy, he moved it with a mechanism worked from his pocket, lurching with an air of enormous strain to pocket sixpence, to say 'It's a fine night'; he looked worn with the awful labour of the trivial act. He said, 'They're goin' up to Peacehaven for a drink. Don't ask me why.' Hand in pocket he pulled the hidden wire and made his unsteady and diagonal way towards a Ford. 'The rain won't hold off long,' his voice came back, and 'Thank you, sir,' and then again the labour of movement as a Morris Oxford backed in, the pulling at the wire.

Dallow stood there hopelessly at a loss. There were buses . . . but everything would be over long before a bus got in. Better to wash his hands of the whole thing . . . after all he didn't *know*; in half an hour he might see the old car coming back past the Aquarium, Pinkie driving and the girl beside him, but he knew very well in his heart that it would never come, not with both of them, that way. The Boy had left too many signs behind him—the message at the shooting-range, at the car-park: he wanted to be followed in good time, in his own time, to fit in with his story. The man came lurching back. He said, 'I thought your friend seemed queer tonight. Sort of lit up.' It was as if he were talking in the witness box, giving the evidence he was meant to give.

Dallow turned hopelessly away . . . fetch Judy, go home, wait . . . and there was the woman standing a few feet away. She'd followed him and listened. He said, 'God's sakes, this is your doing. You made him marry her, you made him . . .'

'Get a car,' she said, 'quick.'

'I've not got the money for a car.'

'I have. You better hurry.'

'There's no cause to hurry,' he said weakly. 'They've just gone for a drink.'

'You know what they've gone for,' she said. 'I don't. But if *you* want to keep out of this, you'd better get that car.'

The first rain began to blow up the parade as he weakly argued. 'I don't know a thing.'

'That's right,' she said. 'You're just taking me for a drive, that's all.' She burst suddenly out at him: 'Don't be a fool. You better have me for a friend . . .' She said, 'You see what's come to Pinkie.'

All the same he didn't hurry. What was the good? Pinkie had laid *this* trail. Pinkie thought of everything, they were meant to follow in due course, and find . . . He hadn't got the imagination to see what they'd find.

9

The Boy stopped at the head of the stairs and looked down. Two
men had come into the lounge: hearty and damp in camel-hair
coats they shook out their moisture like dogs and were noisy over
their drinks. 'Two pints,' they ordered 'in tankards,' and fell suddenly silent scenting a girl in the lounge. They were upper-class,
they'd learned that tankard trick in class hotels: he watched their
gambits with hatred from the stairs. Anything female was better
than nothing, even Rose; but he could sense their half-heartedness.
She wasn't worth more than a little sidelong swagger. 'I think we
touched eighty.'

'I made it eighty-two.'

'She's a good bus.'

'How much did they sting you?'

'A couple of hundred. She's cheap at the price.'

Then they both stopped and took an arrogant look at the girl
by the statuette. She wasn't worth bothering about, but if she ab-
solutely fell, without trouble . . . One of them said something in a
low voice and the other laughed. They took long swills of bitter
from the tankards.

Tenderness came up to the very window and looked in. What
the hell right had they got to swagger and laugh . . . if she was
good enough for him. He came down the stairs into the hall; they
looked up and moued to each other, as much as to say—'Oh well,
she wasn't really worth the trouble.'

One of them said, 'Drink up. We better get on with the good
work. You don't think Zoe'll be out?'

'Oh no. I said I might drop in.'

'Her friend all right?'

'She's hot.'

'Let's get on then.'

They drained their beer and moved arrogantly to the door, taking a passing look at Rose as they went. He could hear them laugh outside the door. They were laughing at him. He came a few steps into the lounge: again they were bound in an icy constraint. He had a sudden inclination to throw up the whole thing, to get into the car and drive home, and let her live. It was less a motion of pity than of weariness—there was such a hell of a lot to do and think of, there were going to be so many questions to be answered. He could hardly believe in the freedom at the end of it, and even that freedom was to be in a strange place. He said, 'The rain's worse.' She stood there waiting; she couldn't answer: she was breathing hard as if she'd run a long way—and she looked old. She was sixteen, but this was how she might have looked after years of marriage, of the childbirth and the daily quarrel: they had reached death and it affected them like age.

She said, 'I wrote what you wanted.' She waited for him to take the scrap of paper and write his own message to the coroner, to *Daily Express* readers, to what one called the world. The other boy came cautiously into the lounge and said, 'You haven't paid.' While Pinkie found the money, she was visited by an almost overwhelming rebellion—she had only to go out, leave him, refuse to play. He couldn't make her kill herself: life wasn't as bad as that. It came like a revelation, as if someone had whispered to her that she was someone, a separate creature—not just one flesh with him. She could always escape—if he didn't change his mind. Nothing was decided. They could go in the car wherever he wanted them to go; she could take the gun from his hand, and even then—at the last moment of all—she needn't shoot. Nothing was decided—there was always hope.

'That's your tip,' the Boy said. 'I always tip a waiter.' Hate came back. He said, 'You a good Roman, Piker? Do you go to Mass on Sundays like they tell you?'

Piker said with weak defiance, 'Why not, Pinkie?'

'You're afraid,' the Boy said. 'You're afraid of burning.'

'Who wouldn't be?'

'I'm not.' He looked with loathing into the past—a cracked bell ringing, a child weeping under the cane—and repeated, 'I'm not afraid.' He said to Rose, 'We'll be going.' He came tentatively across and put a nail against her cheek—half caress, half threat—and said, 'You'd love me always, wouldn't you?'

'Yes.'

He gave her one more chance: 'You'd always have stuck to me,' and when she nodded her agreement, he began wearily the long course of action which one day would let him be free again.

Outside in the rain the self-starter wouldn't work again: he stood with his coat-collar turned up and pulled the handle. She wanted to tell him he mustn't stand there, getting wet, because she'd changed her mind: they were going to live—by hook or by crook, but she didn't dare. She pushed hope back—to the last possible moment. When they drove off she said, 'Last night . . . the night before . . . you didn't hate me, did you, for what we did?'

He said, 'No, I didn't hate you.'

'Even though it was a mortal sin.'

It was quite true—he hadn't hated her; he hadn't even hated the act. There had been a kind of pleasure, a kind of pride, a kind of—something else. The car lurched back on to the main road; he turned the bonnet to Brighton. An enormous emotion beat on him; it was like something trying to get in; the pressure of gigantic wings against the glass. Dona nobis pacem. He withstood it, with all the bitter force of the school bench, the cement playground, the St Pancras waiting-room, Dallow's and Judy's secret lust, and the cold unhappy moment on the pier. If the glass broke, if the beast—whatever it was—got in, God knows what it would do. He had a sense of huge havoc—the confession, the penance and the sacrament—and awful distraction, and he drove blind into the rain. He could see nothing through the cracked stained windscreen. A bus came upon them and pulled out just in time—he was on the wrong side. He said, suddenly, at random, 'We pull in here.'

An ill-made street petered out towards the cliff—bungalows of every shape and kind, a vacant plot full of salt grass and wet thorn bushes like bedraggled fowls, no lights except in three windows. A radio played, and in a garage a man was doing something to his motor-bike which roared and spluttered in the darkness. He drove a few yards in, turned out his headlights, switched off his engine.

The rain came noisily in through the rent in the hood and they could hear the sea battering the cliff. He said, 'Well, take a look. It's the world.' Another light went on behind a stained-glass door (the laughing Cavalier between Tudor roses) and looking out as if it was he who'd got to take some sort of farewell of the bike and the bungalows and the rainy street, he thought of the words in the Mass—'He was in the world and the world was made by Him and the world knew Him not.'

It was about as far as hope could be stretched; she had to say now or never—'I won't do it. I never meant to do it.' It was like some romantic adventure—you plan to fight in Spain, and then before you know the tickets are taken for you, the introductions are pressed into your hand, somebody has come to see you off, everything is real. He put his hand in his pocket and pulled out the gun. He said, 'I got it out of Dallow's room.' She wanted to say she didn't know how to use it to make any excuse, but he seemed to have thought of everything. He explained, 'I've put up the safety-catch. All you need do is pull on this. It isn't hard. Put it in your ear—that'll hold it steady.' His youth came out in the crudity of his instruction: he was like a boy playing on an ash-heap. 'Go on,' he said, 'take it.'

It was amazing how far hope could stretch. She thought: I needn't say anything yet. I can take the gun and then—throw it out of the car, run away, do something to stop everything. But all the time she felt the steady pressure of his will. *His* mind was made up. She took the gun; it was like a treachery. What will he do, she thought, if I don't . . . shoot. Would he shoot himself alone, without her? Then he would be damned, and she wouldn't have her chance of being damned too, of showing Them they couldn't pick and choose. To go on living for years . . . you couldn't tell what life would do to you in making you meek, good, repentant. Belief in her mind had the bright clarity of images, of the crib at Christmas: here goodness ended, past the cow and the sheep, and there evil began—Herod seeking the child's birthplace from his turreted keep. She wanted to be with Herod—if *he* were there. You could win to the evil side suddenly, in a moment of despair or passion, but through a long life the guardian good drove you remorselessly towards the crib, the 'happy death'.

He said, 'We don't want to wait any longer. Do you want me to do it first?'

'No,' she said, 'no.'

'All right then. You take a walk—or better still I'll take a walk an' you stay here. When it's over, I'll come back an' do it too.' Again he gave the sense that he was a boy playing a game, a game in which you could talk in the coldest detail of the scalping knife or the bayonet wound and then go home to tea. He said, 'It'll be too dark for me to see much.'

He opened the door of the car. She sat motionless with the gun on her lap. Behind them on the main road a car went slowly past towards Peacehaven. He said awkwardly, 'You know what to do?' He seemed to think that some motion of tenderness was expected of him. He put out his mouth and kissed her on the cheek; he was afraid of the mouth—thoughts travel too easily from lip to lip. He said, 'It won't hurt,' and began to walk back a little way towards the main road. Hope was stretched now as far as it would go. The radio had stopped; the motor-bicycle exploded twice in the garage, feet moved on gravel and on the main road she could hear a car reversing.

If it was a guardian angel speaking to her now, he spoke like a devil—he tempted her to virtue like a sin. To throw away the gun was a betrayal; it would be an act of cowardice: it would mean that she chose never to see him again for ever. Moral maxims dressed in pedantic priestly tones remembered from old sermons, instructions, confessions—'you can plead for him at the throne of Grace'—came to her like unconvincing insinuations. The evil act was the honest act, the bold and the faithful—it was only lack of courage, it seemed to her, that spoke so virtuously. She put the gun up to her ear and put it down again with a feeling of sickness—it was a poor love that was afraid to die. She hadn't been afraid to commit mortal sin—it was death not damnation which was scaring her. Pinkie said it wouldn't hurt. She felt his will moving her hand—she could trust him. She put up the gun again.

A voice called sharply 'Pinkie' and she heard somebody splashing in the puddles. Footsteps ran . . . she couldn't tell where. It seemed to her that this must be news, that this must make a difference.

She couldn't kill herself when this might mean good news. It was as if somewhere in the darkness the will which had governed her hand relaxed, and all the hideous forces of self-preservation came flooding back. It didn't seem real—that she had really intended to sit there and press the trigger. 'Pinkie,' the voice called again, and the splashing steps came nearer. She pulled the car door open and flung the revolver far away from her towards the damp scrub.

In the light from the stained glass she saw Dallow and the woman—and a policeman who looked confused as if he didn't quite know what was happening. Somebody came softly round the car behind her and said, 'Where's that gun? Why don't you shoot? Give it me.'

She said, 'I threw it away.'

The others approached cautiously like a deputation. Pinkie called out suddenly in a breaking childish voice, 'You bloody squealer, Dallow.'

'Pinkie,' Dallow said, 'it's no use. They got Prewitt.' The policeman looked ill-at-ease like a stranger at a party.

'Where's that gun?' Pinkie said again. He screamed with hate and fear, 'My God, have I got to have a massacre?'

She said, 'I threw it away.'

She could see his face indistinctly as it leant in over the little dashboard light. It was like a child's, badgered, confused, betrayed: fake years slipped away—he was whisked back towards the unhappy playground. He said, 'You little . . .' he didn't finish—the deputation approached, he left her, diving into his pocket for something. 'Come on, Dallow,' he said, 'you bloody squealer,' and put his hand up. Then she couldn't tell what happened: glass—somewhere—broke, he screamed and she saw his face—steam. He screamed and screamed, with his hands up to his eyes; he turned and ran; she saw a police baton at his feet and broken glass. He looked half his size, doubled up in appalling agony: it was as if the flames had literally got him and he shrank—shrank into a schoolboy flying in panic and pain, scrambling over a fence, running on.

'Stop him,' Dallow cried: it wasn't any good: he was at the edge, he was over: they couldn't even hear a splash. It was as if he'd been withdrawn suddenly by a hand out of any existence—past or present, whipped away into zero—nothing.

10

'It shows,' Ida Arnold said, 'you only have to hold on.' She emptied her glass of stout and laid it down on Henekey's upturned barrel.

'And Prewitt?' Clarence asked.

'How slow you are, you old ghost. I just made that up. I couldn't chase over France for him, and the police—you know what police are—they always want evidence.'

'They had Cubitt?'

'Cubitt wouldn't talk when he was sober. And you'd never get him drunk enough to talk to them. Why, this is slander what I've been telling you. Or it would be slander—if *he* were alive.'

'I wonder you don't feel bad about that, Ida.'

'Somebody else would have been dead if we hadn't turned up.'

'It was her own choice.'

But Ida Arnold had an answer to everything. 'She didn't understand. She was only a kid. She thought he was in love with her.'

'An' what does she think now?'

'Don't ask me. I've done my best. I took her home. What a girl needs at a time like that is her mother and dad. Anyway she's got me to thank she isn't dead.'

'How did you get the policeman to go with you?'

'We told him they'd stolen the car. The poor man didn't know what it was all about, but he acted quick when Pinkie pulled out the vitriol.'

'And Phil Corkery?'

'He's talking of Hastings,' she said, 'next year, but I have a sort of feeling there won't be any postcards for me after this.'

'You're a terrible woman, Ida,' Clarence said. He sighed deeply and stared into his glass. 'Have another?'

'No thank you, Clarence. I got to be getting home.'

'You're a terrible woman,' Clarence repeated; he was a little drunk, 'but I got to give you credit. You act for the best.'

'He's not on my conscience anyway.'

'As you say it was him or her.'

'There wasn't any choice,' Ida Arnold said. She got up; she was like a figurehead of Victory. She nodded to Harry at the bar.

'You've been away, Ida?'

'Just a week or two.'

'It doesn't seem so long,' Harry said.

'Well, good night all.'

'Good night. Good night.'

She took the tube to Russell Square and walked, carrying her suitcase: let herself in and looked in the hall for letters. There was only one—from Tom. She knew what that would be about, and her great warm heart softened as she thought: After all, when all's said, Tom an' I know what Love is. She opened the door on to the basement stairs and called, 'Crowe. Old Crowe.'

'You, Ida?'

'Come up for a chat an' we'll have a turn with the Board.'

The curtains were drawn as she had left them—nobody had touched the china on the mantelpiece, but Warwick Deeping wasn't in the bookshelf and *The Good Companions* was on its side. The char had been in—she could see that—borrowing. She got out a box of chocolate biscuits for Old Crowe; the lid had not been left properly on and they were a little soft and stale. Then carefully she lifted out the Board, cleared the table and laid it in the centre. SUIKILLEYE, she thought. I know what that means now. The Board had foreseen it all—Sui, its own word for the scream, the agony, the leap. She brooded gently with her fingers on the Board. When you came to think of it, the Board had saved Rose, and a multitude of popular sayings began to pass together into her mind. It was like when the points shift and the signal goes down and the red lamp changes to green and the great engine takes the accustomed rails. It's a strange world, there's more things in heaven and earth . . .

Old Crowe came peering in. 'What's it to be, Ida?'

'I want to ask advice,' Ida said. 'I want to ask whether maybe I ought to go back to Tom.'

II

Rose could just see the old head bent towards the grill. The priest had a whistle in his breath. He listened—patiently—whistling, while she painfully brought out her whole agony. She could hear the exasperated women creak their chairs outside waiting for confession. She said, 'It's *that* I repent. Not going with him.' She was defiant and tearless in the stuffy box; the old priest had a cold and smelt of eucalyptus. He said gently and nasally, 'Go on, my child.'

She said, 'I wish I'd killed myself. I ought to 'ave killed myself.' The old man began to say something, but she interrupted him. 'I'm not asking for absolution. I don't want absolution. I want to be like him—damned.'

The old man whistled as he drew in his breath. She felt certain he understood nothing. She repeated monotonously, 'I wish I'd killed myself.' She pressed her hands against her breasts in the passion of misery. She hadn't come to confess, she had come to think; she couldn't think at home where the stove hadn't been lit and her father had got a mood and her mother—she could tell it in her sidelong questions—was wondering how much money Pinkie . . . She would have found the courage now to kill herself if she hadn't been afraid that somewhere in that obscure countryside of death they might miss each other—mercy operating somehow for one and not for the other. She said with breaking voice, 'That woman. She ought to be damned. Saying he wanted to get rid of me. *She* doesn't know about love.'

'Perhaps she was right,' the old priest murmured.

'And you don't either,' she said furiously, pressing her childish face against the grill.

The old man suddenly began to talk, whistling every now and

then and blowing eucalyptus through the grill. He said, 'There was a man, a Frenchman, you wouldn't know about him, my child, who had the same idea as you. He was a good man, a holy man, and he lived in sin all through his life, because he couldn't bear the idea that any soul could suffer damnation.' She listened with astonishment. He said, 'This man decided that if any soul was going to be damned, he would be damned too. He never took the sacraments, he never married his wife in church. I don't know, my child, but some people think he was—well, a saint. I think he died in what we are told is mortal sin—I'm not sure: it was in the war: perhaps . . .' He sighed and whistled, bending his old head. He said, 'You can't conceive, my child, nor can I or anyone the . . . appalling . . . strangeness of the mercy of God.'

Outside the chairs creaked again and again—people impatient to get their own repentance, absolution, penance finished for the week. He said, 'It was a case of greater love hath no man than this that he lay down his soul for his friend.'

He shivered and sneezed. 'We must hope and pray,' he said, 'hope and pray. The Church does not demand that we believe any soul is cut off from mercy.'

She said with sad conviction, 'He's damned. He knew what he was about. He was a Catholic too.'

He said gently, 'Corruptio optimi est pessima.'

'Yes, father?'

'I mean—a Catholic is more capable of evil than anyone. I think perhaps—because we believe in Him—we are more in touch with the devil than other people. But we must hope,' he said mechanically, 'hope and pray.'

'I want to hope,' she said, 'but I don't know how.'

'If he loved you, surely,' the old man said, 'that shows there was some good . . .'

'Even love like that?'

'Yes.'

She brooded on the idea in the little dark box. He said, 'And come back soon—I can't give you absolution now—but come back—tomorrow.'

She said weakly, 'Yes, father . . . And if there's a baby . . .'

He said, 'With your simplicity and his force . . . Make him a saint—to pray for his father.'

A sudden feeling of immense gratitude broke through the pain—it was as if she had been given the sight a long way off of life going on again. He said, 'Pray for me, my child.'

She said, 'Yes, oh yes.'

Outside she looked up at the name on the confessional box—it wasn't any name she remembered. Priests come and go.

She went out into the street—the pain was still there, you couldn't shake it off with a word; but the worst horror she thought was over—the horror of the complete circle—to be back at home, back at Snow's—they'd take her back—just as if the Boy had never existed at all. He had existed and would always exist. She had a sudden conviction that she carried life, and she thought proudly: Let them get over that if they can; let them get over that. She turned out on to the front opposite the Palace Pier and began to walk firmly away from the direction of her home towards Frank's. There was something to be salvaged from that house and room, something else they wouldn't be able to get over—his voice speaking a message to her: if there was a child, speaking to the child. 'If he loved you,' the priest had said, 'that shows . . .' She walked rapidly in the thin June sunlight towards the worst horror of all.

Brighton Rock

The classic film adaptation of *Brighton Rock* was released in 1947. Graham Greene and Terence Rattigan wrote the screenplay. The film was produced and directed by the Boulting Brothers. Richard Attenborough starred as the razor-wielding Pinkie in perhaps his most iconic onscreen role. Famously, The British Board of Film Censors requested that Greene soften the story's memorably cruel ending. Despite this change, *Brighton Rock* is widely viewed as one of the best British *film noirs*.

A remake is scheduled for release in 2010, featuring Sam Riley and Helen Mirren. Director Rowan Joffe plans to shift the setting from the 1930s to 1960s to give it a more modern feel.

Certificate: PG
Running Time: 92 minutes